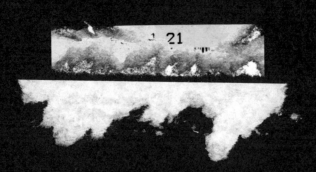

21

NEWTON'S
APPLE

NEWTON'S APPLE

Isaac Newton and the English Scientific Renaissance

PETER AUGHTON

WEIDENFELD & NICOLSON · A WINDRUSH PRESS BOOK

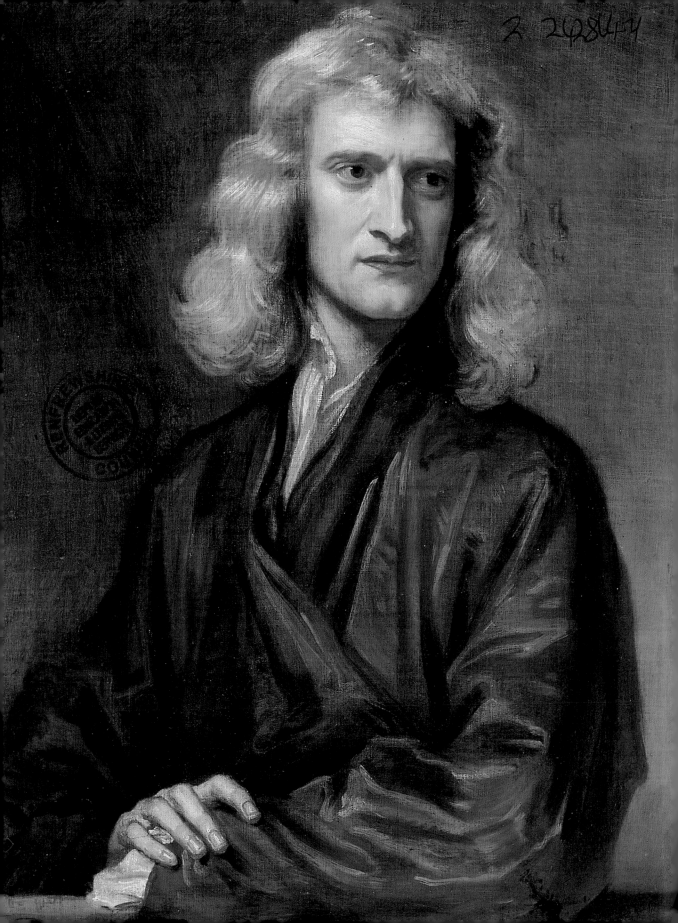

CONTENTS

PROLOGUE

FOR I DIPT INTO THE FUTURE,
      FAR AS HUMAN EYE COULD SEE,
SAW THE VISION OF THE WORLD,
AND ALL THE WONDER THAT COULD BE.

Alfred, Lord Tennyson (1809-1892)

IT WAS A NEW CENTURY and a new millennium. A wealth of information was available to the whole world through artificial satellites and computers. News and pictures travelled from continent to continent at the speed of light. Grandparents could see and speak to their grandchildren on the other side of the planet. Wealthy households in every nation owned horseless carriages which could carry them at great speed and in great comfort to the market centres, places of sport and entertainment, and to cities far afield. Silver craft flew high in the sky, soaring above the mountains and the clouds, carrying merchants to distant lands and conveying inquisitive travellers to exotic locations.

Houses were supplied with piped water, with gas for heating, with thin glass fibres to carry pictures and data, with the electric current to power the magical machines that helped with the cleaning and cooking in home and kitchen. Heating and lighting were provided at the touch of a switch. Waste water and sewage were piped away invisibly and hygienically to processing plants far away.

None of the city dwellers and very few of the country people worked on the land. They had no need to give up their spare time in the summer months to help bring home the harvest. Crops were gathered in by a handful of people with a wonderful array of machines to sow the seed, to cut the corn, and to thresh, bale, and bag the produce of the land. Food arrived at the market place fresh, hygienically packaged, and ready to eat. Medical treatments were assisted by marvellous diagnostic equipment that could create

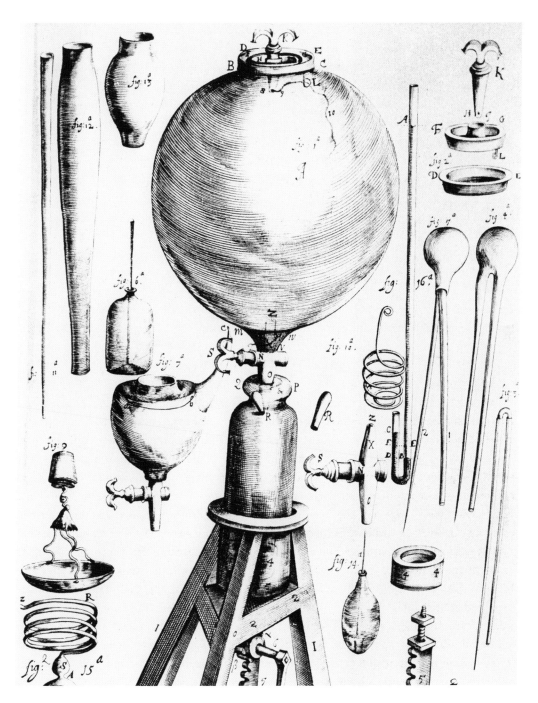

ABOVE Robert Boyle's air pump, as illustrated in his book *New Experiments Physio-Mechanical*. Robert Boyle was one of the pioneers of modern science. His law and experiments earned him the title of Father of modern chemistry.

a three-dimensional image of the inside of the human body. Cures were available for many diseases, and the understanding and prevention of these diseases kept illness to a minimum. The unravelling of the structure of the DNA molecule, the decoding of the chromosomes and the human genes, were rapidly unlocking the secrets of life itself.

Those of us who live in the third millennium know that our world is not a Utopia. The selfish use of energy in the developed world and the great pressures which over-population has created on our environment are quickly using up resources that have taken millions of years for nature to create. The relentless increase in the world's population has led to pollution in the industrialized world and to war and famine in the third world. Even so, to our ancestors living on the same planet a mere dozen generations ago, the twenty-first century with its technological miracles would appear as a Utopia.

There are times when we must stand aside and ask how our brave new world came to evolve. Where did the knowledge, the understanding, and the techniques originate which enable us to harness the forces of nature so effectively? In the space of a single lifetime the elderly have seen living standards improve beyond all recognition, and the same sentiments were expressed a hundred years ago. Many nationalities and many sciences have made important contributions to the technological progress but where was the starting point and what were the significant advances? Did it all begin in the ancient world? Was it born in the Renaissance? Was it the harnessing of power and the Industrial Revolution that marked the turning point? Was it the understanding of electricity and electronics? In the twentieth century the development of the digital computer was a key factor. All these have played their part but, before significant progress could be made, knowledge had to advance beyond the empirical methods of the ancient world. The laws of nature, the laws which governed the chemical, physical, and biological reactions, had to be discovered, formulated, and applied before the world could advance beyond the hand-to-mouth existence of the Middle Ages.

The horseless carriage is powered by a gas, rapidly compressing and exploding in a controlled fashion inside a cylinder. The changes in temperature, volume, and pressure are too complex to be explained by Boyle's law but it was the Irish physicist and chemist, Robert Boyle (1627–91), who took a critical first step towards the formulation of the gas laws. The suspension of the carriage, which gives the occupants a smooth ride over the roughest terrain, is designed by computer software using finite element analysis to define and analyse the stress and strain relationships. The calculations are far in advance of the simple law concealed in an anagram by the English scientist, Robert Hooke (1635–1703), but Hooke's law defines the basic principle from which the characteristics of any flexible structure can be calculated. What are the torque and thrust generated by the engine of the car and what are the forces on the vehicle that determine its speed, acceleration, and cornering? What exactly do we mean by the terms thrust, force, and acceleration? We can go on to ask the same questions of the aeroplane which flies at great height and great speed across the skies even though it is heavier than the air in which it flies. What are the laws that govern the aerodynamics of the aircraft?

What of the communications' satellite transmitting data from its place high above the Earth? What are the laws which govern its orbit and which determine its position above the surface of the earth? What is the action and reaction principle of the rocket that puts the satellites into orbit, the same rocket motors which launch the space probes to explore the world outside the Earth, the planets of the Solar System, and the space beyond?

Those who lived only a dozen generations ago inhabited a world where the tending of animals and crops created full-time employment for the great majority of the population. A bad year and a bad harvest made the difference between survival and starvation. Fuel had to be collected and stockpiled for the winter, and only the wealthy had more than one hearth with which to heat their homes. Lighting for the rich was by candle, for the poor it was the rush-light, the firelight, or the moonlight. The risk of plague and fire was always present for rich and poor alike, particularly in the cities and the centres of population. Wooden sailing ships had crossed the world's oceans but neither the new seas nor the new lands were fully explored. The new world across the Atlantic was slowly being explored and settled but those who were literate enough to write to their cousins in the American colonies were fortunate to get a reply in a matter of months if they ever received one at all.

In the seventeenth century there existed an elite few who could spare the time to be interested in the study of natural phenomena. The universities had good libraries where the thoughts and experiments of earlier workers were published for those who were fortunate enough to have access to the books but they did not offer degrees in engineering, science, or even in natural philosophy. Some had the vision and the foresight to know that it was possible to create a better world for future generations. The more practical among them wanted to improve agriculture and manufacturing processes, the more philosophical wanted to discover the laws that governed the Universe. Although they used the words 'natural philosophy' rather than 'science' to describe the laws of nature, they have a claim to be the founding fathers of modern science. Among the first philosophers of the Renaissance were the astronomers Copernicus (1473–1543), Kepler (1571–1630), and Galileo (1564–1642). Early in the seventeenth century Italy was far ahead of its rivals but the concern of the Roman Catholic Church stifled progress, and the main thrust of the scientific Renaissance moved from the Mediterranean countries to northern Europe. The Dutch, the Germans, the French, and others all made important contributions to the new knowledge and a few lesser contributions had been made by the British nations. By the middle of the seventeenth century, however, the English had progressed so rapidly that, for several generations, England became the main contributor to the new knowledge.

This is a story of the English scientific Renaissance.

I

WOOLSTHORPE

THE BABE WHOSE BIRTH EMBRAVES THIS MORN,
MADE HIS OWN BED ERE HE WAS BORN.

Richard Crashaw (1613-1649)

IT WAS LATE ON CHRISTMAS EVE 1642 when Hannah Newton first felt the contractions. The child would be premature for it was not expected to arrive until January or February. But the contractions became regular and persistent – it became obvious that the child would be born very soon. Hannah's mother, Margery Ayscough, hurried over from the nearby village of Market Overton to assist with the birth, and the festive preparations had to be shelved as Christmas Day approached. The babe entered the world in the small hours of the morning. The infant was a male child. He was small and weak and his head sagged limply to one side. He was so tiny that it seemed as though his little body would fit into a quart jug.

Two local midwives were despatched from the Manor House at Woolsthorpe to the house of Lady Packenham in North Witham to obtain supplies for the premature new arrival. The parish registers tell their own story of the terrible and inevitable infant mortality rates of the seventeenth century. There were plenty of women around who had borne ten or twelve babies of whom only one or two, or sometimes none at all, survived for more than a few days. The women were in no hurry for the supplies, they probably dawdled at the stile and exchanged gossip as they walked. They thought it very unlikely that Hannah Newton's frail infant would still be alive on their return.

When the midwives returned to Woolsthorpe their fears proved unfounded. The baby was still breathing. Christmas Day, the sabbath, came and passed by and Hannah Newton's child was still alive. He needed a bolster to support his head; he was small and frail, but having entered the world, he had inside him the will to live. On the first day of January the local parson arrived at the Manor House to baptize the child. It was very natural that his mother should name him after his deceased father, Isaac Newton.

The cold midwinter of 1642 was not the best of times to be born. Civil war had broken out in England and it was the dominant and most pressing problem of the times. Families and local communities were deeply divided in their loyalties to the Crown or to Parliament. Parties of soldiers and deserters foraging for food and shelter were all too common in the village of Woolsthorpe, which lay on the Great North Road, and in the surrounding countryside where minor skirmishes were breaking out all the time. Hannah Newton could have done without the problems of the Civil War; she belonged to the silent majority of people who prayed only for peace. Emotionally she needed Isaac, her firstborn child; he was

ABOVE Woolsthorpe Manor. A rural painting from the eighteenth century. Woolsthorpe was a substantial farmhouse but a small manor house. The house still retains its original character but the dormer windows in the roof have been removed. Compare this picture with the modern photograph on page 57.

all she had left from a marriage that had been all too short. She had married Isaac Newton in the April of 1642, the marriage was consummated soon afterwards but, after only six months of married life, she became a widow. She experienced marriage, bereavement, and birth in the space of nine months.

The manor of Woolsthorpe lay in the parish of Colsterworth, deep in the countryside of south Lincolnshire. It was near the source of the River Witham which flowed through Woolsthorpe to Grantham and from there it meandered on to Lincoln where it fed the Roman Fossdyke canal and helped to drain the Lincolnshire Fens before entering the sea at the Wash near Boston. The Great North Road branched off from the Roman road of Ermine Street at Woolsthorpe and met the Witham again at Lincoln. The character of the land was one of low rolling hills and rich green valleys, very different from the flat and watery landscape of the fenlands which began a few miles to the East. The occasional exposed hill boasted a windmill and some of the streams drove a water mill though wind power was beginning to replace water for grinding the corn.

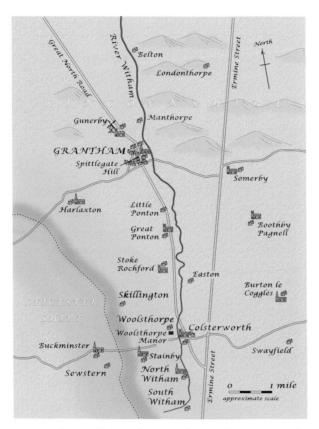

ABOVE A map of Newton's county, showing three routes to the North, Ermine Street, the Viking Way and the Great North Road. Most of the places shown are mentioned in the text.

The Newtons' manor of Woolsthorpe was very typical of the area, it consisted of good arable and pastoral farmland.

The late Isaac Newton, husband of Hannah, was Lord of the Manor of Woolsthorpe. It sounded a grand title and it was sufficient to place him on the lowest echelon of the country gentry, but Woolsthorpe was a very small manor and, in practice, within the social pecking order in seventeenth-century England, the Newtons were little more than yeoman farmers. But the family was well established in the area and, when Isaac Newton was born in 1642, he became the sixth generation of settlement in Woolsthorpe and the third generation to own the manor. The family name probably originated from Newton-le-Willows in Lancashire, but they had been farming in Colsterworth Parish at least since 1561 when John Newton of Westby is recorded as purchasing a cottage with a few acres of land at Woolsthorpe. The land descended from John Newton to his son John, from John the second to his son Richard, and from Richard Newton to his son Robert. Each generation prospered through hard rural toil and, by the time Robert Newton became an adult, he was wealthy enough to purchase the Woolsthorpe Manor. It was Robert's son Isaac who married Hannah Ayscough in 1642. When Isaac Newton Senior died, his goods and chattels were valued at £459 12s 4d, he had a flock of 234 sheep, 46 head of cattle, and a good harvest of oats, barley, and malt. This would have been seen as a small but significant sum by the peers of the realm but, at a time when the average farm labourer took home ten to fifteen pounds a year, it was a fortune by the standards of the poor. Hannah Newton had domestic servants and she had labourers to work the farm. She had a substantial and well-built stone manor house. She had a supportive family. She was therefore of independent means, and she was able to spend a little on small luxuries and time in bringing up her infant son. Nothing seemed less likely than the idea that Hannah Newton's small child could change the world. Neither his father's nor his mother's side could boast a relative higher in the social order than a country parson. They had no aspirations to politics or leadership, business or commerce, literature or art – they were the rural yeoman farmers who for generations had scraped a living from the soil. Every developing child displays an interest in the world around, the inquisitive examination of the world by sight, sound, and touch, the pleasure of toys and trinkets and pretty rounded pebbles from the seashore. So it must have been with Hannah Newton's child, but his curiosity about the world around him was far beyond the normal. When he matured he was driven by an insatiable desire to know more about the physical nature of the world and of the universe into which he was born.

For three years young Isaac enjoyed the undivided attention of his doting mother but Hannah Newton did not grieve for her deceased husband for ever. She was still of child-bearing age and her looks attracted the attention of one Barnabas Smith, the rector of the neighbouring parish of North Witham. Rector Smith was sixty-three years old and he too was alone and a widower. His advanced age and marital experience, however, did nothing to improve his confidence with the fair sex, and his idea of wooing was decidedly unromantic. There do not seem to have been any preliminaries to his courtship. He wanted to make an approach to Hannah but he did not have the nerve to do so. He eventually got as far as writing a letter asking Hannah if she would marry him but he lacked the confidence to deliver the letter himself and he paid his servant a day's wages to deliver the marriage proposal on his behalf.

In the small community of Woolsthorpe, Barnabas Smith was not a stranger to Hannah Newton. He was a wealthy man and, when she received his proposal of marriage, she did not accept or reject it immediately. It seems that she decided to treat it as a commercial proposition. She consulted her family, particularly her brother William Ayscough who was the incumbent of the neighbouring parish of Burton Coggles, and her parents James and Margery Ayscough. The family got together and thrashed out the pros and cons. Barnabas Smith was an elderly man with a considerable estate and he would probably not live for many years. His case was supported by a substantial income of 500 pounds a year over and above his rector's salary. The family negotiated a businesslike deal, Hannah was to marry Rector Smith and move to North Witham, but the plan was for three-year-old Isaac to remain in the Newton home at Woolsthorpe with his grandparents, James and Margery Ayscough. It cannot have been welcome news to young Isaac that he was to lose his mother's affections to an older male, particularly if his mother abandoned him to his grandparents, as appears from the arrangements. Some psychologists, eager to prove the hypothesis that Isaac Newton's phenomenal intellectual output was due to a great trauma in his early childhood, have interpreted this incident as the main reason for Newton's outstanding intellectual achievements. Others have taken an almost opposite view: that such a creative genius was the result of a close and lasting personal relationship between mother and son.

It seems unlikely that Barnabas Smith, who was too diffident to make a direct approach to Hannah for her hand in marriage, would risk offending his new wife by putting his foot down and refusing to have her precocious three-year-old in the house. Hannah Newton was certainly not the type of woman completely to abandon her first-born child – at that time her only child – at such a tender age. It made sense for the married couple to live at North Witham where the rectory came with Barnabas Smith's job, but it also made sound economic sense to keep on the manor house at Woolsthorpe. Barnabas Smith paid for repairs to the house, and Hannah's parents moved in to live there, but the house belonged to the Newtons and as it was the legacy of Isaac's father, it would therefore belong to young Isaac when he inherited from his mother. A more plausible theory than the total abandonment hypothesis is that young Isaac lived with his parents at North Witham until he was old enough to attend the dame schools at Skillington and Stoke Rochford. He may then have lived mainly with grandparents at Woolsthorpe because it was nearer to the schools. In practice the manor house at Woolsthorpe was little over a mile from the rectory at North Witham, there were duties to be performed at both places, and the most likely scenario is that the houses were jointly occupied by three generations of Ayscoughs, Newtons, and Smiths – a typical

Newton of Woolsthorpe and Colsterworth

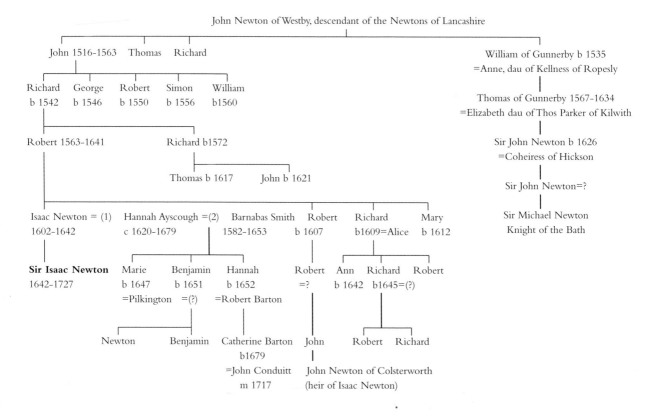

extended family of the period.

It was true, that at the age of three young Isaac no longer enjoyed his mother's total attention, but at that age a father figure and the stimulus of other children would be good for his development. At the age of nineteen he kept a private journal in which he listed fifty-one sins written in Shelton's shorthand (the very same shorthand that Samuel Pepys used for his private diary). It was obvious that, as a young man, Isaac Newton still felt guilty about many incidents from his childhood. Perhaps the worst of these was 'Threatening my father and mother Smith to burn them and the house over them' – an incident that had

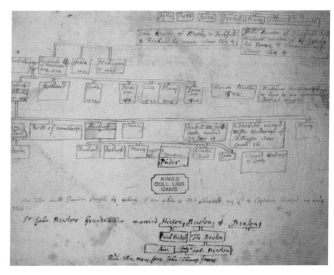

ABOVE A manuscript showing some of Newton's own genealogical researches. It is now in King's College Library, Cambridge. Keynes Ms 112/4

probably generated one of the harshest parental rebukes in his young life. He was only ten when his stepfather died so the incident was an outburst of childish anger. His other sins are more trivial and they shed light on some of the domestic scenes which show that his mother (and not his grandparents) was the dominant figure in his childhood. They include 'robbing my mother's box of plums and sugar', 'peevishness with my mother', 'punching my sister', 'refusing to go to the close at my mother's command', and 'falling out with the servants'. He shows a great obsession with the Sabbath, and his listed sins included 'eating an apple in Thy house', 'Making a mousetrap on Thy day', 'Twisting a cord on Sunday morning', and 'squirting water' on the Sabbath – he does not tell us with what or at what he squirted the water! He confesses to 'idle discourse on Thy day and at other times', 'Not loving Thee for Thyself', 'Fearing man above Thee', and many other sins against God. These adolescent misdemeanours read like the results of a strict Puritan upbringing. They are thoughts rather than actions, but many of Newton's contemporaries would have seen them as sinful and they throw some light on the deep religious upbringing of the times. Even in his first year at Cambridge, when he helped a colleague to make a 'water watch', he considered this friendly action to be a sin because the time was after midnight on a Saturday, it was the Sabbath!

Most of Newton's biographers have assumed that he hated his stepfather but, if we exclude the ambiguous sin of 'Wishing death and hoping it to some' then the only evidence to support this theory is his childish threat to burn down the house. It is possible that Barnabas Smith was actually a good role model for Isaac Newton.

The rector certainly had an excellent library of books, which Newton eventually inherited, and he must have been the major factor in Newton's devout religious upbringing and his puritanical beliefs. Barnabas Smith probably also contributed to Isaac Newton's high moral principles and his fascination with theology. The fact that, when in his sixties, Barnabas Smith fathered three children by Hannah Newton implies a successful marriage. Isaac Newton always accepted his half brother and half sisters as part of his family even after he had left them far behind on the social scale. Isaac did not reject everything his stepfather stood for.

At the little dame schools in Skillington and Stoke Rochford, Isaac Newton learnt the basics of reading, writing, and elementary arithmetic. It was during these years of early education that he acquired a stepsister Marie (b. 1647), a stepbrother Benjamin (b. 1651), and a second stepsister Hannah (b. 1652). Barnabas Smith died in the year after his third child was born. The rectory at North Witham then became the residence of the new rector. Thus, from 1653, Woolsthorpe Manor became the only home of the Smith/Newton/Ayscough family.

Isaac did not show exceptional promise at his first schools but, at the age of twelve, two years after the death of his stepfather, his academic standard was sufficient to gain him entrance to the Free Grammar School of King Edward VI at Grantham. The school at Grantham was not as grand as its title may suggest. It certainly taught Latin and perhaps some Greek grammar as did all the country schools aspiring to the title of 'grammar' schools. It had only one master – in Newton's time the post was filled by John Stokes – and the academic standard varied every time a new schoolmaster took office. The school received a charter under Edward VI, but it had been in existence for perhaps two centuries before the reign of the boy king and three centuries before Isaac Newton attended. In Newton's time, the building appears to have consisted of only a single schoolroom and the number of pupils fluctuated greatly but it was never more than one master could handle on his own. By comparison with other country schools in the area, Grantham had a good reputation. William Cecil was an old boy of the school and, just before Newton's time, Henry More, whom Newton came to know when he went up to

LEFT A stark view of one of the rooms at Woolsthorpe Manor. Showing the fireplace and a recess or cupboard in the far wall.

Cambridge, was educated there.

The market town of Grantham lay about 8 miles north of Woolsthorpe. It was too far from Isaac's home for a comfortable daily journey, and he was therefore provided with lodgings at the premises of an apothecary, Mr Clark, who lived next door to the George Inn on the High Street. The apothecary was married to a Mrs Storer, and living in the household were the three Storer children Arthur, Edward, and Catherine – they were Mrs Storer's children from her previous marriage and therefore stepchildren to Mr Clark. The new school and new surroundings were a great stimulus to young Isaac and the children provided him with new companions. The apothecary's shop held many fascinations for him, and it seems that Mr Clark was generous and patient in teaching his new, keen-eyed and inquisitive lodger about his trade.

Isaac Newton quickly made an impression on his schoolmaster, John Stokes, who discovered that his latest charge was a very capable but rather eccentric student. The boy could learn very quickly when he decided to apply himself but, for most of the time, he seemed to become deeply involved in schemes of his own which had little or nothing to do with the school curriculum. He got along tolerably well with his school-fellows but he was picked upon by the school bully from the class above him. The account is given by John Conduitt, one of Newton's early biographers who, out of a misguided sense of respect, always refers to him as 'Sir Isaac' in deference to a knighthood that was conferred fifty years later:

> *As soon as the school was over he challenged the boy to fight, & they went out together into the church yard, the schoolmaster's son came to them whilst they were fighting and clapped one on the back & winked at the other to encourage them both. Though Sir Isaac was not so lusty as his antagonist he had so much more spirit and resolution that he beat him 'til he declared he would fight no more, upon which the schoolmaster's son bad him use him like a coward, and rub his nose against the wall & accordingly Sir Isaac pulled him along by the ears and thrust his face against the side of the church.*[1]

The bullying episode does not seem quite in character for a boy with a nature as studious as that of Isaac Newton but, in his list of his sins, he recorded 'beating Arthur Storer' as one of them. This entry seems not only to confirm that the story was true but we also discover that the school bully lived in the same household as Isaac Newton – he was none other than the stepson of Mr Clark the Grantham apothecary. A second anecdote shows another side of his relationship with his schoolfellows. The story is told by William Stukeley and it can be dated precisely to the day that Oliver Cromwell died in September 1658; it is therefore a later episode describing Newton as a youth of fifteen. Stukeley has the same problem as Conduitt in that he also insists on calling the boy 'Sir' Isaac.

On the day that Oliver Cromwell dy'd, there was a very great wind or tempest over the whole king-
dom. That day, as the boys were playing, a sett of them were leaping. Sir Isaac, tho' not otherwise
famous for his activity at that sport, yet observing the gusts of the wind, took so proper an advantage
of them as surprizingly to outleap the rest of the boys.[2]

Once again the story has the ring of truth to it and the exact day adds to the authenticity. Stukeley is probably correct to assume that Isaac Newton normally took little
interest in sport. It is, however, very much in character for him to work out the pattern in the gusts of wind. Perhaps he was aware of the wind rustling through a nearby copse of trees as it approached. He was able to predict correctly when the wind
would reach its maximum strength and to use his knowledge to outleap his
competitors.

At the nearby village of Gonerby a new windmill was under construction, and it
became a pleasant excursion for people from Grantham to walk to Gonerby to watch
the building work. Young Newton was fascinated to see the method of construction,
the gearing of the mill, and how the power of the wind was harnessed to grind the
corn. It seems that the millwrights were happy to answer the boy's many questions:

A walk to this new windmill was the usual amusement of the town of Grantham. The multitude
return'd with some satisfaction to their curiosity, but little improvement in their understanding, and it
was the common rendezvous of the schoolboys. Newton's innate fire was soon excited. He was early
with the workmen, carefully observed the progress, the manner of every part of it, and the connexion
of the whole. He obtain'd so exact a notion of the mechanism of it, that he made a true and perfect
model of it in wood; and it was said to be as clean a piece of workmanship as the original.[3]

The anecdote shows clearly where the boy's interests were focused. Isaac loved making models of all kinds, and he acquired saws, hammers, chisels, and a complete set of
woodworking tools. The model windmill worked well, and he decided to modify the
mill to his own designs. He replaced the sails with a treadmill and installed a mouse to
grind the corn. He complained jokingly that the miller ate up all his profits.

Young Newton loved to carve figures and diagrams on wood and stone. His garret
room in Grantham High Street was covered with carvings, with pictures of birds,
beasts, men, ships, plants, and with mathematical figures. In the best adolescent tradition he carved his initials on the desks and forms at school, a pastime that doubtless
got him into trouble with John Stokes. His home at Woolsthorpe contained handiwork
from his earlier childhood, including a very simple wall carving of a post mill which
may have been the mill at Gonerby, and a church which is thought to be St Wulframs
at Grantham. The long-suffering Clark family of Grantham also had to put up with his
first forays into astronomy. Pegs were driven into the walls, strings were attached to the

pegs, and lines were drawn all over the walls. Any wall which received sunshine during the day was given the peg and string treatment, and Isaac was then able to tell the time to within a quarter-of-an-hour whenever the sun shone and whatever the season of the year. He was already making a detailed study of the Sun's motion through the sky.

> ...*tying long strings with running balls upon them, and the like contriveances, in order to find out the periods and conversions and elevations of the luminary: and [he] made a sort of almanac of these lines, knowing the day of the month by them, and the suns entry into signs, the equinoxes and solstices. So that Isaacs dyals, when the sun shined, were the common guide of the family and neighbourhood.*[4]

His mechanical ingenuity appeared again when he constructed a wooden clock powered by weights. It was a copy of an existing clock but, as with the model windmill, he wanted to modify the design and he went on to construct a clock on an entirely different principle – a water clock regulated by the flow of water from a cistern. The mechanism was very simple, with a float driving a rack-and-pinion motion, but it was said to keep very good time. He built a second clock on a similar principle but he discovered that there was a limit to the accuracy which could be obtained with a water clock. 'The chief inconvenience attending it was this', he claimed much later in his life. 'The hole thro' which the water drops must necessarily be extremely small, therefore it was subject to be furr'd up by impuritys in the water. So hour-glasses made with sand will wear the hole thro' which it is transmitted bigger. These inconveniences in time spoil the use of both instruments.'

Young Newton's total involvement in his mechanical projects tended to make a recluse out of him. On holidays he was busy cutting and sawing at his latest project rather than playing on the common with his schoolfellows. We now know that Newton purchased a book called *The Mysteries of Nature and Art* by John Bate which described how to make many of the contrivances that he constructed. This discovery lessens his precocity to some extent but, like the list of sins, it is valuable in confirming the accuracy of many of the childhood anecdotes. He was very creative at making improvements to the models and, when his schoolfellows took to flying kites, Isaac was quick to join them, characteristically producing some of his own improvements and novelties:

> *He was particuarly ingenious at improving all their usual diversions; for instance in the fabrick of their paper kites, in finding out their proportions, figure, the best point of fastning the string, in how many places, the length of the tail, and the like. And as an omen of the sublimity of his discoverys, he invented the trick of a paper lanthorn with a candle in it, ty'd to the tail of a kite. This wonderfully affrighted all the neighbouring inhabitants for some time, and caus'd not a little discourse on market days, among the country people, when over their mugs of ale.*[5]

Isaac Newton's closest friend during this formative part of his life was not one of his schoolfellows but Catherine Storer, the apothecary's stepdaughter. She was about two years his junior, and he enjoyed using his creative skills to make little cupboards, tables, and chairs on which Catherine and her friends could put their dolls and trinkets. It was a role that he seemed to enjoy, possibly because there was none of the competitiveness that could sometimes make him unpopular with other boys.

Young Newton's creative talents were developing rapidly when his enjoyable school-days came to a sudden end. In 1659, when Isaac was sixteen, his mother Hannah decided that he was old enough to be taught the running of the farm which was to be his future. The boy had reached a most difficult age: he suffered from all the problems associated with adolescence and, in addition, absent-mindedness. His first duty, was look-ing after the sheep and his second was the weekly excursion to Grantham on market day to sell the farm produce and to make purchases for the household and the farm. His idea of looking after the sheep was to hide under a bush with his nose in a book or to take his knife and to fashion a part for his latest wooden water mill. On 28 October 1659 the manorial records of Colsterworth fined Isaac Newton 3s 4d for 'suffering his sheep to break the stubbs of 23 loes [loose] furlongs'. When Isaac was sent to the Saturday market at Grantham to sell the farm produce and to buy the necessities for the follow-ing week, he left one of the farmhands to transact the business while he visited his friend Mr Clark at the apothecary's shop. The good-natured Mr Clark had recently inherited some books from his brother and he allowed Isaac free access to them. On subsequent visits to the market Isaac simply stopped under a hedge to read while his servant transacted the business for him.

One day the youth arrived home carrying the horse's bridle but without the horse which should have been attached to it. Isaac had dismounted to lead the horse up Spittlegate Hill on the road out of Grantham but his mind was so immersed in some problem of his own that he had walked all the way back in a trance without even notic-ing that the horse had slipped the bridle. These incidents must have driven poor Hannah to her wits' end. She had lost two husbands and now, as soon as her oldest child had reached an age to take on some responsibility, he was constantly causing problems, los-ing valuable sheep and essential horses, and incurring fines at the manorial court. The youth hardly ever managed to turn up on time for meals for he was always so absorbed in his own childish thoughts and projects which he should have outgrown at the age of sixteen. What was she to do with the boy? She discussed the matter with her brother William Ayscough and also with Isaac's former schoolmaster John Stokes.

Perhaps they could make a parson out of him? But he didn't seem to have the nec-essary common touch. Perhaps he could become a schoolmaster? John Stokes spoke highly of Isaac's academic ability and pressed Hannah to let the boy try for university. Stokes was full of enthusiasm for the idea and he was even prepared to waive the school fees of forty shillings. William Ayscough, Hannah's brother, supported the schoolmaster's plans for his nephew. Despite his adolescent problems, Hannah did not want to lose her boy but she eventually agreed that university was a way forward and luckily she had no real financial problems about furthering his education. Isaac seemed to agree willingly enough to this suggestion. John Stokes was so pleased to have Isaac back again that he took him as a boarder in his own house. In 1660, when most boys would have been delighted to see the back of their schooling, Isaac Newton returned to Grantham, the oldest boy in the school, under special tuition to gain entry into Cambridge.

It was a great year for the Royalist supporters when Charles II returned from exile to claim his throne as King of England. It was also a good year for Isaac Newton. He had tasted the fruit from the tree of knowledge and he willingly accepted the help given to him by John Stokes and by his own family. As the oldest boy in the school, he was a little isolated but he had always been something of a loner and this did not trouble him. He enjoyed being able to see the Clark family again and he had access to the apothecary's library as well as any books that John Stokes could procure for him. His friendship with Catherine Storer blossomed to such an extent that they contemplated marriage. Stukeley gives us a glimpse of Catherine Storer much later in life, showing that the friendship lasted long after Isaac Newton left home:

> Sir Isaac and she being thus brought up together, it is said that Sir Isaac entertained a passion for her when they grew up; nor does she deny it. 'Tis certain he always had a great kindness for her. He visited her whenever in the country, in both her husbands days, and gave her, at a time when it was useful to her, a sum of money. She is a woman but of middle stature, of a brisk eye, and without difficulty we may discern that she has been very handsome.[6]

Thus Catherine claimed to be engaged to Isaac Newton when he left home for Cambridge, and there seems no reason to deny her claim. But, as his career developed, Catherine Storer's fiancé developed other passions which left him with little time for the opposite sex. For some reason the engagement seems to have been broken by mutual consent but they still retained the friendship of their childhood. Stukeley's phrase 'in both her husbands days' refers to Catherine's two marriages – she became firstly Mrs Bakon and later Mrs Vincent but never Mrs Newton.

In the summer of 1661 Isaac was offered a place at Trinity College, Cambridge. His childhood and his adolescence were over, and his entry into the adult world, after his failure as a farmer, was still an undergraduate life away. It was July when the country boy left his home and his family for the journey of fifty miles to Cambridge. As Hannah Newton Smith saw her son leave the security of the home on the road to the south she must have wondered and hoped that her first born would make something out of himself in the great world outside Woolsthorpe.

2
OXFORD

TIME WILL COME, WHEN THE INDEAVOURS OF AFTER AGES, SHALL
BRING SUCH THINGS TO LIGHT AS NOW LIE HID IN OBSCURITIE. ARTS
ARE NOT YET COME TO THEIR SOLSTICE. BUT THE INDUSTRIE OF
FUTURE TIMES, ASSISTED WITH THE LABOURS OF THEIR FOREFATHERS,
MAY REACH THAT HEIGHT WHICH WEE COULD NOT ATTAINE TO.

John Wilkins (1614-1672)

OUR STORY MOVES not to Cambridge but to her great rival Oxford.

Oxenford was the place where the River Thames became the Isis and where the waters of the Cherwell joined a confluence of riverlets to create a myriad of lesser streams and a complex of green watery meadows. Travellers from the east entered the city over the arches of Magdalene Bridge to find themselves in the High Street, leading to the Carfax at the central crossroads of the town. The Carfax was surrounded by a complex of narrow medieval streets. The towers and spires of the colleges, churches, and chapels huddled in these straggling lanes competing with one another for their learning and their antiquity. The waterside meadows and the spacious quadrangles of the colleges contrasted sharply with the busy and crowded streets. The university was the second oldest in Europe, acknowledging only the Sorbonne in Paris as an earlier foundation and, in the seventeenth century, it could already claim four hundred years of academia.

Oxford could also boast to have held a Royal Court. This was not by choice. It was thrust upon the people in the troubled times of the English Civil War when Charles I made the city his headquarters. Loyalty to the Crown had to be penalized during the Interregnum, and heads rolled as town and gown took time to reorganize and to recover from the ordeal of being on the losing side. By the middle of the 1650s, however, some semblance of normality was beginning to return to the university town.

The Oxbridge philosophy was that universities existed for Divinity, Law, and Physic in that order, and the idea of studying anything outside this curriculum was alien to the members of the old school. Anthony à Wood may not be the best authority on Oxford during the Interregnum, but he is certainly the most entertaining. In his autobiography, he criticizes the 'new learning', by which he meant the great ferment of religious and political ideas that circulated at Oxford during and after the time of the Civil War. The new philosophies were an inevitable outcome of the Cromwellian regime:

> 'Tis well knowne that the Universities of this land have had their beginnings and continuances to noe other end but to propagate religion and good manners and supply the nations with persons chiefly professing the three famous faculties of Divinity, Law, and Physick. But in these late times when the dregs of people grew wiser then their teachers, and pretended to have received revelations, visions, inspirations, and I know not what, and, therefore, above all religion ordinarily profest, nothing could satisfie their insatiable desires but aiming at an utter subversion of them, church, and schooles, or those places that they thought might put a curb to their proceedings. Intelligent men knew and saw verie well that it was their intent to rout up all and to ruine those things that smelt of an Academy, never rejoycing more then when they could trample on the gowne and bring humane learning and arts into disgrace...
>
> Some there were also that made it their common practice to preach against them, stiling them 'the nurseries of wickedness, the nest of mutton tuggers, the dens of formall droanes'; ever and anon stiling the Colledges and Halls 'cages of uncleane birds'; and such like. Nay there were not wanting some also that said the like expressions, or to that purpos, publickly from the pulpit even in the Universities themselves . . .[1]

The ancient seats of learning were certainly great centres of old learning but, by the seventeenth century, Oxford and Cambridge could no longer claim a monopoly of the intellectual activity in England. In London, Gresham College had been founded in 1598 as an establishment very different from Oxford and Cambridge. Gresham College had professors but no undergraduate students. It offered public lectures on a wide variety of subjects. It was founded with the object of advancing useful knowledge such as navigation and manufacturing processes. There was common ground with the astronomy and mathematics taught at Oxford and Cambridge but not with the classics and theology.

The Oxbridge graduates could quote Virgil and Horace at great length. They could regurgitate long tracts from the Bible, correctly quoting book, chapter, and verse. They could enter into interminable theological controversies and long debates on Greek philosophy but, when it came to practical knowledge, the upstart Gresham College put them to shame. The Londoners were well aware of the fact that in many fields of knowledge they were well ahead of the traditional universities. Their view of the Oxbridge pedagogues is expressed in the 'Ballad of Gresham Colledge', coloured by the wit of Joseph Glanville:

The Colledge, Gresham, shall hereafter
Be the whole world's Universitie,
Oxford and Cambridge are our laughter;
Their learning is but Pedantry.
Those new colleagues doe assure us,
Aristole's an Asse to Epicurus.

The noble learned Corporation
Not for itselfe is thus combyn'd
But for the publique good oth' Nation
And general benefit of Mankynd.
These are not men of common mould;
They covet fame but contemn gold.
Joseph Glanville[2]

In the 1640s when the Civil War created a divided England, a small group of enthusiasts began to meet in London to discuss matters of natural philosophy. The group consisted mainly of academics from Gresham College, and it became known as the 'invisible college' because it had people but no buildings and no material possessions. Early in the 1650s two of the group's most active members, John Wallis and John Wilkins, were given new posts at Oxford to replace some of the unfortunate academics who supported the losing side during the Civil War. These two newcomers were the prime movers in setting up the Oxford Philosophical Society. The Invisible College continued to meet in London for a few years after the departure of Wallis and Wilkins to Oxford, but the philosophical interests in London declined rapidly without these leading lights. At this time it happened that there were a number of brilliant men at Oxford and, for about a decade, the tables were turned and it was Oxford which became the leading centre of 'scientific' activity.

In his *History of the Royal Society* Thomas Sprat acknowledged the importance of the Oxford group as a forerunner of the Royal Society, and his history records the names of the prominent men among their number:

Nor were the good effects of this conversation, onely confin'd to Oxford: But they have made them-
selves known in their printed Works, both in our own, and in the learned Language: which have much
conduc'd to the Fame of our Nation abroad, and to the spreading of the profitable light, at home. This
I trust, will be universally acknowledge'd, when I shall have nam'd the Men. The principle, and most
constant of them, were Dr Seth Ward, the present Lord Bishop of Exeter, Mr Boyl, Dr Wilkins, Sir
William Petty, Mr Matthew Wren, Dr Wallis, Dr Goddard, Dr Willis, Dr Barthurst, Dr Christopher
Wren, Mr Rook: besides several others , who joyn'd themselves to them, upon occasion...[3]

As well as boasting the earliest university college in England, Oxford claimed a first with a lesser establishment – in this same decade it boasted the first coffee houses in the country. Oxford's first coffee drinker was a Cretan called Nathaniel Conopius of Balliol College who imported the coffee beans and made his own coffee. Conopius was 'sent hither' in 1648 for the terrible sin of consuming caffeine but, by that time, it was too late to stamp out the habit, coffee was still being consumed by others, and a public coffee house was opened by Jacob the Jew in 1651. Jacob was sufficiently notorious to gain a mention in the Life and Times of Anthony à Wood:

> This year [1651] Jacob a Jew opened a coffey house at the Angel in the parish of S. Peter, in the East Oxon; and there it was by some, who delighted in noveltie, drank. When he left Oxon he sold it in Old Southampton buildings in Holborne neare London, and was living in 1671.[4]

Anthony à Wood mentions four 'berrys' at the University of Oxford. One is Arthur Berry of Exeter College, known as 'black-berry' because of his dark complexion; another is Amos Berry, alias 'ale-berry', a great 'ale bibber' of Corpus Christi; the third is Richard Berry, 'goose-berry', of Christ Church described by Wood as 'a simple hot-headed coxcombe'; and lastly there is Phineas Berry, alias 'coffey-berry' who is a great coffee drinker and who was a fellow of Wadham College. The coffee bean was usually referred to as the 'coffee berry' at this time and we shall see that Phineas Berry was a pioneer in what became a great tradition of his college. It was predictable that Cromwell's Puritans would not approve of the new Turkish drink. The real problem was not the caffeine, it was the fact that, from its very inception, the coffee house was a place for freedom of speech. It was an ideal place to spend a few hours holding the meeting after the meeting of the day and to argue the pros and cons of the current topics of the times. It seemed to provide something that the tavern did not provide – or perhaps the tavern supplied alcohol which the coffee house did not supply and this was the reason why philosophical debates were more productive when they were fuelled by coffee rather than by the strong ales of the tavern. In the eyes of the Puritans free speech was an even greater sin than alcohol and the reputation of the coffee house was as bad, if not worse, than that of the tavern. They saw it as a place where heretical creeds and dangerous political theories could be expounded, and they were outraged by the vain and carefree attitude of the coffee drinkers. Cromwell's regime tried to stamp out the free speech by closing down all the coffee houses but, luckily for those who had become addicted to the new habit, the Restoration came along before the new laws could be put into effect.

Fellows and students alike took to the new fashion and, in 1655, an apothecary called Arthur Tillyard, who had a reputation as a 'great Royalist', opened a coffee house near All Souls College. Among the caffeine addicts was a promising youth of twenty-one called Christopher Wren – he had graduated from Wadham College four years earlier and became a fellow of All Souls in 1653. Christopher Wren came from a family with very good connections and with strong ecclesiastical traditions. His father, who was the rector of East Knoyle in Wiltshire, was made chaplain to Charles I and, later in life, became the Dean of Windsor. The son's greatest contribution to Oxford, the Sheldonian Theatre, was still several years in the future and, in his youth, Christopher saw himself as a mathematician and an astronomer rather than a designer of buildings. In the 1650s his architectural skill was very much in its infancy but he had designed a glass beehive which was one of several conversation pieces at Wadham College.

Wren was a slightly built young man of average height and straight carriage, but his fellow coffee drinker appeared a far less promising prospect. His name was Robert Hooke, a young man about three years Wren's junior who entered Oxford as a Christ Church chorister but who had yet to acquire a degree. Hooke was a sickly looking youth. His body was slightly deformed and he had lank, mousy hair but his appearance was misleading: his eye was bright and he had a very sharp and active mind. In spite of his ailing health, Hooke still managed to be a man bristling with energy, full of new ideas and enthusiasm. Both men were educated at Westminster School before coming to Oxford. Wren left school at about the same time as Hooke arrived at Westminster but their schooling, their university connections, and their common interests created a bond between them that lasted a lifetime.

Like Wren, Hooke came from an ecclesiastical family. He was born at Freshwater on the Isle of Wight where his father was the local minister. As a child he suffered from persistent headaches which made his father despair of his plans to train his son for the ministry. When left to his own devices, the boy showed a great talent for making mechanical devices. He constructed a working wooden replica of a clock and a model man-of-war which could sail fully rigged and fire a salvo. When his father died in 1648, Hooke's family sent the thirteen-year-old boy to London where he had a stroke of good fortune. He was befriended by Richard Busby, one of the masters of Westminster School, who recognized the boy's potential and took him into his home to tutor him privately. Robert Hooke easily matched up to Busby's expectations. He mastered Latin and Greek, and his passion for geometry was such that he devoured the first six books of Euclid within a week. He claimed that he could play twenty pieces on the organ and that he had invented thirty different ways of flying. His flying machines never advanced beyond the drawing board but his talents were recognized by his tutors and, in 1653, at the age of eighteen, he was accepted as a chorister at Christ Church Oxford.

Wren and Hooke were the youngest members of the Oxford Philosophical Society, also known as the Oxford Experimental Club, a body of enthusiasts who held regular meetings at Wadham College. The meetings took place in the rooms of John Wilkins, the master of the college. Wadham College was founded in 1612 by Nicholas Wadham; in the 1650s it was the second youngest college in the university and only Pembroke (1642) was of a more recent foundation:

Nicholas Wadham, founder of Wadham Coll. Oxon., was wont often to say to one Mr. Orang a neighbor of his (who was accounted a wise discrete man in that country) that 'he had a good estate and had noe children to leave it too, and his kindred to whome he thought to leave his estate did not care for him.' 'Why' (said Mr. Orang) 'doe as Sir Tho. Bodley hath lately done. As he hath built a library, soe you build a College and you shall be remembred every day. It will last from generation to generation.' Soe Mr. Wadham proceded and did all according to his counsell.[5]

It is perhaps no great surprise to find that Nicholas Wadham's college was the most forward-thinking college of its time – one reason being that it was not as steeped in ancient learning as were many of the older colleges. John Wilkins was keen to embrace new and radical ideas, not in the fields of religion and politics but in natural philosophy. As we have seen, he had been a member of the Invisible College in London and he was one the academics from Gresham College who moved to Oxford in the late 1640s to replace the unfortunate Royalists who lost their livings at the close of the Civil War. Wilkins' character is glowingly described by his half brother, Walter Pope:

…he was a Learned Man, and a Lover of such; he was of a Comely aspect and Gentleman-Like Behaviour…He had nothing of Bigottry, Unmannerliness, or Censoriousness, which were then in the Zenith amongst some of the Heads, and Fellows of Colleges in Oxford. For which reason many Country Gentlemen, of all Persuations, but especially those then stiled Cavaliers and Malignants, for adhering to the King and the Church, sent their Sons to that College [Wadham] that they might be under his Government.[6]

John Wilkins was certainly very open minded in matters of politics and religion, a very rare philosophy for these troubled times. He was well known to have Royalist sympathies and this was the reason why Cavalier families chose to send their sons to Wadham College – but it was no secret that, despite his Royalist leanings, he was married to the sister of Oliver Cromwell! Anthony à Wood, his contemporary at Oxford, described Wilkins in less glowing terms, as a smooth-talking flatterer, and he gives us a brief résumé of his subsequent career after leaving Oxford:

Dr John Wilkins, a notorious complyer with the Presbyterians (from whom he obtained the wardenship of Wadham); with the Independents: and Cromwell himself, by whose favour he did not onlie get a dispensation to marry (contrary to the College statute) but also (because he had married his [Cromwell's] sister) Master of Trinity College in Cambridge. From which being ejected at the restauration, faced about and by his smooth language, insinuating preaching, flatteries, and I know not what, got, amongst other preferments, the deanery of Rippon; and at length (By the commendation of George Viliers duke of Buckingham, a great favourer of fanaticks and atheists) the bishoprick of Chester.[7]

The fact that John Wilkins eventually became Bishop of Chester shows that his religion was orthodox, but his greatest asset was that he was against political and religious persecution of any kind. This was the main reason why his career advanced during the Interregnum and after the Restoration. Thomas Sprat described how Wilkins helped to create the Oxford Philosophical Society:

> It was therefore, some space after the end of the Civil Wars at Oxford, in Dr. Wilkins his lodgings, in Wadham College, which was then the place of resort for Vertuous and Learned Men, that the first meetings were held which laid the foundation of all this that follow'd. The University had, at this time, many Members of its own who had begun a free way of reasoning; and was also frequented by some Gentlemen, of Philosophical Minds, whom the misfortunes of the Kingdom, and the security and ease of a retirement amongst Gown-men had drawn thither. Their first purpose was no more, then onely the satisfaction of breathing a freer air, and of conversing in quiet one with another, without being engaged in the passions and madness of that dismal Age…
>
> …invincibly armed against the enchantments of Enthusiasm…For such a candid and impassionate company as that was, and for such a gloomy season, what would have been a better subject to pitch upon than Natural Philosophy? To have been always tossing about some Theological question would have been to have made that their private diversion the excess of which they themselves disliked in the public.[8]

By the 'gloomy season' Sprat meant the Commonwealth years.

The Oxford Philosophical Society was greatly influenced by the book *Novum Organum* [New Methodology] written by Francis Bacon (1561–1626) and published in 1620, and also by Bacon's later works such as the *New Atlantis* which was published in 1626. Bacon's thinking was very advanced for his times. He supported the heliocentric theory of Copernicus and he performed a number of scientific experiments on a wide range of subjects. He conducted experiments on heat using a primitive thermometer and he tried to focus heat rays using a burning glass based on the same principle as the magnifying glass. He discovered that water could not be compressed. He put forward a tentative theory of planetary wind circulation based on the heating influence of the Sun. His interests were wide and he made calculations of the national wealth.

Francis Bacon's genius was that he was able to recognize the shortcomings of the academic world of his time. The academics would spent a lifetime studying the ancient world and arguing about Greek philosophy. The story was told that they would spend hours discussing the number of teeth owned by a horse but they would not condescend to look in the horse's mouth and count them. The thought of examining nature itself or of gaining knowledge from practical experiments was believed by the Greeks to be a perfectly good occupation for underclasses and slaves, but it was considered beneath the aristocracy. The method of the Greek philosopher, Aristotle (384–322 BC) was to state a set of assumptions and use them to arrive at a conclusion. Aristotle had been the tutor of Alexander the Great and Alexander had conquered the whole of the civilized western world. This was the reason why the teachings of Aristotle were carried across the whole of the Hellenistic world and they were considered sacrosanct for nearly two thousand years. But Francis Bacon recognized that Aristotle's assumptions were frequently wrong and, in these cases, the conclusions drawn from them were of no use at all. He made the very obvious suggestion that knowledge should be advanced by the study of nature rather than by reading the works of the ancients and studying pure philosophy. He saw the academics of his time as having advanced very little beyond the medieval monks in their monastic cells. In academic terms the cloisters of the Oxbridge colleges were akin to those of the monasteries that Henry VIII had dissolved in the previous century:

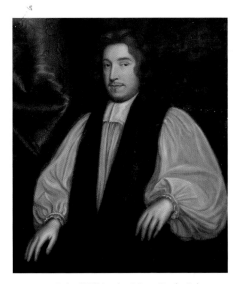

ABOVE John Wilkins by Mary Beale. John Wilkins was the master of Wadham College and in the 1650s the pioneering Oxford Philosophical Society met in his rooms. The gatherings included John Wallis, the young Christopher Wren, Robert Hooke and Robert Boyle all of whom went on to become active members of the Royal Society.

This kind of degenerate learning did reign chiefly amongst the Schoolmen: who, having sharp and strong wits and abundance of leisure, and small variety of reading, but their wits being shut up in the cells of a few authors (chiefly Aristotle, their dictator), as their persons were shut up in the cells of monasteries and colleges, and knowing little history, either of nature or time, did out of no great quantity of matter and infinite agitation of wit, spin out unto us those laborious webs of learning which are extant in their books. For the wit and mind of man, If it work upon matter, which is the contemplation of the creatures of God, worketh according to the stuff, and is limited thereby; but if it work upon itself, as the spider worketh his web, then it is endless, and brings forth, indeed, cobwebs of learning admirable for the fineness of thread and work, but of no substance or profit.[9]

Bacon was impressed by practical men like Columbus, who had sailed into the unknown and discovered a new continent, and by Galileo who had reinvented the telescope and used it to discover new worlds in the skies and to provide a practical aid to seamen. His belief in the radical philosophy of expanding knowledge, by making unbiased observations of natural events, was a field of knowledge that became known as Natural Philosophy.

ABOVE Robert Boyle by Johann Kerseboom. Robert Boyle came to Oxford in 1656 and some of the meetings of the Oxford Philosophical Society were held in his rooms on the High Street. He is well known for his law relating the volume and the pressure of a gas, but he acknowledged that Richard Towneley was the discoverer of the law.

Returning from Francis Bacon to John Wilkins, we find that some of his early scientific contributions included pioneering work on a universal language. In 1638 Wilkins wrote a *Discourse on the Discovery of a New World in the Moone* in which he created a great controversy in theological circles by claiming that the Moon could be another inhabited world! In this book, which was very far reaching in its scope, he gives his own opinion of Aristotle and put the philosophy of the new science very clearly into perspective. At one point he refers to standing on the shoulders of the ancients, which makes it appear that Isaac Newton must have read and been influenced by the passage. Newton would certainly agree with Wilkins's sentiments that there were still many things left in nature to be discovered:

I thinke the world is much beholden to him [Bacon] for all its sciences. But yet 'twere a shame for these later ages to rest our selves meerly upon the labours of our forefathers, as if they had informed us of all things to be knowne, and when we are set upon their shoulders, not to see further than they themselves did. 'Twere a superstitious, a lazie opinion to think Aristotles works the bounds and limits of all humane invention, beyond which there could be no possibility of reaching. Certainely there are yet many things left to discovery, and it cannot be any inconvenience for us, to maintaine a new truth or rectifie an ancient errour.[10]

The Oxford Philosophical Society did not keep formal minutes, and we are therefore lacking in detailed accounts of their meetings, but we have an excellent description of some of the members from the pen of the diarist John Evelyn (1620–1706)who visited Oxford in July 1654. Wren's glass apiary with its 'castles and palaces' was already a conversation piece, as was Wilkins's curious talking statue of which Evelyn soon discovered the secret. Evelyn was so taken with the glass beehive that John Wilkins generously presented him with a spare one for his own use. The diarist met the architect of the apiary, Christopher Wren – he evidently made a good impression for the 'prodigious' young scholar presented him with a white piece of marble artistically stained with a red dye:

We all din'd, at that most obliging and universaly Curious Dr Wilkins, at Waddum, who was the first who shew'd me the Transparent Apiaries, which he had built like Castles and Palaces, and so order'd them one upon the other as to take the Hony without destroying the Bees: These were adorn'd with variety of Dials, little Statues, Vanes etc: very ornamental…

He had also contriv'd an hollow Statue which gave a Voice, and utterd words, by a long conceal'd pipe that went into its mouth, whilst one spake thro it at a good distance, and which at first was very Surprizing:

He had above in his Gallery and Lodgings variety of Shadows, Dyals, Perspe[c]tives, places to introduce the Species, and may other artificial, mathematical, Magical curiosities; A Way-Wiser, a Thermometer, a monstrous Magne[t]s, Conic and other Sections, a Balance on a demie Circle, most of them of his owne and that prodigious young Scholar, Mr Chr: Wren, who presented me with a piece of White Marble, which he had stain'd a lively red, very deepe, as beautiful as if it had been naturall.[11]

Prominent among the Oxford members was Robert Boyle who hosted some of the early meetings of the Oxford Philosophical Society at his house on High Street. Boyle spent many of his early years in Geneva, and he was twenty-nine years old when he arrived at Oxford in 1656. It was natural that he should join the Philosophical Society for he had been influenced by Bacon to such an extent that he made what many would consider an heretical claim – that he could learn more about stones by talking to masons and stonecutters than from the writings of Pliny and Aristotle.

Boyle knew of Otto Guericke's experiment in 1654 with the Magdeburg Hemispheres. Guericke constructed two large hollow bronze hemispheres which fitted closely together with a seal. He extracted the air from between the hemispheres, then harnessed two teams of eight horses to pull them apart, but the sixteen horses could not separate the hemispheres against the pressure of the air. Boyle knew that Guericke had constructed a pump to extract the air from the hemispheres, and he made it one of his first tasks to design a similar pump of his own. Boyle's pump had a glass chamber so that it could be used to observe experiments in a low-pressure environment. With Robert Hooke as his assistant, Boyle constructed a successful air pump and, in one of his first experiments, he was able to prove that air was needed for life and for combustion. There was much discussion at the time about the character of a vacuum: many believed that nature abhorred a vacuum and that an empty space could not exist. Boyle showed that the space over a column of mercury, as demonstrated by the Italian physicist, Evangelista Torricelli (1608–47), at the Accademia del Cimento in Florence, was indeed empty and that it was a better vacuum than he could achieve with his air pump. Boyle's first publication of his work was his *New Experiments Physico-Mechanicall, Touching the Spring of the Air and its Effects* which was printed in 1660, and it is valuable as a description of many of the experiments originally performed at the Oxford Philosophical Society.

Robert Boyle is remembered from his law relating the pressure and the volume of a gas. His law and his experiments earned him the title of the father of modern chemistry. It was he who first conceived the world as a piece of clockwork. 'Like a rare clock, where all things are so skilfully contrived, that the engine being once set a Moving all things proceed according to the Artificer's first design . . .' He wrote that the world behaved 'as if there were diffused through the universe an intelligent being'. Boyle's years in Geneva had left him as a very religious man, and in his will he left money for what he called the 'confutation of atheism'.

Robert Hooke tells us a little about the meetings of the Society and, in particular, Boyle's 'Pneumatick Engine' which was demonstrated in 1655. He expresses his reservation that much of the knowledge gained by these researches was lost because no minutes were taken. The results were not written up for posterity and consequently knowledge was continually having to be rediscovered:

> At these meetings, which were about the Year 1655 (before which time I knew little of them) divers Experiments were suggested, discours'd and try'd with various successes, tho' no other account was taken of them but what particular Persons perhaps did for the help of their own Memories; so that many excellent things have been lost, some few only by the kindness of the Authors have since made publick; among these may be reckon'd the Honourable Mr Boyle's Pneumatick Engine and Experiments, first printed in the Year 1660.[12]

Anthony à Wood gives us a very entertaining glimpse of Wadham College some years later when he was invited to dine there by the courtesy of a Mr Lloyd. Wood had recently published his book *Athenae Oxonienses* with its priceless anecdotes of seventeenth-century life in Oxford, but his writing was so blunt that he gave offence to many of the people to whom he referred. He makes mention of John Wilkins, who by then had become the Bishop of Chester, and also Thomas Sprat who wrote the first history of the Royal Society. It appears that the host chased his guest around the room brandishing the spit from the roasting meat:

> I sup'd with the warden of Wadham at his lodgings, Mr. Lloyd being with me. He desir'd Mr Lloyd to bring me with him. He gave me roast meat and beat me with the spit. He told me that my book was full of contumelies, falsities, contradictions, and full of frivolous stuff, viz. what need was there of saying that Dr. John Wilkins was married, or that he was promoted to the bishoprick of Chester by commendation to the king of the duke of Bucks, or that Dr. Thomas Sprat was chaplain to the duke of Bucks, etc. : that every snivelling fellow should undertake to write of secret matters of state' (meaning that I should, forsooth, take notice of Buckingham's commendation of Wilkins). He also said that 'if he had been vice-chancellour, he would (instead of buying and printing the book) have caused it to be burned.' He had the book there and read it scornfully.

After wee had sup'd and all took away and servants gone. Mr Warden drunk to Mr Lloyd, and told him that ; 'he should pledge him in claret': but the bottle being set on the side table, I was made an offer to fetch it. Whereupon he said 'twas clownish, rude and uncivill to doe so': that 'Scholars were generally clownes.' But who was more clowne? I, or the warden? – he, for abusing me and my book in his lodgings; I, for my humility. A fool. Puppie, child![13]

It is not possible to assign a specific date to the scientific renaissance in Europe, and each country would want to assign a different date to honour its leading contributors. We remember only the successful experiments and those that led on to greater things. We forget the frequent negative results, many of which were essential in pointing the way forward by a process of elimination. It is evident that by 1660 there were many who were struggling to embrace a scientific method into their research. The Oxford group brought together some brilliant men and achieved great fame and leadership for a short decade, and their failure to continue as leaders is attributed to the breaking up of the group. There were other reasons that seem obvious with hindsight. Seth Ward, for example, realized that the Society did not have a proper catalogue or index of the work already carried out in the various fields of philosophy, and he set about trying to create a scientific catalogue of all the works in the Bodleian Library. At no time did the Society take any formal minutes and record the details of its meetings. The Society had no publication in which to advertise its findings to parties who did not attend their meetings nor to those outside Oxford who were interested in their achievements. The ferment of ideas needed more than demonstrations and enthusiasm, it needed a formal structure for the recording and distribution of knowledge.

Later in the 1650s the Oxford Group began to split up. Robert Hooke moved to London where he eventually became professor of geometry at Gresham College. Others were also drawn to London for various reasons. In 1657 Christopher Wren moved to Gresham College as professor of astronomy but he returned to Oxford four years later when he was offered the Chair of Savilian Professor of Astronomy. Years later he again moved back to London and eventually he became President of the Royal Society.

It was in the following decade, the 1660s, that a philosophical society was formed which undertook all the formalities of minutes and publications that were lacking at Oxford. The new society was formed in the largest centre of population in England where the wealthiest patrons lived and where there was access to centres of trade and industry as well as to centres of learning such as Gresham College. The stage was set in England for the next chapter of the scientific revolution. The new society also enjoyed the status of royal patronage. In 1660 the monarchy had been restored and England was ready for the creation of the Royal Society.

3

THE ROYAL SOCIETY

I HAVE TAKEN ALL KNOWLEDGE TO BE MY PROVINCE.

Francis Bacon (1561-1626)

FEW CITIES HAVE EXPERIENCED the turmoil that London suffered in the seventeenth century. But, in spite of the English Civil War, religious conflicts, interregnums, restorations, plague, and pestilence, the population of London increased steadily throughout the century and, by 1660, the number of inhabitants exceeded four hundred thousand. The city had long since burst out of its medieval city walls and had sprouted suburbs on all sides – predominantly on the north and west. Within the old city the streets, lanes, and alleyways contained thousands of timber-framed houses ranging from spacious town houses to cramped, depressing slums, often with rich and poor living cheek by jowl. A wealthy person owned a whole house which, if he or she was lucky, was set back from the street frontage with a private garden at the rear. The poor were fortunate to have more than one dingy room in a shared house. Merchants, artisans, tradesmen, and craftsmen lived side by side and plied their trade in a thousand tiny premises: they were all part of the teeming mass of humanity that inhabited the capital city of England. Painted wooden gables overhung the cobbled streets where the upper stories jettied out to overhang the pavements below. Inn trade signs swung overhead: the grasshopper of the money changers, the three balls of the pawnbroker, the metalwork of the ironmonger, and the scissors of the tailor. Conduits of wood and stone carried water to the houses, and an open drain in the centre of the street carried refuse and sewage away to the river. A hundred small churches shared the cramped streets with the houses and taverns, and every hour heard a great cacophony of sound as all the churches' clocks chimed in and out of unison. Public buildings stood alongside the company halls of the many jealously guarded guilds of the city. The alleyways by the river – above and below the solitary bridge – led to a ramshackle collection of wooden wharves where the cargoes of merchandise were unloaded at the riverside to supply the ever-increasing

ABOVE The view from Southwark across the Thames to London in about 1660, drawn by N de Visscher. Old St Pauls dominates the skyline with over a hundred lesser churches in the city. The artist shows plenty of period detail of the housing, London Bridge and the shipping in the Thames.

needs of London. The wider thoroughfares were frequented by coaches transporting the wealthy – they competed for road space with pedestrians, horses, mules, sedan chairs, labouring carts carrying humble provisions of all kinds, and sheep, cattle, and poultry on their way to the slaughterhouse.

On Ludgate Hill St Paul's Cathedral presided over its flock of a hundred parish churches. Old St Paul's, originated as a Norman cathedral of great beauty, had stood for nearly six centuries but it had undergone many changes in that time. The spire originally rose to a towering 450 feet (137 metres) above ground level but it had been struck by lightning in the previous century and only the supporting tower remained. The east nave had been rebuilt in a later Perpendicular style with impressive flying buttresses but much of the older fabric was badly in need of restoration. Inigo Jones (1573–c. 1652) designed a new west front, built of Portland stone, in the greatly admired modern style of the Renaissance. The new west front could hardly have been better designed to show a horrendous clash of architectural styles. It looked like a carbuncle on the old Norman cathedral but most people thought it a great improvement for few, if any, were prepared to recognize the architectural merits of any building from the Middle Ages. A much happier example of the new architecture was Inigo Jones's Banqueting House in

ABOVE Old St Paul's Cathedral by Wenceslaus Hollar. The picture dates from 1656, the perpendicular style can be seen on the right of the tower, the old Norman nave to the left. The tower originally carried a spire rising to 450 feet but in the sixteenth century it fell after a strike by lightening.

Whitehall, the finest building of its time, where thousands of Londoners still remembered seeing the execution of Charles I in 1649.

Westminster just managed to hang on to a semblance of countryside. The western suburbs, from the River Fleet to Westminster, were spacious and salubrious but Lincoln's Inn and everything to the west of it lay outside the city liberties. The eastern limit of the city of London was dominated by a building even older than St Paul's. Here the Tower of London stood sentinel, rising high above the nearby houses and still dominating the city around it, just as William the Conqueror had planned it should do six centuries earlier.

Half-a-mile upstream from the Tower was the only river crossing in London. It consisted of a motley collection of nineteen arches of assorted sizes, supporting a street of mismatched houses with smoking chimneys and gaps like missing teeth where houses had been demolished. The houses varied between solidly fashioned stone buildings of five stories to ramshackle wooden constructions of three or four floors, each with a built-on appendage overhanging the river at the rear and giving the only advantage of living on the bridge – the most efficient sewage-disposal system in London. The finest of these houses was Nonsuch House of seven stories with four cupolas, one at each corner, flying a flag at the highest point of the bridge. It dated from the time of Good Queen Bess and had been brought in sections from Holland for assembly on the bridge. The massive supporting bridge piers – fashioned by masons in an age when sheer bulk was the only solution to a structural problem – each had its own wooden surround, called a 'sterling' or 'starling', to protect against boats and current. The bridge was almost a dam. As the trapped river water tried to follow the outgoing tide, the rush of water through the narrow arches was like a mill-race and it took all the skill of the boatmen to take their craft through one of the arches. Indeed, at the northern end two arches were supplied with undershot water wheels where river and tidal power were used for several hours a day to raise the water into the conduits for distribution around the city. In the midst of the chaos was the chapel of St Mary Overie for travellers to rest and pray before entering the city from the south.

With the seething mass of humanity, livestock, horses, geese, and chickens, it took so long to pass across the bridge that it was far quicker to use one of the ferries to cross the river. Nobody, except the poor and the inquisitive with leisure time to spare, used the bridge by choice. Travellers were molested by beggars, paupers, hucksters, and peddlers. At the Southwark end the prostitutes joined the throng of hustlers. Here were the bear gardens, bull-baiting pits, places of sport and entertainment, taverns, whorehouses, and playhouses. Here, too, was the old gateway to the bridge, used since time immemorial to display to the public the rotting heads of traitors. Five hundred years earlier, and a hundred years later, London Bridge was still the only crossing of the River Thames – it was a bridge that managed at the same time to be the ugliest and most fascinating in the world!

London did not boast a university. But, as we have seen, at the end of the sixteenth century, Gresham College was founded with the legacy of Thomas Gresham (1519–79), the wealthy Tudor Merchant who founded the Royal Exchange. Gresham College was housed in solid stone premises at Bishopsgate, and built around a quadrangle in a similar style to the Oxford and Cambridge colleges. The college provided London with a badly needed centre of learning, and regular weekly lectures were given by resident professors on seven chosen subjects as diverse as Astronomy, Divinity, Music, Law, Medicine (Physic), Geometry, and Rhetoric. The college was well equipped and among its scientific instruments it boasted a telescope 36 feet (11 m) long. It survived the traumas of the Civil War and the Interregnum but such was the uncertainty of the times that, after the death of Oliver Cromwell (1658), the college was taken over as a barracks. Luckily this phase was short-lived and at the Restoration it returned again to its former function as an educational establishment. In 1658 Thomas Sprat wrote to Christopher Wren describing the terrible state of the college after the soldiers had left:

This day I went to visit Gresham College but found the place in such a nasty condition, so defil'd, and the Smells so infernal, that if you should now come to make use of your Tube, it would be like Dives looking out of Hell into Heaven.

Dr Goddard of all your colleagues, keeps Possession, which he could never be able to do, had he not before prepared his nose for Camp Perfumes, by his voyage to Scotland, and had he not such excellent Restoratives in the Cellar.

The soldiers by their Violence which they put on the Muses Seats have made themselves odious to all the ingenious world...[1]

The place had to be scrubbed, cleaned, and disinfected before the college could resume its previous function but, soon after the Restoration, a philosophical society began to meet at Gresham College on Wednesdays and Thursdays. The diarist John Evelyn was a member of this society and, in 1660, he attended the first meeting. He was nominated as a fellow of the society and because his nominee was the new king, Charles II, his election was a foregone conclusion:

I was now chosen (And nominated by his Majestie for one of that Council) by Suffrage of the rest of the Members, a Fellow of the Philosophical Society, now meeting at Gressham Coll: where was an assembly of divers learned Gent: It being the first meeting since the returne of his Majestie in Lond: but begun some years before at Oxford, and interruptedly here in Lond: during the Rebellion...[2]

Evelyn was well acquainted with King Charles and he was a major influence in obtaining royal patronage for the new Philosophical Society. In May 1661 the king was shown the Society's great telescope and, using it, he was able to see Jupiter with its satellites and the mysterious rings around the planet Saturn. The king was obviously impressed with what he had seen and the next week John Evelyn obtained a personal audience with him. 'His Majestie was pleased to discourse with me concerning severall particulars relating to our Society, and the planet Saturn etc: as he sat at supper in the withdrawing room to his Bed-Chamber', reads Evelyn's diary.

The king continued to show a great interest in the proceedings of the Philosophical Society and, in 1662, he granted a charter and allowed it to call itself the 'Royal Society of London for the promotion of Natural Knowledge'. A second charter was granted in the following year, and the Royal Society was granted a coat of arms and acquired a grand silver mace weighing 150 ounces (4.25 kg) after the fashion of Cromwell's 'bauble', the parliamentary mace. As a council member, John Evelyn was present on the occasion when Lord Brounker was appointed as the first president:

20 August 1662

I was this day admitted and then Sworne one of the present Council of the Royal Society, being nominated in his Majesties Original Graunt, to be of this first Council, for the regulation of [the] Society, and making of such Laws and statutes as were conducible to its establishment and progresse: for which we now set a part every Wednesday morning, 'till they were all finished: My Lord Viscount Brounchar being also, by his Majestie, our Founders, nomination, our first [President]: The King being likewise

pleas'd to give us the armes of England, to beare in a Canton, in our armes, and send us a Mace of
Silver guilt of the same fashion and bignesse with those carried before his Majestie to be borne before
our President on Meeting-daies etc: which was brought us by Sir Gilbert Talbot, master of his
Majesties Jewelhouse.[3]

The king himself attended an occasional meeting but he did not always display a great depth of knowledge on the subjects under discussion. When he discovered that Robert Boyle intended to demonstrate and measure the weight of the air, Charles found the idea very amusing. The king 'mightily laughed at Gresham College for spending time only in weighing of ayre and doing nothing else since they sat', wrote Samuel Pepys. The king was not alone in his ridicule, the pundits came up with some amusing rhymes to support him:

> *Their learned speculations*
> *And all their constant occupations,*
> *To measure wind, and weigh the air,*
> *And turn a circle to a square.*
> Samuel Butler

The charter instructed the society to elect its council and officers on St Andrew's Day, 30 November. This, too, generated some witty criticisms:

'Methought 'twas not so well that we should pitch it upon the Patron Saint of Scotland's Day', said John Aubrey to William Petty. 'We should rather have taken St George or St Isidore.' Isadore was a saint who also happened to be a philosopher.

'No', replied Petty who had his own view of the aims of the society. 'I had rather have had it been on St Thomas's Day, for he would not believe till he had seen and putt his fingers into the holes; according to the motto *Nullius in Verba.*'

The honour of being Europe's first scientific academy belonged to the Accademia del Cimento in Florence, founded in 1657. The Royal Society was founded in 1662 and claimed to be second. The French were close behind when the Académie des Sciences was founded in 1666. Several societies were formed in Germany but only the Berlin Academy, co-founded by the philosopher and mathematician Gottfried Leibniz (1646–1716), acquired international acclaim. All the societies were interested in the work of the others. There was an unwritten agreement that their knowledge should be published and shared but, at the same time, they were all intensely patriotic and jealous about their own claims to priority. It was common for leading members of one society to subscribe to one or more of the others and, when the Royal Society became well established, foreign visitors were common and they were invariably given a warm welcome.

The range of interests in the Royal Society was very wide. Many thought it was too wide for any society to encompass but the royal assent provided a marvellous boost, and membership increased among the social élite and the wealthy members of London society. Robert Hooke was appointed as the first curator. It was Hooke's job to provide experiments and demonstrations for every weekly meeting. The task of curator was an arduous and exacting one but Hooke was the ideal person for it and he carried out his duties very efficiently. Initially Hooke received no salary for his duties and it is difficult to see how he made a living in the first few years, but his efforts were recognized and, in 1664, he was voted an allowance of thirty pounds per annum plus expenses for his lodgings. This, together with his allowance of fifty pounds a year on his appointment as the Gresham Professor of Geometry, gave him an adequate income.

Among the early experiments were repetitions from the Oxford days, such as demonstrations of Torricelli's vacuum and Boyle's air pump. There were many anatomical and biological experiments and it was common for industrial processes, such as brewing, mining, and cloth refining, to be demonstrated. Some of the demonstrations were very bloody affairs. Dissections were common and vivisection was sometimes practised. Blood transfusions were carried out between different species and, on one occasion, a man was given sheep's blood without any obvious ill effects. There was a lot of interest in the origins and creation of life. The production of maggots from dead animals was studied in detail as an example of what some thought was a spontaneous generation of life. The boundary between science and folklore was still unknown. Medical cures were claimed by using the magnetism of the lodestone and, at one meeting, the Society solemnly sat around a table to see if a spider could escape from a circle of what was claimed to be powdered unicorn horn! The horn had been supplied by the Duke of Buckingham who obtained it from some unknown source. Its authenticity was not questioned, and items purporting to be parts of mythical beasts were readily available from the hucksters on many of the stalls of the fairs and street markets, having been brought from overseas by inquisitive or gullible sailors. The Royal Society adhered closely to its scientific principles, and experiments in pseudo-science became less and less common. Astrology was never practised and, though alchemy was still respectable, it was treated with caution because it was known to be rife with dubious recipes and practices. The charter defined the object of the Society as 'the improving of Natural Knowledge by experiment' and the word 'natural' was significant for it excluded the study of all things 'supernatural'. The two subjects forbidden at the Royal Society were politics and religion – in a century where both were in such great turmoil, it was obvious that nothing would be achieved unless these contentious topics were banned from the syllabus. It is not so obvious to understand why logic was also banned unless it was a deliberate attempt to exclude Aristotle. The second charter of the Society reads as follows:

> *To improve the knowledge of all naturall things, and all useful Arts, manufactures, Mechanick practises, Engines and Inventions by Experiments – (not meddling with Divinity, Metaphysics, Moralls, Politicks, Grammar, Rhetoric or Logick).*
> *To attempt the recovery of such allowable arts and inventions as are lost.*
> *To examine all the systems, theories, principles, hypotheses, elements, histories, and experiments of all things naturall, mathematicall and mechanicall, invented, recorded, or practised by any considerable authors ancient or modern. In order to the compiling of a complete system of solid philosophy for explicating all phenomena produced by nature or art, and recording a rationall account of the causes of things.*[4]

The Society stated clearly that it would not support any doctrine or hypothesis unless it had been proved by debate and experiment to the satisfaction of its members:

> *In the meantime this Society will not own any hypothesis, system or doctrine of the principles of natural philosophy, proposed or mentioned by any philosopher ancient or modern, nor the explication of any phenomena whose recourse must be had to originall causes (as not being explicable by heat, cold, weight, figure and the like as effects produced thereby); nor dogmatically define nor fix axioms of scientificall things, but will question and canvass all opinions, adopting nor adhering to none, till by mature debate and clear arguments, chiefly such as are deduced from legitimate experiments, the truth of such experiments be demonstrated invincibly.*[5]

The charter tried to control the direction of the research by choosing relevant topics and avoiding debate until sufficient experimental facts had been demonstrated:

> *And till there be a sufficient collection made of experiment, histories, and observations there are no debates to be held at the weekly meetings of the Society concerning any hypothesis or principle of philosophy, nor any discourse made for explicating any phenomena, except by the special appointment of the Society, or allowance of the President. But the time of the assembly is to be employed in proposing and making experiments, discoursing of the truth, manner, grounds, and use thereof, reading and discoursing upon letters, reports and other papers concerning philosophicall and mechanicall matters, viewing and discoursing of curiosities of nature and art, and doing such other things as the Council or President shall appoint.*[6]

Henry Oldenburg was appointed secretary and, on his own account, he began to publish the *Philosophical Transactions of the Royal Society* in March of 1665. This was an important innovation. The 'Transactions' included papers and abstracts by members of the society, correspondence and controversy, and notices of newly published scientific books. The *Philosophical Transactions* circulated throughout the scientific world. It was also common for members to produce their own publications, sometimes at their own

ABOVE Portrait of Henry Oldenburg by Jan van Cleef. Oldenburg was the first secretary of the Royal Society. He began to publish the *Philosophical Transactions* in 1665. He was an indefatigable correspondent and tried to generate interest and discussion in philosophical matters

expense and sometimes wholly or partly sponsored by the Royal Society. Thus, John Evelyn was interested in the lack of suitable timber for shipbuilding, and his book, *Sylva – a Discourse on Forest Trees*, was published in 1664. Hooke's masterpiece was his *Micrographia* which was published in 1665. It contained drawings of his observations through a microscope and was the first treatise to show details such as the cellular structure of cork. Hooke made full use of the microscope to show insects drawn in great detail: his readers were impressed with a 16-inch (40-cm) drawing of a louse attached to a human hair as well as an incredibly detailed picture of a common house-fly showing its compound eye. He described the creatures he saw through the microscope:

[the flea] The strength and beauty of this small creature, had it no other relation to man, would deserve description…But, as for the beauty of it, the microscope manifests it to be all over adorned with a curiously polished suit of sable armour, neatly jointed and beset with multitudes of sharp pins, shaped almost like porcupine's quills or bright conical steel bodkins…It has two…biters…shaped very like the blades of a pair of round-topped scissors and were opened and shut just after the same manner. With these instruments does this busy little creature bite and pierce the skin and suck the blood out of an animal, leaving the skin inflamed with a small round red spot.[7]

Christopher Wren assisted Hooke with his microscopic observations and he may well have made the illustrations – they were certainly of a very high standard of draughtsmanship. By this time, Wren was already very involved with architecture and, in 1663, he exhibited a model of the Sheldonian Theatre to the Royal Society. Wren was based back in Oxford as the Savilian Professor of Astronomy and, in this capacity, he had constructed a three-dimensional model of the Moon, complete with mountains and craters made to scale:

He has essay'd to make a true Selenography by Measure; the World having nothing yet but Pictures, rather than Surveys or Maps of the Moon. He has stated the Theory of the Moon's Libration as far as his Observations could carry him. He has composed a Lunar Globe representing not only the spots and various Degrees of Whiteness upon the Surface but the Hills, Eminences and Cavities moulded in solid work. The Globe thus fashioned into a true Model of the Moon, as you turn it to the Light represents all the menstrual phases with the variety of Appearances that happen from the Shadow of the Mountains and Vallies.[8]

John Evelyn was not the only diarist in the society. His friend, Samuel Pepys, became a member on 15 February 1665. With his job at the Navy Board, Pepys was a busy man. He was not a scientist; in fact, he had to employ a mathematician to teach him his multiplication tables, and his spare time was spent on theatres and mistresses rather than in scientific research. He was, however, a very able administrator and many years later, in the 1680s, he rose to become President of the Society. His diary is very valuable in that we sometimes meet members of the Society socially. It is through Pepys, for example, that we pick up gossip about Lord Brounker the first president, with whom he worked very closely at the Navy Office. Pepys could not help but observe the relationship between Lord Brounker and Mrs Abigail Williams, 'Who without question must be my Lord's wife, else she could not follow him wherever he goes and kiss and use him publicly as she doth'. Lord Brounker never married Mrs Williams but they had a stable and long-term relationship. Brounker died a bachelor but left most of his estate to 'Mrs Abigail Williams alias Cromwell'. Pepys had no right to criticize Lord Brounker's social life, for he had many mistresses of whom one Bagwell, the wife of a humble Deptford carpenter, was one of his favourites. Pepys could not resist her, and broke into pidgin French when he came to describe his attentions to her:

…finding Mrs Bagwell waiting at the office after dinner, away elle and I to a cabaret where elle and I have été before; and there I had her company toute l'après-dîner had mon plien plaisir of elle – but strange to see how a woman, notwithstanding her greatest pretences of love à son mari and religion, may be vaincu.[9]

Feeling that he had stepped over the line with Mrs Bagwell, Samuel Pepys resolved to contain his passions in the future but he did not have the willpower to make his resolution last for more than a month:

So I back again and to my office, where I did with great content faire a vow to mind my business and laisser aller les femmes for a month; and am with all my heart glad to find myself able to come to so good a resolution, that therby I may fallow my business, which, and my honour therby, lies a-bleeding[10]

In his diary he recorded his election to the Royal Society and, true to form, he adds plenty of gossip. His close association with Lord Brounker makes it appear that his lordship's name rhymed with 'drunkard' for Pepys refers to him with the consistent spelling 'Brunkard'. It is through Pepys that we discover the name of the Tavern behind the Royal Exchange to which the members adjourned for supper when the meeting was over. And we are also given a short potted opinion of the curator Robert Hooke.

Thence with Creed to Gresham College – where I had been by Mr. Povy the last week proposed to be admitted a member; and was this day admitted, by signing a book and being taken by the hand of the President, my Lord Brunkard, and some words of admittance said to me. But it is a most acceptable thing to hear their discourses and see their experiments; which was this day on the nature of fire, and how it goes out in a place where the ayre is not free, and sooner out where the ayre is exhausted; which they showed by an engine on purpose. After this being done, they to the Crowne tavern behind the Change, and there my Lord and most of the company to a club supper – Sir P. Neale, Sir R Murrey, Dr. Clerk, Dr. Whistler, Dr. Goddard, and others of eminent worth. Above all, Mr. Boyle today was at the meeting, and above him Mr Hooke, who is the most, and promises the least, of any man in the world that I ever saw.[11]

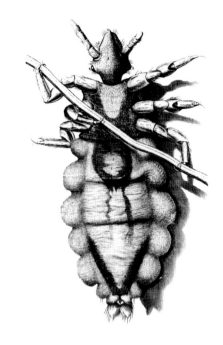

ABOVE Drawing of a louse from Hooke's *Micrographia*. Hooke was one of the first men make use of the microscope. When his greatly magnified drawings of insects and other objects were published in 1665 they showed details never seen before and made a great impression on the public.

John Aubrey, the author of Brief Lives, also knew Hooke personally. He gives us a description of his appearance which is in general agreement with that given by Pepys:

He is but of middling stature, something crooked, pale faced, and his face but little below, but his head is large; his eye full and popping, and not quick; a grey eye. He has a delicate head of hair, brown, and of an excellent moist curl. He is and ever was very temperate, and moderate in diet etc.[12]

Samuel Pepys had very recently purchased Hooke's *Micrographia* with its amazing pictures of insects as seen through the microscope. He was suitably impressed and described the work as 'the most ingenious book that I ever read in my life'. Hooke did not see Pepys as a rival and he graciously accepted the praise. Consequently, they were able to get along with each other on good terms. Pepys and Hooke were both of a sociable, gossipy nature, frequenters of taverns and coffee houses, always picking up the latest ideas and exchanging views with others. This was the best side of Robert Hooke: he was always full of enthusiasm and he was an excellent communicator, a jack of all trades and master of some. Pepys gives us a nice little anecdote about a casual meeting with Hooke on the street:

> ...discoursed with Mr Hooke a little, whom we met in the street, about the nature of Sounds, and he did make me understand the nature of Musicall sounds made by strings, mighty prettily; and told me that having come to a certain Number of Vibracions proper to make any tone he is able tell how many strokes a fly makes with her wings (those flies that hum at their flying) by the note that it answers to in Musique during their flying. That I suppose was a little too much raffined; but his discourse in general of sound was mighty fine.[13]

Some of Hooke's experiments had to be made outside the premises of Gresham College, such as when he wanted to prove that bodies weighed more when they were nearer to the centre of the Earth. He climbed one of the towers at Westminster Abbey and placed a set of scales high above the ground with a lump of iron and a long length of pack thread in one pan, and an exact balancing weight in the other. The iron was then carefully lowered on the thread almost to the ground with the thread tied to the balance. He could detect no increase in the weight of the iron. He repeated the experiment in St Paul's Cathedral but the result was still negative. The church authorities seemed to be very co-operative about using their buildings to further the cause of science. The weight difference he sought did, in fact, exist but it was far too small for him to be able to measure.

There remained much work to be done to shake off the prejudices of the Middle Ages. A new outlook was dawning but the new knowledge had done nothing to alleviate the sufferings of the poor, and living standards in London had changed very little since Tudor times. Medical understanding was minimal, it was almost impossible to sort out the sound knowledge from the folklore, and medical experimentation had made very little progress in the understanding of infectious diseases. The plague had last struck London in 1636 when ten thousand died, but only the middle-aged were old enough to remember it. Those over fifty remembered a worse outbreak in 1625 when the death toll reached 25,000 but no one thought that such a terrible epidemic could strike again. One day in June of 1665 Samuel Pepys noticed that some houses in Drury Lane each had a red cross painted on the door:

> This day, much against my Will, I did in Drury-lane see two or three houses marked with a red cross upon the doors, and 'Lord have mercy upon us' writ there – which was a sad sight to me, being the first of that kind that to my remembrance I ever saw. It put me into an ill conception of myself and my smell, so that I was forced to buy some roll-tobacco to smell to and chew – which took away the apprehension.[14]

It was early summer and, though the death rate from the plague was high, it was not significantly higher than at any other time. As the hot summer progressed, however, the number of plague victims increased steadily. July saw a noticeable increase in numbers and, by August, the disease had reached epidemic proportions with thousands dying every week:

> *Thus the month ends, with great sadness upon the public through the greatness of the plague, everywhere through the Kingdom almost. Every day sadder and sadder news of its encrease. In the city died this week 7496; and of them 6102 of the plague. But it is feared that the true number of the dead this week is near 10000 – partly from the poor that cannot be taken notice of through the greatness of the number, and partly from the Quakers and others that will not have any bell rung for them.*[15]

The plague had yet to reach its climax. Soon there were bonfires in the street every day as the goods and bedding from stricken homes were burned in an attempt to stamp out the pestilence. People were fleeing from the city by the thousand, some by boat and barge along the river, others with carts and wagons along the roads to the country. Funeral processions had to queue as they followed one after the other at each of the city's parish churches. Communal burial pits were dug outside the walls where the corpses of the poor were carried by cartload for burial. Pepys was able to move out of his house in Seething Lane to Woolwich where he could continue to perform his duties for the Admiralty, but he was still obliged to make regular visits to London and he was horrified by what he saw:

> *…to London to pack up more things thence; and there I looked into the street, and saw Fires burning in the street, as it is through the Whole City by the Lord Mayors order. Thence by water to the Duke of Albemarle. All the way fires on each side the Thames; and strange to see in broad daylight two or three Burialls upon the Bankeside, one at the very heels of another – doubtless all of the plague – and yet at least 40 or 50 people going along with every one of them.*[16]

The plague did not reach its climax until September. John Evelyn was appalled and frightened by the scenes that greeted his eyes in London. We discover that the *Duke of Albemarle*, mentioned by Pepys, was a hospital ship moored on the Thames; John Evelyn went to visit the ship:

> *Came home, there perishing now neere ten thousand poore creatures weekely: however I went all along the Citty and suburbs from Kent streete to St James's, a dismal passage and dangerous, to see so many Cofines exposed in the steetes and the street thin of people, the shops shut up, and all in mournefull silence, as not knowing whose turne might be next: I went to the D[uke]: of Albemarle for a Pest-ship, to waite on our infected men, who were not a few…*

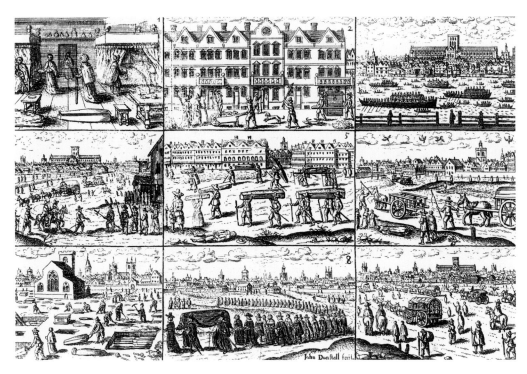

ABOVE In 1665 the worst plague since the Black Death struck London. Nine scenes are depicted here by John Dunstall. 1. Domestic household with sick bed and coffin. 2. Wheelbarrow carrying the humble dead. 3. Funerals of the wealthy on the Thames. 4. Fleeing from the stricken city. 5. Coffins and burials which occurred daily. 6. Carts, apparently carrying coffins. 7. A communal burial pit. 8. A long line of tall hatted mourners. 9. Returning to London after the plague.

...I went thro the whole Citty, having occasion to alight out of the Coach in severall places about business of money, when I was invironed with multitudes of poore pestiferous creatures, begging almes, the shops being universally shut up, a dreadful prospect...[17]

John Evelyn estimated that the death rate had risen to ten thousand a week. It was an overestimate but not a gross exaggeration. The council kept very detailed records within every parish showing that the rate peaked in the week of the twelfth to the nineteenth of September: the number of deaths reached 7690 of which 6544 were plague victims.

Shops and trading points were closed as tradesmen left the city. Many of those who stayed behind to trade contracted the plague themselves and died. The summer of 1665 was the worst in living memory. The death toll was more than seventy thousand in London alone and it far exceeded all the other plagues since the Black Death. Parliament moved out to Oxford, the Royal Exchange was closed, and the Royal Society was unable to meet again until the plague had done its worst.

4
CAMBRIDGE

YE FIELDS OF CAMBRIDGE, OUR DEAR CAMBRIDGE, SAY,
HAVE YE NOT SEEN US WALKING EVERY DAY?

Abraham Cowley (1618-1667)

A RECORD SURVIVES of Isaac Newton's expenses for his first journey from Woolsthorpe to Cambridge:

IMPENSIA PROPRIA[1]

	£	s	d
Sewsterne	0	1	0
Stilton	0	2	0
Cambridge White Lion	0	2	6
Carriage to the College	0	0	8
A chamber pot	0	2	2
A table to set down the number of my clothes in the wash	0	1	0
A paper book	0	0	8
For a quart bottle and ink to fill it	0	1	7
Income for a glass and other things to my Chamberfellow	0	0	9
	0	**12**	**4**

The chamber pot was an obvious necessity for a new student. Sewstern, the first place Newton mentions, was only about 3 miles from Woolsthorpe. Before he was born the land belonged to the Ayscoughs and it had been given to him by his mother. It lay just over the county boundary in Leicestershire and would give him an income of £50 per annum on the occasion of his coming of age. Stilton, situated on Ermine Street, was about half-way between Woolsthorpe and Cambridge, and is evidently the point where Isaac broke his journey. He may have chosen to ride all the way but the mention of the

ABOVE Trinity College, Cambridge in the seventeenth century from David Loggan's *Cantabrigia Illustrata* (1690). Newton's room was to the right of the gatehouse with an outside staircase and a garden to walk in. Cambridge University Library Ii 9.3

White Lion in Cambridge and the cost of carriage to his college implies that he made the journey by carrier.

In Tudor times the number of students at Cambridge was only a fraction of the number at Oxford but, by the time Isaac Newton arrived as a fresh-faced sizar, the numbers at Cambridge had increased four or five fold and there was no longer any significant difference between the university undergraduate populations. Trinity College was one of the main reasons for the increase: it had been generously endowed in the time of Henry VIII and it had grown to become the largest college in Cambridge. The neighbouring college of St John's was numerically second but it exercised great influence over Trinity by supplying the first four masters of the larger college. Newton's first impression of Trinity would have been the great gatehouse that guarded the large quadrangle and, in his time, most of the college buildings surrounded the quadrangle which was the main court of the college. The court was laid out with formal gardens, flanked on one side by the college chapel designed by Ralph Symons, and on the other three sides by living quarters, the library, common rooms, and other college buildings. The centre piece of the court was an elaborate hexagonal fountain dating from the earliest years of the century, with water supplied by a conduit passing beneath the river. The main court had changed very little when Celia Fiennes visited Cambridge later in the century:

> ...the town which lyes in a bottom and marshy ground all about it severall miles which is garnish'd with willows; the Buildings are old and indifferent and the Streets mostly narrow except near the Market place which is pretty spacious, there stands the University Church.
>
> Trinity Colledg is the finest yet not so large as Christchurch College in Oxford; in the first court there is a very fine fountaine in the middle of the Quadrangle with a carved top and Dyals around...the river runs at the back side of most of the Colleges; they have fine stone bridges over it and gates that lead to fine walks, the rivers name is Cam...[2]

Newton's room at Trinity College was shared with another fresher by the name of Francis Wilford: he is the 'chamber fellow' mentioned in the account, and a person about whom we know very little. In his list of sins (see Chapter 1), Newton admitted to 'Using Wilford's towel to spare my own', which is certainly a sin but, on the positive side, it might be taken to imply that he washed slightly more frequently than the average first-year student. Isaac Newton, a raw youth from the provinces, did not make a great impression on his fellows in his years as an undergraduate. He entered as a subsizar, which meant that he had to pay his way by performing menial tasks and errands for one of the fellows of the college. He was a reserved, fatherless country boy, and his accent and mannerisms would make no impression at all on the overconfident public school products who dominated the university and looked down their noses with contempt at any student who had to make his way through the college as a sizar. Those students who did not enter as sizars and subsizars were known as pensioners, a confusing nomenclature for those so young, but the term was used in the sense that their board and lodging were paid for and provided. The wasted years when his well-meaning mother tried to make a farmer out of him meant that Newton was eighteen and therefore about two years older than most of his fellow students. He was of a serious nature and he was more mature and studious than the typical first-year student. The high-living student life and the freedom enjoyed by the wealthy were not things in which he was able to participate fully and it may have been difficult for him to make friends. We are not certain for whom he sizared but it was probably Humphrey Babington, who was related by marriage to Mr Clark, the apothecary on the High Street in Grantham. If this is true then young Newton was fortunate, for Babington was not only personally acquainted with Newton's family but he also spent very little time in college.

Isaac Newton soon discovered that new students were not considered suitable people to borrow books from the library. The minimum requirement for a borrower was a Master of Arts degree, and his access to the library's great fund of knowledge which he so passionately desired was restricted to a few hours a week. His Grantham connections and his old school furnished him with introductions to certain of the Cambridge fellows, however, and it seems likely that Humphrey Babington and another Grantham acquaintance, the philosopher Henry More, were prepared to borrow books on his behalf. Newton's isolation in his first years at university probably did not trouble him unduly. He was not of a sociable nature, he was very self-sufficient and he enjoyed having time to himself to meditate. He was content to be lost in a book absorbing knowledge. Isaac's circle of friends was small. He did not appear to hit it off with his room-mate but he was accepted by Babington and More and he mixed well with the older fellows. His earliest surviving personal letter shows that he had at least one other close but unknown friend:

> *Loving Friend.*
> *It is commonly reported that you are sick. Truly I am sorry for that. But I am much more sorry that you got your sickness (for they say that too) by drinking too much. I earnestly desire you first to repent of your having been drunk and you to seek to recover your health. And it please God that you ever be well again, you have a care to live healthfully and soberly for time to come. This will be very pleasing to all your friends and especially to*
> *Your very loving friend*
> *I N.*[3]

If Newton himself did not pitch in with the university high life, then it seems from the letter that one of his friends did participate. Here we get a glimpse of the straight-principled Newton admonishing a colleague for being drunk. The undergraduates were banned from going to the local taverns but most of them had no problem about getting around the ban. There is no direct evidence that Newton himself frequented the taverns as an undergraduate but entries in his later accounts show that he was a customer in his early graduate years and it is therefore likely that he was familiar with more than one Cambridge tavern before that time.

By the time of Newton's second year at Trinity he had tired of sharing a room with Francis Wilford. He wanted privacy and he took to wandering around the walks and the quadrangles to meditate and to get time on his own. It was there that he met another student in a similar predicament: both were wandering aimlessly around the college grounds. This student was John Wickins whose father was the master of Manchester Grammar School. We are indebted to Wickins's son Nicholas for providing a second-hand account of the meeting between his father and Isaac Newton:

My father's intimacy with him came by mere accident. My father's first chamber-fellow being very dis-
agreeable to him, he retired one day into the walks, where he found Mr. Newton solitary and dejected.
Upon entering into discourse, they found their course of retirement the same, and thereupon agreed to
shake off their present disorderly companions and chum together, which they did as soon as they could,
and so continued as long as my father staid at college.[4]

Even though Wickins was a pensioner and Newton a mere subsizar who had to work
for his pension, the two struck up a very close friendship. The class distinctions between
students were generally upheld but there must have been plenty of exceptions to the
rule. John Wickins stayed at the college for twenty years. He was evidently a good-
natured and long-suffering friend for he put up with his room-mate's long periods of
absent-mindedness, he frequently assisted Newton with his many experiments, and in
later years he served as a copyist for some of his lengthy correspondence. Wickins does
not leave behind a first-hand description of Newton and, again, the account we have is
told many years later by John Wickins's son but it shows that eating and sleeping took
second place to Newton's search for knowledge:

I have heard my father say that he has been a witness of what the world has so often heard of Sir
Isaac's forgetfulness of his food when intent upon his studies; and of his rising in pleasant manner with
the satisfaction of having found out some proposition without any concern for seeming want of his
night's sleep, which he was sensible he had lost thereby.[5]

We know that Newton mastered most of the books required for his course. They included Sanderson's *Logic*, Kepler's *Optics,* and the works of Francis Bacon who was a graduate of the same college as Newton. Like many of his fellow students, Newton became
well acquainted with the local fairs and markets about Cambridge for these were the best
places to make purchases for his growing interests. He wanted to know more about
astrology and he purchased a book on the subject. The book gave instructions on how
to calculate the positions of the planets using Kepler's laws but Newton found that he
could not follow the mathematics. He was not convinced by the astrology but he made
it his business to read up on the mathematics, eventually leading to his discovery and
mastery of the new *Analytical Geometry* written by the brilliant French philosopher and
mathematician, René Descartes (1596–1650).

   He also read very widely outside his syllabus – probably too widely from the point
of view of his degree for, when he came to be examined for his Bachelor of Arts, his
performance was not impressive and, in fact, he was put into 'second posing':

I have heard it said, as a tradition, whilst I was a student at Cambridge, that when Sir Isaac stood for
Bachelor of Arts degree, he was put into second posing, or lost his groats, as they term it; which is

ABOVE Newton, with his room mate John Wickens, studying the spectrum in his room at Cambridge.
A nineteenth century engraving by Louis Figuier from '*Vies des Savants Illustres du XVIII Siecle*', Paris 1874

look'd upon as disgraceful. I can't tell whether it be true or not; but it seems no strange thing at that
time of day, notwithstanding Sir Isaacs great parts; for he was to busy in the solid track of learning
and the sublime pursuit of mathematical philosophy, to allow for time enough to be master of words
only, or the trifling niceties of technical logic and school subtleties, which was then the chief test of
proficiency in academic learning and qualification for a degree.[6]

Like most of the stories of Newton's early years, the information is second hand.
Stukeley, who was at Cambridge himself, quotes the anecdote as a story that was circulated among the students many years after the event. Even so, it may well be correct, or
at least the echo of something close to the truth. The 'groat' referred to was a small silver coin worth four old pence (less than 2p) and it ceased to be legal tender after 1662,
three years before the incident described. The tradition was for each candidate to back
his exams with a few groats and, if he did badly, then the groats were not returned.
A tradition developed that it was the works of Euclid on which Newton failed. He had
mastered the more difficult work of Descartes but he did not know the fundamental
classical geometry of the ancient world. On his first perusal of Euclid's Elements, he
decided that most of them were too obvious to be worthy of his time and he therefore
decided to ignore the rest of the work. A copy of Euclid exists, however, that is

thoroughly scrutinized and fully annotated in Newton's hand, so either the story is apocryphal or at some stage Newton changed his mind about the value of Euclid.

After his graduation in 1665 we begin to get a fuller picture of Newton's life, and we discover some of the other items that he purchased at the local fairs. In the same year he began to keep an account of his expenditure and this continued until 1669.[7]

	£	s	d
Drills, gravers, a hone, a hammer, and a mandril	0	5	0
A magnet	0	16	0
Compasses	0	3	6
Glass bubbles	0	4	0
My Bachelor's account	0	17	6
At the tavern several other times	1	0	0
Spent on my cousin Ayscough	0	12	6
On other acquaintance	0	10	1
Cloth, 2 yards, and buckles for a vest	2	0	0
Philosophical Intelligences	0	9	6
The Hist of the Royal Society	0	7	0
Gunter's Book and Sector to Dr Fox	0	5	0
Lost at cards twice	0	15	0
At the tavern twice	0	3	6
I went into the country, Dec 4 1667			
I returned to Cambridge, Feb 12 1667 [ie 1668 NS]			
Received of my mother	30	0	0
My journey	0	7	6
For my degree to the College	5	10	0
To the proctor	2	0	0
To three prisms	3	0	0
Four ounces of putty	0	1	4
Lent to Dr Wickens	1	7	6
Bacon's Miscellanies	0	1	6
Expenses caused by my degree	0	15	0
A Bible binding	0	3	0
For oranges for my sister	0	4	2
Spent on my journey to London, and 4s or 5s more which my mother gave me in the country	5	10	0
I went to London, Wednesday, August 5th and returned to Cambridge on Monday, September 28 1668			
Lent Dr Wickens	0	11	07

We notice the two entries, 'At the tavern twice' and 'At the tavern several other times'. He also lost at cards twice, so that his mathematical ability was evidently of little practical advantage against the card sharps, but the entries do seem to indicate that he was a normal student socializing at the tavern to a moderate degree. The practical items of drills, gravers, hammer, and mandrel were the small tools to assist him with his hobby of constructing models. The magnet shows his wish to know more about the strange phenomenon of magnetism. The three expensive prisms, at a pound each, show an early interest in his passion to understand the nature of light, and the glass bubbles could have helped him to understand the theory of the rainbow. The 'Philosophical Intelligences' may or may not be the *Philosophical Transactions* of the Royal Society but there can be no doubt that the 'Hist. of Royal Society' is Thomas Sprat's history of which Newton thought highly enough to purchase his own copy. The purchase of Bacon's *Miscellanies* shows that, at this time, he was already absorbing the doctrine of Francis Bacon.

The accounts show a contribution of thirty pounds from his mother and a further small gift from her when he undertook his first journey to London in 1668. A brief letter, from his mother Hannah and written in May 1665, survives. Unfortunately, the edge of the page is cut away so that some of the words are missing but the close relationship between mother and son is very evident in the wording and 'loving mother' appears only two lines later than the words 'love to you with my motherly love':

Isack
received your leter and I perceive you . . .
letter from mee with your cloth but . . .
none to you. Your sisters present thai . . .
love to you with my motherly lov . . .
you and prayers to god for you I . . .
your loving mother
Hanah
Wollstrup may the 6. 1665[8]

His sisters Hannah and Mary were the daughters of Barnabas Smith, his half sisters by his mother's second marriage, and his account book seems to show that he favoured one sister with oranges but not the other. Was it Hannah or Mary who had the passion for oranges? Was the singular a slip of the pen and did the sisters in fact share the oranges?

Less than two months after she wrote to her son, Hannah Smith's firstborn was back home again. News arrived at Cambridge of a terrible plague that was ravaging London. It was not only the capital which had been hit but also some of the provincial towns, particularly Colchester where, as a proportion of the population, the number of deaths was even higher than in London. In the summer the university decided to close down because of the threat of the plague and the students were sent home. Thus, we find Newton absent from Cambridge from 1 August 1665 until the following March. In 1666 outbreaks of the plague were still appearing. Newton left the university in June, returning again in March 1667. For about two years he spent more time at Woolsthorpe than he did at Cambridge.

We do not know what Newton's mother thought of her son when he returned home from his first year at college. He spent a lot of time in his study at Woolsthorpe, especially on the bright sunny days, with the shutters closed, using his prism to project rainbow colours on to the walls. He would take himself for long walks in the country to be alone with this thoughts, and sometimes he would sit in the garden contemplating the apple trees. Some things had moved on very little since the disastrous attempt to make a farmer out of him; he still wandered around in a trance and he still forgot to turn up on time for his meals. Perhaps he discussed his findings with his mother but probably he did not. Perhaps she had maternal instinct enough to know that her son was trying to uncover the secrets of the universe but, even if Hannah knew something of the thoughts that occupied him, she could not have known of their depth and vision.

At Cambridge in 1663, when he was making notes on the works of Aristotle and read Aristotle's famous quotation '*Amicus Plato, sed magis clinica veritas*' [I am a friend of Plato, but truth is my greater friend] Newton stopped in mid page. He expanded the quote and used it as a title for his notes. The Greek methods were excellent as far as they went but he did not consider them to be infallible – his burning desire was to know the absolute truth. He had reached the point at which Francis Bacon had arrived in the same Cambridge college about forty years before him. But what were these truths that he pondered so much and which he so desperately sought to find?

At Trinity College Newton began to keep a notebook in which he jotted down philosophical questions which were of interest to him. The book not only gives us a good idea of what occupied his mind at the time but it also points the way to his future discoveries and shows some early developments of his philosophy. Under the heading 'Of ye first matter' he tried to envisage something smaller than the atom but his thinking always led to a contradiction and he concluded that only the atom could be the 'first' matter. He wondered about the nature of a vacuum: did empty space exist if there was nothing to fill it? He wondered about the spaces between the atoms and how close the atoms could approach one another. He knew that a soap bubble grew thinner and thinner as the liquid ran to the bottom, until the wall was invisible and the light came through undisturbed, yet the bubble still did not burst. Was the wall of the bubble so thin that it was the thickness of an atom? And what of the brilliant rainbow colours in the bubble before it became invisible? Were these the same as the colours seen in a film of oil on the surface of water? How were the colours created and why were they the same as the colours of the rainbow? Why was it that these same bright colours were created

ABOVE Newton's birthplace still retains much of the character as he knew it. In the foreground is a scion of Newton's original apple tree.

from sunlight in so many entirely different ways? Could the rainbow be explained by calculating the path of a ray of light through a small drop of water in the sky?

The nature of light and colour fascinated him, and he wished to understand more about it. His thoughts turned to moving objects and he philosophized on the cause and nature of motion. What was the matter of the heavens and of what matter was the Sun? Of what were the stars, the planets, and the comets made? What were the laws of motion on the Earth where everything ran down to rest, and why were these laws different from those of the planets which enjoyed perpetual motion? What was the nature of sound? What was the sensation of touch? What was the reason for sleep and what was the meaning of dreams? What was the nature of heat and cold? What was the strange force that drew everything to the ground? What was the cause of magnetic attraction which

ABOVE The Spectrum. Newton wondered why it was that all the colours of the rainbow could be produced from white sunlight using no more than a simple prism.

seemed only to work on metals, and what were the electrical forces that seemed to draw small, light bodies to charged objects? What was time and what was eternity? He reflected on God, the soul, and the Creation. How were the world and the universe created? With a few reservations, he was happy to accept the account in Genesis for the creation of the world.

At Cambridge he had gathered much knowledge from the libraries, and he had read the views of the great thinkers before him. Woolsthorpe gave him a quiet country retreat to ponder on his theories and to try out some of the many experiments that he had formulated in his mind. Early in the year he had been working on mathematics. He had developed the binomial theorem which showed how the sum $(a + b)$ of two variables could be expanded to any power, even negative and fractional values. He discovered a method of calculating the tangents to curves. The mathematics he needed to solve the secrets of the universe did not exist. There was no way to handle quantities in a state of flux which changed with time. His thoughts therefore moved on to develop the method of fluxions which could handle these flowing quantities. By January 1666 he was performing his experiments on light and he formulated his theory of colours. Later in the year he began to think about the Earth's gravity extending to the Moon. He tells us in his own words about his *annus mirabilis*:

In the beginning of the year 1665 I found the Method of approximating series and the Rule for Reducing any dignity of any Binomial into such a series. The same year in May I found the method of Tangents of Gregory and Slusius, and in November had the direct method of fluxions and the next year in January had the Theory of Colours and in May following I had entrance into ye inverse method of fluxions. And the same year I began to think of gravity extending to the orb of the moon, and having found out how to estimate the force with which a globe revolving within a sphere presses the surface of the sphere, from Kepler's rule of the periodical times of the planets being in a sesquialterate proportion of their distances from the centre of their orbs I deduced that the forces which keep the planets in their orbs must [be] reciprocally as the squares of their distances from the centres about which they revolve: and thereby compared the force requisite to keep the moon in her orb with the force of gravity at the surface of the earth and found them to answer pretty nearly. All this was in the two plague years of 1665 and 1666, for in those days I was in the prime of my age for invention, and minded mathematics and philosophy more than at any time since.[9]

There are so many great discoveries in this passage that it is too much to take in at a single reading. There was the binomial theorem with its many applications to probability theory and infinite series; the fluxions which were the origins of the differential and integral calculus; the theory of light and colour; and the universal theory of gravitation. They were all conceived in less than two years by this one genius working in isolation.

Newton described his experiments with the prism: how at first he delighted in the bright colours produced from the sunlight by the glass, and how he determined to study the phenomenon of the colours more closely and to discover how they were produced. In a letter to Henry Oldenburg at the Royal Society, he gave the date when he made his first experiments on light as 1666, a date that agrees with the one given in the extract above. At this time, he was home in Woolsthorpe but some of the later experiments were probably executed at Cambridge. It seems certain that he performed experiments in light at both places over a period that could have been a year or more:

I procured me a Triangular glass-Prisme, to try therewith the celebrated Phenomena of Colours. And in order thereto having darkened my chamber, and made a small hole in my window-shuts, to let in a convenient quantity of the Sun's light, I placed my Prisme at his entrance, that it might thereby be refracted to the opposite wall. It was at first a very pleasing divertisment, to view the vivid and intense colours produced thereby; but after a while applying myself to consider them more circumspectly, I became surprised to see them in an oblong form; which according to the received laws of Refraction, I expected should be circular.[10]

Many people had seen the colours before Newton. His fairground purchase was no more than a toy which was designed to show the bright colours, and others knew that they were somehow inherent within the prism or the sunlight. Newton experimented time and again with the colours produced by the prism. He noticed that part of the light was reflected from the surface of the prism and he wondered why both reflection and refraction took place at the glass surface. He tried to split the colours further by passing the coloured light through a second prism. He also brought the beams of different colours back together again and found that he could recreate the white light. He focused the beams with lenses, and he took painstaking measurements of the degree of refraction of each colour. He passed the light through coloured films and other media:

I have refracted it with Prismes and reflected with it Bodies which in Day-light were of other colours; I have intercepted with the coloured film of Air interceding two compressed plates of glass; transmitted it through coloured Mediums, and through Mediums irradiated with other sorts of Rays, and diversely terminated it; and yet could never produce any new colour out of it.

But the most surprising, a wonderful composition was that of Whiteness. There is no one sort of Rays which alone can exhibit this. 'Tis ever compounded, and to its composition are requisite all the aforesaid primary Colours, mixed in a due proportion. I have often with Admiration beheld, that all the Colours of the Prisme being made to converge, and thereby to be again mixed, reproduced light, intirely and perfectly white. Hence therefore it comes to pass, that Whiteness is the usual colour of light; for, Light is a confused aggregate rays indued with all sorts of Colors, as they are promiscuously darted from the various parts of luminous bodies.[11]

He was particularly interested to discover how the light was propagated. Did the light move as a wave motion in a fashion similar to a sound wave or did light consist of tiny particles? The planets had no air to impede their motion, therefore there was no air between the Earth and the Sun. He concluded that the light could not be carried by the air. The light required a medium which pervaded the whole of space. The existence of this medium had been suggested by other philosophers and it was known as the ether. It had some very special qualities which made it almost undetectable. But perhaps the light consisted of particles? If so then it should be possible to impart a spin to the parti-

ABOVE A crude sketch of Newton's *experimentum crucis* to analyse the colours of the spectrum by passing them through a second prism.

cles and he would expect to see a curved path as they passed through a resisting medium. He used the analogy of the curved trajectory of a spinning tennis ball. But no amount of careful observation showed anything other than a straight line for the path of light.

It was not simply light that occupied Newton's thoughts. There was so much to learn and to be discovered. He wanted to know more about the laws of nature. What were the laws that governed the universe? The planets followed their elliptical orbits according to the laws formulated by Kepler. The system delighted astrologers because it was excellent for predicting the positions of the planets in the night sky but Kepler had not attempted to explain the mechanism behind the motion. Kepler and others before him knew that the planetary orbits were governed by a force of some kind emanating from the Sun but to explain the mechanism mathematically, when even the concept of force could not be defined, presented a very difficult problem. The motion of a body in a straight line had to be explained before the curved orbits of the planets could be expounded. Galileo had made great progress on the former problem but it was necessary to explain terms such as force and velocity more precisely, and also to define the more difficult concept of acceleration, the change in speed and velocity.

Newton realized that the mathematics of his time did not have the means he needed to solve the problem of the motion of the planets. Properties such as speed and direction were in a constant state of flux, always changing with time but with varying rates of change. A new branch of mathematics was needed to handle these concepts. Newton had been working for some time on the problems of drawing tangents to curves, and the calculation of areas and the lengths of curves. This was where the key lay to the method of the fluxions – later known as the calculus – a tool so powerful that it opened up many new directions in mathematics. It was in the plague years of 1665 and 1666 that Newton developed his method of the fluxions to the point where he was able to use it to prove many far-reaching conclusions in mechanics and astronomy.

Characteristically, he made no attempt to publish his method and, having derived the results he wanted, he then reworked his results appealing to limiting cases of classical geometry so that the rest of the world could follow his conclusions. But this lay far in the future: in the 1660s he kept these things to himself and pondered on them.

What was the force that drew the falling apple towards the ground? This force was obviously directed towards the centre of the Earth. Was this the same as the force that kept the Moon in its orbit, and was the force on the Moon also directed towards the centre of the Earth? If the Moon was drawn to the Earth, then why didn't it fall to the ground? Did the planets obey the same laws of motion as bodies on the surface of the Earth? Many had studied the motion of the projectile and the curved trajectory followed by the cannon ball but no one thought the motion of the cannon ball obeyed the same laws as the heavenly bodies. The Moon and the planets remained in the heavens, they did not fall back to the Earth like the cannon ball.

ABOVE Isaac Barrow (1630–1677) was Newton's tutor at Cambridge and he was the first to realise Newton's mathematical genius. In 1663 he relinquished the Lucasian chair of mathematics in favour of his prodigy, but he went on to become master of Trinity College.

'I deduced that the forces which keep the planets in their orbs must [be] reciprocally as the squares of their distances from the centres about which they revolve', he wrote. '. . . and thereby compared the force requisite to keep the moon in her orb with the force of gravity at the surface of the earth and found them to answer pretty nearly.'

Much has been made of Newton's words 'pretty nearly'. His result was too small by about one-eighth. He knew that his value for the radius of the Earth was only approximate, and he knew, too, that the orbit of the Moon was not a circle as he supposed but could be more accurately described as an ellipse. When he wrote 'pretty nearly' he meant exactly those words, the result pretty nearly proved the inverse square law of gravitation. A lesser man would have published the result and made a claim to the discovery, and, at first sight, it seems strange that Newton did not publish in 1666.

He had his own reasons for keeping the calculation to himself, however. Firstly, he was only twenty-four years old and he had never before published a mathematical paper. He had not yet been awarded his Master's Degree. A few years later he did have good support from his tutor Isaac Barrow and others at the university but, if we are to believe the story that he lost his groats, then in 1665 Barrow had been less than impressed by his mathematical ability. Isaac Newton was a very sensitive young man and he did not have the self-confidence to press for a publication. There were other problems in his work that the critics could latch on to. He knew that to calculate the force on the apple, he had taken the distance from the apple to the Earth as the distance to the centre of the Earth. He had made the assumption that a sphere should be treated as though all its mass was concentrated at a single point at its centre. He also had to show that the inverse square law would predict that the planets move around the Sun in ellipses with a constant areal velocity, in obedience to the laws first formulated by Kepler and universally accepted as fact. He had to show that a two-body system, such as the Sun and Jupiter, revolved around their common centre of gravity and that this system still satisfied Kepler's laws. He had to tackle the far more difficult three-body problem. If the Moon was attracted by the Earth and by the Sun then what kind of orbit could be expected of it? Some of the problems he could solve by his new method of the fluxions but how could he get the world to accept the results of such a radical new concept in mathematics? The foundations of a marvellous new system had been laid but they existed only in the mind of one man. There was still much to be done and many of the great questions were still without an answer.

What *was* the system of the world?

5

FIRE

THE ROYAL SOCIETY held an informal meeting on 1 January 1666, followed by a council meeting on 21 February, but the first full meeting after the plague did not take place until 14 March. There were still isolated outbreaks of plague in London and full precautions had to be taken all through the year. The summer was uncommonly hot and dry. At the end of August, a select gathering met at St Paul's Cathedral to examine the state of the church fabric. Messrs Chichley and Pratt, surveyors, were present with the Dean of St Paul's and the Bishop of London. Christopher Wren and John Evelyn were also present. The building was in a terrible state of repair and the walls of the cathedral were leaning dangerously outwards. John Evelyn recorded the findings in his diary; he was not impressed with Chichley and Pratt:

> …we went about, to survey the generall decays of that antient & venerable Church, & to set downe the particulars in writing, what was fit to be don, with the charge thereof: giving our opinion from article to article: We found the maine building to recede outward: 'It was Mr Chichley's & Prats opinion that it had been built ab origina for an effect in Perspective, in reguard of the height; but I was with Dr Wren quite of another judgement, as indeede ridiculous, & so we entered it: We plumbed the Uprights in severall places:[1]

The steeple had fallen more than a century earlier but Evelyn refers to the tower which once supported it as the steeple. The tower had deteriorated to such an extent that it was no longer safe. Evelyn and Wren were better informed than their colleagues but they were not beyond criticism. There seemed to be no question in their minds of making any repairs which were sympathetic to the original Early English style of old St Paul's.

ABOVE Great Fire of London by Philippe Jacques de Loutherbourg. A scene framed in one of the arches on London Bridge, showing the flames of the great fire about to engulf St Paul's cathedral.

The general feeling was for a fashionable cupola to complete the garish clash of architectural styles already achieved by Inigo Jones's greatly admired carbuncle on the new West Front:

> When we came to the steeple, it was deliberated whither it were not well enough to repair it onely upon its old foundation, with reservation to the 4 Pillars: This Mr Chichley & Prat were also for; but we totally rejected it & persisted that it requir'd a new foundation, not onely in reguard of the necessitie, but for that shape of what stood was very meane, & we had a mind to build it with a noble Cupula, a forme of church building, not as yet knowne in England, but of wonderful grace: for this purpose we offerd to bring in a draught & estimate, which (after much contest) was at last assented to, & that we should nominate a Committee of able Workmen to examine the present foundation: This

concluded we drew all up in Writing, and so going with my L: Bishop to the Deanes, after a little refreshment, went home.[2]

It appears that a decision of some kind was taken on the day and it was acted on very quickly for we know that a week later there was a substantial amount of scaffolding around the structure so that the major task of repairs could begin.

Only five days after this meeting, Samuel Pepys was awakened at three in the morning by his maid Jane. She had seen a fire from her window and wanted to draw her master's attention to it. Pepys slipped on his night-gown and stared sleepily out of his maid's window. He decided the fire was a long way off across the city and he went back to bed. He was up again at seven, he dressed himself and went to look again at the fire. The morning sun shed its rays on the city and the fire

ABOVE Samuel Pepys by Godfrey Kneller. Only a minority of the fellows of the Royal Society were actively engaged in research. Many others, like Samuel Pepys, joined the society to come to the lectures and for reasons of social status. Pepys was not a scientist but he was a very able administrator and in the 1680s he became president.

looked less in the daylight than it had appeared in the night. Pepys decided it was not so large as it seemed earlier and it looked to be further away than before.

It was Sunday and he was setting about his day's business when Jane burst in with the news that there were three hundred houses blazing in Fish Street near London Bridge. Samuel Pepys had no doubt that this was a ridiculous exaggeration but he felt obliged to take this latest information seriously. He donned his coat and, accompanied by a small boy, the son of a neighbour, he hurried from Seething Lane to the nearby Tower of London where they climbed a stone staircase to get a better view. What he saw from the Tower changed his mind completely. He was sufficiently disturbed to hire a boat and go to see the situation for himself. One reason for his concern was that his former mistress, Sarah, lived on London Bridge:

...and there I did see the houses at that end of the bridge all on fire, and an infinite great fire on this and the other side the end of the bridge – which, among other people, did trouble me for poor little Michell and our Sarah on the Bridge. So down, with my heart full of trouble, to the Lieutenant of the Tower, who tells me that it begun this morning in the King's bakers house in Pudding Lane, and that it hath burned down St Magnes church and most part of Fishstreet already. So I down to the water-side and there got a boat and through bridge, and there saw a lamentable fire. Poor Michell's house, as far as the Old Swan, already burned that way and the fire running further, that in a very little time it got as far as the Stillyard while I was there. Everybody endeavouring to remove their goods, and fling-ing into the River or bringing them into lighters that lay off. Poor people staying in their houses as long as till the very fire touched them, and running into boats or clambering from one pair of stair by the watere-side to another. And among other things, the poor pigeons I perceive were loath to leave their houses, but hovered about the widows and balconies till they were some of them burned their wings and fell down.[3]

He remained for about an hour near the fire and he watched helplessly as it raged to and fro. People were desperately trying to save their goods and possessions but everywhere there was a great sense of shock and no effort was being made to put the fire out. The drought had made everything very dry and combustible. There was a high wind that was fanning the flames completely out of control so that even the stone buildings were catch-ing fire. Having already passed through the bridge, Pepys decided to carry on up the river to Whitehall to get a message to the king about the emergency. He arrived at the Court with news of the fire and people pressed about him asking for details. He was escorted to the royal bedchamber to see King Charles and the Duke of York, both of whom expressed great concern at the news. They all knew that the only way to stop the fire was to pull down houses and to create a fire break. The king sent Pepys back to the city with orders to the Lord Mayor giving him powers to demolish any house that stood in the path of the fire. He would be supplied with as many soldiers as he needed to carry out his task.

Samuel Pepys made his way back to the fire, this time by road in a coach provided by Captain Cocke. It was a terrible sight to see the people running from the fire. The streets were busy with carts full of personal goods and poor people with loads on their backs trying to save their belongings. Even the sick and infirm were being carried on their beds through the streets as their homes perished in flames behind them. He left the coach and frantically searched the streets for Sir Thomas Budworth, the Lord Mayor of London. Eventually he found a very harassed Sir Thomas in Canning Street – he had a handker-chief around his neck. Pepys delivered the royal message to him. 'Lord, what can I do?', cried Sir Thomas like a fainting woman. 'I am spent. People will not obey me. I have been pulling down houses. But the fire overtakes us faster than we can do it.' The Lord Mayor had certainly done his duty. He had been up all night trying to create a firebreak but no one was prepared to lose their house to stop the fire. Sir Thomas Budworth had had a long, exhausting night with nothing to show for it.

Pepys had obeyed the royal command and delivered his message to the mayor, so he decided to walk home. Most people were still too shocked by the ferocity of the fire to think about any means of quenching it. At the heart of the fire, to the north of the bridge, the houses were built very close together. Near the banks of the Thames there were many warehouses full of inflammable goods. Pitch and tar were stored in Thames Street, and the neighbouring streets had warehouses full of oil, tallow, timber, wine, and brandy. Samuel Pepys saw Mr Isaac Houblon at his door at Dowgate, 'prettily dressed' but covered in smuts – he was receiving some things from his brother whose house was on fire. The churches were filling up with people clutching their treasured possessions, Londoners who thought they had found sanctuary and who, on any other Sunday, would have been quietly sitting at the morning service.

In the afternoon Pepys walked out again through the panic-stricken city. The chaos was worse than before. The streets were crowded with people, horses, and carts laden with goods, all in such a panic that they were ready to run over one another. Some were moving goods from one burned house only to find that the house to which they had moved them was itself soon threatened with fire. Goods were being moved from houses in Canning Street, where they had been taken that morning, to Lombard Street and further afield. Accompanied by a Mr Carcass and his brother, whom he had met casually in the street, Pepys went to a wharf where he had booked a boat. They passed through one of the arches of London Bridge and, from the river, they could see the extent of the fire above and below the bridge. It was obvious that the fire was still gaining and there seemed to be no way to stop it. The king and Duke of York were present in a royal barge, and the boats went together to Queenshithe. The king's orders were to pull down the waterside houses below the bridge but the fire came up on them so quickly that there was no time to carry out the demolition. Attempts were made to stop the fire at the Three Cranes above London Bridge and at Botolph's Wharf below it, but there was no stopping the inferno as the high wind drove it still further into the city. The Thames was full of lighters and boats taking in goods of all kinds. Personal belongings were floating in the water. The fire advanced effortlessly from one house to the next, the angry flames leaping easily across the narrow alleyways:

> So near the fire as we could for smoke; and all over the Thames with one's face in the wind you were almost burned with a shower of Firedrops – this is very true – so as houses were burned by these drops and flakes of fire, three or four, nay five or six houses, one from another. When we could endure no more upon the water, we came to a little ale house near the Three Cranes and stayed till it was dark almost and saw the fire grow; and as it grow darker, appeared more and more, and in corners and upon steeples and between churches and houses as far as we could see up the hill of the City, in a hor-

rid malicious bloody flame, not like the fine flame of an ordinary fire.

... We stayed till, it being darkish, we saw the fire as only one entire arch of fire from this to the other side of the bridge, and in a bow up the hill for an arch of above a mile long. It made me weep to see it. The churches, houses, and all on fire and flaming at once, and a horrid noise the flames made, and the cracking of houses at their ruine. So home with a sad heart, and there find everybody discoursing and lamenting the fire.[4]

Night was falling. It was warm weather and there was a bright moon. How could the inferno be stopped? It seemed only a question of time before the whole of London would be ablaze. Pepys did the neighbourly thing and invited Tom Hater, whose house had burned down on Fish Street Hill, to stay at his house in Seething Lane. The ferocious cracking and roaring of the fire during the night made it impossible to get any sleep. Every moment the conflagration seemed to be drawing closer. In the moonlight Samuel Pepys and his family carried their goods into the garden. With the help of Tom Hater they moved all the money and iron chests into the cellar thinking it to be the safest place for the valuables. In his office were bags of gold which he made ready to carry away with his legal documents and his papers of accounts. One of the neighbours, William Batten, arranged for carts to come out of the country to take his goods to safety that very night.

On the Southwark side of the Thames, John Evelyn, with his wife and son, arrived by coach. The night was so bright with the great fire raging that it was almost as light as day. On Ludgate Hill he could see the brilliant red flames creeping ominously towards St Paul's Cathedral:

...went to the bank side in Southwark, where we beheld that dismal speectaccle, the whole Citty in dreadful flames neere the Water side, & had now consumed all the houses from the bridge all Thames Streete & up-wards towards Cheape side, downe to the three Cranes & so returned exceedingly astonishd, what would become of the rest.

The fire having continud all this night (if I may call that night, which was as light as day for 10 miles round about after a dreadful manner) when consp[ir]ing with a fierce Eastern Wind, in a very drie season, I went on foote to the same place, when I saw the whole South part of the Citty burning from Cheape side to the Thames, & all along Cornehill (for it likewise kindled back against the Wind, as well [as] forward) Tower-Streete, Fen-church-street, Gracious [Grace Church] Streete & so along to Bainard Castle, and was now taking hold of St Paules-Church, to which the Scaffalds contributed exceedingly: The Conflagration was so universal, & the people so astonished, that from the beginning (I know not by what desponding or fate) they hardly stirr'd to quench it, so as there was nothing hearde or seene but crying out & lamentation, & running about like distracted creatures, without at all attempting to save even their goods; such a strange consternation there was upon them, so as it burned both in breadth & length, The Churches, Publique Halls, Exchange, Hospitals, Monuments, & orna-

ments, leaping after a prodigious manner from house to house & streete to streete, at greate distance one from the other, for the heate (with a long set of faire & warme weather) had even ignited the aire, & prepared the materials to conceive the fire, which devoured after a incredible manner, houses, furniture & everything: Here we saw the Thames coverd with goods floating, all the barges and boates laden with what some had time & courage to save, as on the other, the carts &c carrying out to the fields, which for many miles were strewed with movables of all sorts, & tents erecting to shelter both people &c what goods they could get away: O the miserable & calamitous speectacle, such as happily the whole world had not seene the like since the foundation of it, not to be out don, 'til the universal Conflagration of it, all the skie were of a fiery aspect, like the top of a burning Oven, and the light seene above 40 miles round about for many nights: God grant mine eyes may never behold the like, who now saw above ten thousand houses all in one flame, the noise & crakling & thunder of the impetuous flames, the shreeking of Women & children, the hurry of people, the fall of towers, houses and churches was like an hideous storme, & the aire all about so hot and inflam'd that at the last one was not able to approch it, so as they were forced [to] stand still, and let the flames consume on which they did for neere two whole mile[s] in length and one in bredth: The Clowds also of Smoke were dismall, & reached upon computation neere 50 miles in length: Thus I left it this afternoone burning, a resemblance of Sodome, or the last day: it call'd to mind that of 4 Heb: non enim hic habemus stabilem Civitatem: the ruines resembling the picture of Troy: London was, but is no more.[5]

The next day the fire was still raging. John Evelyn went into the city on horseback. The fire had got as far as the Inner Temple. All Fleet Street was in flames. The buildings in Old Bailey, Ludgate Hill, Warwick Lane, Newgate, Paules Chaine, and Watling Street were burning where they had not already been reduced to ashes. At St Paul's cathedral the heat of the fire caused the stones to crack and fly 'like grenades'. A river of molten lead was flowing down the streets. It was so hot that the very pavements were glowing a fiery red and neither human nor horse was able to tread on them. All the narrow passageways around the cathedral had been blocked by the demolition work. There was no respite. The easterly wind was driving the flames ever onwards:

Nothing but the almighty power of God was able to stop them, for vaine was the help of man: on the fifth it crossed towards White-hall, but O the Confusion was then at that Court: It pleased his Majestie to command me among the rest to looke after the quenching of fetter-lane end, to preserve (if possible) that part of Holborn, whilst the rest of the Gent: tooke their several posts, some at one part, some at another, for now they began to bestirr themselves, & not 'til now, who 'til now had stood as men interdict, with their hands a crosse, & began to consider that nothing was like to put a stop, but the blowing up of so many houses, as might make a wider gap, than any had yet ben made by the ordinary method of pulling them downe with Engines; This some stout seamen proposed early enough to have saved the whole Citty; but some tenacious & avaritious Men, Aldermen, &c. would not permitt, because their houses must have been [of] the first: It was therefore now commanded to be prac-

tised, & my concerne being particularly for the Hospital of St. Bartholemews neere Smithfield, where I
had many wounded & sick men, made me the more diligent to promote it; nor was my care for the
Savoy lesse: So as it pleased Almighty God by abating of the Wind, & the industrie of people, now
when all was lost, infusing a new Spirit into them (& such as had if exerted in time undoubtedly pre-
served the whole) that the furie of it began sensibly to abate, about noone, so as it came no further
than the Temple West-ward, nor than the enterance of Smithfield North.[6]

At last there was a concerted effort to control the fire. It broke out again at Temple but
the demolition gang was well organized and the men were able to contain it by blowing up houses with gunpowder. But this was no more than a temporary respite. The wind
changed direction and the fire began to move eastwards, towards Cripplegate and the
Tower. Coal and timber yards were soon blazing furiously, and Evelyn claimed that it was
so hot that it was impossible to get within a furlong of the fire. At last, worn out by his
fire-fighting efforts, he left the 'smoking & sulltry heape, which mounted up in dismall
clowds night & day' and he described the plight of those who had lost their homes and
belongings in the fire:

…the poore Inhabitants dispersed all about St Georges, Moore filds, as far as higate, & severall miles
in Circle, Some under tents, others under miserable Hutts and Hovells, without a rag, or any necessary
utinsils, bed or board, who from delicatnesse, riches & easy accommodations in stately & well furnished
houses, were now reduced to extreamest misery & poverty: In this Calamitious Condition I returned
with a sad heart to my house, blessing & adoring the distinguishing mercy of God, to me & mine,
who in the midst of all this ruine, was like Lot, in my little Zoar, safe and sound…[7]

The smoke from the fire was seen as far away as Oxford where Anthony à Wood first saw
it on the Monday. By Tuesday 'the sunshine was much darkened' and at night the moon
was darkened by the clouds of smoke and took on a reddish hue. Wood was not an eye
witness to the Great Fire but his account still adds valuable detail about those who lost
everything in it:

Soe suddenly did it come and therby caused such distraction and severall forgot their names when they
with their money or goods their armes were examined by the watch that then immediately was
appointed. Others that had occasion to write letters a day or 2 after it ended, forgat the day of the
mounth and the mounth of the year. Others quite distracted for the generall loss they have received.
Thousands utterly undone that had houses there. Those that had a house today were the next glad of
the shelter of an hedge or pigstie or stable. Those that were this day riding wantonly in coaches, were
the next glad to ride in dungcarts to save their lives. Those that thought the ground too unworthy to be
touched by their feet, did run up to the knees in dirt and water to save themselves from the fury of the
fire or the falling of houses. Those that faired deliciously this day and nothing curious enough to satiate

their palatts were within a few days following glad of a browne crust. Those that delighted themselves
in downe bedds and silken curteynes, are now glad of the shelter of a hedge.[8]

At four o'clock in the morning Samuel Pepys was loading up a cart, lent by Lady Batten,
to carry away all his money and valuables to Sir William Rider's at Bethnal Green. He
rode on the cart, attired in his night-gown, to protect his treasures. Never had the city
seen such feverish activity in the middle of the night. The streets and the highways were
crowded with people, some running, some riding, and others driving carts to take away
their belongings. Sir William Rider was tired of being called up in the middle of the
night to receive things from all his friends. The house at Bethnal Green was full of goods
but this was of little concern to Pepys who was well pleased to have secured his valuables. There was no sleep for Samuel and his wife: all the household had to return to
London and to rescue the rest of their belongings. They carried their possessions over
Tower Hill and down to the riverside where Pepys had arranged for a lighter to take
them. By this time, it seemed the whole world was carrying household goods over Tower
Hill. The lighter lay in the next quay above the Tower Dock, and Pepys offered to take
with him a few of things for his neighbour, Mrs Buckworth, who was there with her
'pretty child'. But there was such a crush at the postern gate that no one could get
through to the riverside. The Duke of York came to the Admiralty Office and spoke to
the occupants; he rode with his guard up and down the City to keep the peace. Unable
to get to the river, Pepys and his wife returned and lay down on a borrowed quilt in the
office at Seething Lane. They fed upon the remains of yesterday's dinner 'having no fire
nor dishes, nor any opportunity of dressing anything'.

   The next day (Tuesday, 4 September) he was up at the break of day to load the
remainder of his things. It took him until the afternoon but, eventually, he got them all
away by water. The flames were getting perilously close and he went to Tower Street with
Sir William Penn to see the latest situation for himself. The fire was burning fiercely on
both sides of the narrow street. The neighbours were all busy digging pits in their garden to bury wine and other belongings. Pepys followed suit and buried his Parmesan
cheese with his wine. All seemed lost when, at last, Pepys came up with a sensible suggestion to contain the fire. He reasoned that the Admiralty Office was of great value to
the country and, therefore, if the men from the yards at Woolwich and Deptford could
be brought to fight the fire, it might be possible to make a firebreak and save the office.
The Duke of York had the authority to give permission for the destruction of houses for
the firebreak. William Penn agreed to the suggestion and rushed off to find the Duke of
York. That night, with their neighbour Mrs Turner, the Pepyses dined on a shoulder of
mutton 'without any napkin or anything'. The fire was still creeping ominously closer:

   …now and then walking in the garden and saw how horridly the sky looks, all on fire in the night,

was enough to put us out of our wits; and endeed it was extreamly dreadfull – for it looks just as if it
was at us, and the whole heaven on fire. I after supper walked in the dark down to Tower-street, and
there saw it all on fire at the Trinity house on that side and the Dolphin tavern on this side, which
was very near us – and the fire with extraordinary vehemence. Now begins the practice of blowing up
of houses in Tower-street, those next the Tower, which at first did frighten people more then anything;
but it stop[ped] the fire where it was done, it bringing down the houses to the ground in the same
places they stood, and then it was easy to quench what little fire was in it though it kindled nothing
almost. W. Hewer this day went to see how his mother did, and comes late home, but telling us how he
hath been forced to move her to Islington, her house in pye-Corner being burned. So that it is got so far
that way and all the Old Bayley, and was running down to Fleetestreete. And Pauls is burned and all
Cheapside. I wrote to my father this night; but the post-house being burned, the letter could not go.[9]

Pepys had to sleep in his office for another night – he was so tired that he could hardly
stand up. At two in the morning he was awakened by yet another cry of 'fire!', this time
from his wife. The ancient Saxon church of All Hallows Barking at the bottom end of
Seething Lane was in flames. This was surely the end of Samuel Pepys' house, and the
time had come for the household to flee their home. Samuel hurriedly gathered up his
two thousand pounds in gold and, with a heavy heart, the little party made their way
down to the river. They took a boat to Woolwich where he had arranged accommodation. As they sailed down the Thames in the moonlight, they could see the whole city
on fire. All the way down the river to Woolwich they gazed back at the scene in awe and
dismay. The gates of the Woolwich house were locked when they arrived and there was
no one guarding the premises. Samuel somehow managed to open the gates and to lock
his gold safely away. He set off back to London yet again, leaving his wife Elizabeth and
his clerk William Hewer with strict instructions never to leave the room and the valuables unattended night or day.

Pepys arrived back at Seething Lane fearing to see his house as a blackened, burnt-
out shell. For the first time in three terrible days there was good news:

Home, and wheras I expected to have seen our house on fire, it being now about 7 a-clock, it was not.
But to the Fyre, and there find greater hopes than I expected; for my confidence of finding our office on fire
was such, that I durst not ask anybody how it was with us, till I came and saw it not burned. But going to
the fire, I find, by the blowing up the houses and the great help given by the workmen out of the King's
yards, sent up by Sir W Penn, there is a good stop given to it as well as at Marke-lane end as ours – it
having only burned the Dyall of Barking Church, and part of the porch and was there quenched. I up to
the top of Barkeing steeple, and there saw the saddest sight of desolation that I ever saw. Everywhere great
fires. Oyle-cellers and brimstone and other things burning. I became afeared to stay there long; and therefore
down again as fast as I could, the fire being spread as far as I could see it, and to Sir W. Penn's and there
eat a piece of cold meat, having eaten nothing since Sunday but the remains of Sunday's dinner.[10]

The fire at the east end of the city was contained for the present. Samuel Pepys walked down Fenchurch Street, Gracechurch Street, and Lombard Street. Ashes and dust were everywhere. The Royal Exchange was a sad sight: the beautiful open piazza was a desolate ruin and the statues of the worthies of England were fallen and all broken bar one. The effigy of Thomas Gresham, founder of the Exchange and benefactor of Gresham College, had somehow remained intact. Pepys walked into Moorfields, with his feet burning on the smouldering pavement, to find it full of homeless people, poor wretches huddled together protecting their valuables. The only blessing was that the weather was fine enough for them to sleep out in the night. He was able to buy a drink and to buy a plain penny loaf for two pence.

Pepys turned homeward through Cheapside and Newgate Market where all the houses were burned to ashes. He saw his friend Anthony Joyce's house still on fire. He took up a piece of melted glass from Mercer's Chapel to keep as a souvenir. He saw a poor cat taken, still alive, from a hole in the chimney in the wall of the Exchange with all the hair burned from its body. He was compelled to search out Salisbury Court off Fleet Street to find his father's house where he had lived as a child. He could find no more than a heap of ashes. He staggered home and went to see the dock workers who were sleeping in the Admiralty Office where drinks and bread and cheese were provided for them. He lay down and slept. So much had happened since Sunday that he had almost forgotten the day of the week.

On the Thursday he was up at five and he heard the news that fire had broken out anew in Bishopsgate. This time the fire was soon extinguished. He praised the way the women worked at sweeping the water, but then 'they would scold for drink and be as drunk as devils'. The river was a sad sight with not a house or a church to be seen intact before reaching the western limit of the fire at Temple. There was much talk about the fire being a plot by the Dutch, the French or the Papists but no one could decide which foreign power to blame and no evidence emerged to support the sabotage theory.

It was Friday, 7 September when John Evelyn made a tour of London to survey the damage for himself. He walked from Whitehall as far as London Bridge, through the remains of Fleet Street, up Ludgate Hill, past the ruins of St Paul's, down Cheapside, and past the Exchange; then to Bishopsgate, through Aldersgate, out to Moorfields, and on to Cornhill. Everywhere he had to clamber over mountains of smoking rubbish, frequently finding himself wondering which street he was in because the familiar landmarks had been lost for ever. The ground beneath his feet was so hot that he was in a continual sweat as the hot stones and ashes burned the soles of his shoes. He thought it a miracle that the Tower of London, which was used to store ammunition and gunpowder, did not take fire. He described the desolation that was St Paul's cathedral, a blackened and burnt-out shell with no roof and with even the floor of the choir fallen into the chapel below:

> *In the meantime his Majestie got to the Tower by water, to demolish the houses about the Graft, which being built intirely about it, had htye [it] taken fire, and attaq'd the white Towre, where the Magazines of Powder lay, would undobtedly have not onely beaten down and destroyed all the bridge, but sunke and torne all the vessels in the river, and rendred the demolition beyond all expression for several miles even about the country at many miles distance: At my return I was infinitely concern'd to find that goodly Church st. Paules now a sad ruine, and that beautiful Portico (for structure comparable to any in Europ, as not long before repaird by the late King) now rent in pieces, flakes of vast Stone Split in sunder, and nothing remaining intire but the inscription in the Architrave which shewing by whom it was built, had not one letter of it deface'd: which I could not but take notice of: It was aston-*

ABOVE John Evelyn by Godfrey Kneller. An excellent likeness of John Evelyn. Evelyn, like Pepys, kept a diary and was a member of the Royal Society. Evelyn was interested in conservation and he is holding a copy of his book *Sylva – A Discourse on Forest Trees*

> *ishing to see what immense stones the heat had in a manner Calcin'd, so as all the ornaments, Columns, freezes, Capitels and proetures of massie Portland stone flew off, even to the very roofe, where a Sheete of Leade covering no lesse than 6 akers by measure, being totally mealted, the ruines of the Vaulted roofe, falling break into St Faithes, which being filled with the magazines of bookes, belonging to the Stationer, and carried thither for safty, they were all consumed burning for a weeke following: It is also observable, that the lead over the Altar at the East end was untouch'd; and among the diverse monuments, the body of one Bishop, remain intire. Thus lay in ashes that most venerabe Church, one of the [most ancient] Pieces of early Piety in the Christian World, beside neere 100 more [smaller churches]…*[11]

The heat had not only melted the lead, but also bells, church plate, and even some of the ironwork. He walked through the shell of the Royal Exchange, he saw the ruins of Christ Church, and he noticed the sad remains of the many Company Halls – sumptu-ous buildings reduced to dust and rubble. The fountains were dried up and ruined but, remaining in their basins, a few still had water so hot it was near to boiling. Some of the subterranean cellars, wells, and basements were still burning and giving out a nauseous stench, dark clouds of smoke belching from them like the entrance to Hell. Like Pepys, Evelyn noticed how Thomas Gresham's statue had survived, and he tells of iron gates scorched so hot that the iron melted on their hinges. His feet were burnt and his hair singed by the heat, and he could not get through the narrower streets because the heat was still too intense:

...so as people who now walked about the ruines, appeared like men in some distant desart, or rather in some great Citty, lay'd wast by an impetuous and cruel Enemy, to which was added the stench that came from some poore Creaturs bodys, beds, and other combustible goods: Sir Tho: Gresshams Statue, though falln to the ground from its nich in the Ro: Exchange remain'd intire, when all those of the Kings since the Conquest were broken to pieces; also the Standard in Cornehill, and Q[ueen]: Elizabeths Effigies, with some armes on Ludgate continud with but little detriment, whilst the vast yron Chaines of the Cittie streetes, vast hinges, barrs and gates of Prisons were many of them mealted, and reduc'd to cinders by the vehement heats: nor was I yet able to passe through any of the narrower streetes, but kept the widest, the ground and aire, smoake and fiery vapour, continud so intense, my haire being almost seinged, and my feete unsufferably surbated: The bielanes and narrower streetes were quite fill'd up with rubbish, nor could one have possibly knowne where he was, but by the ruines of some church, or hall, that had some remarkable towre or pinnacle remaining...[12]

In Islington and Highgate about two hundred thousand homeless people camped out with what few belongings they had saved from the holocaust. Evelyn was impressed with their pride. There were no beggars among them. The King and the Council were making every effort to rehouse them but the job ahead could not be more formidable:

I then went towards Islington, and high-gate, where one might have seene two hundred thousand people of all ranks and degrees, dispersed, and laying along by their heapes of what they could save from the Incendium, deploring their losse, and though ready to perish for hunger and destitution, yet not asking one penny for reliefe, which to me appeard a stranger sight, than any I had yet beheld: His Majestie and Council indeede tooke all imaginable care for their reliefe, by Proclamation, for the Country to come in and refresh them with provisions: when in the middst of al this Calamity and confusion, there was (I know not how) an Alarme begun, that the French and Dutch (with whom we were now in hostility) were not onely landed, but even entring the Citty; there being in truth, great suspicion some days before, of those two nations joyning, and even now, that they had been the occasion of firing the Towne: This report did so terrifie, that on a suddaine there was such an uprore and tumult, that they ran from their goods, and taking what weapons they could come at, they could not be stop'd from falling on some of those nations whom they casualy met, without sense or reason, the clamor and perill growing so excessive, as made the whole Court amaz'd at it, and they did with infinite paines, and great difficulty reduce and apease the people, sending Guards and troopes of souldiers, to cause them to retire into the fields againe, where they were watched all this night when I left them pretty quiet, and came home to my house, sufficiently weary and broken: There spirits thus a little sedated, and the affright abated, they now began to repair into the suburbs about the Citty, where such as had friends or opportunite got shelter and harbour for the Present; to which his Majesties Proclamation also invited them. Still the Plague, continuing in our parish, I could not without danger adventure to our Church.[13]

Gone was the old London of timber frames, wattle and daub, high overhanging gables, narrow alleyways, cobbled passages, and medieval courtyards. Pepys's House and the Navy Office were situated in a narrow strip of London that survived inside the ancient city walls. Gresham College escaped by a similarly narrow margin. West of the city the easterly winds carried the fire beyond the ancient boundary and as far as Fetter Lane. It was remarkable that two of the oldest structures in London survived the fire. London Bridge survived almost intact, it had suffered an earlier fire in 1633 which burnt down about twenty houses at the London end. The gap had not been filled and the bridge therefore had its own firebreak. The other was the Tower of London. Despite having been used to store explosives, William the Conqueror's great keep still presided over the East End of London and added the great fire to its long store of memories.

The Great Fire of London was a turning point and it represented a symbolic ending of an era. Old London was gone. As the ashes smouldered on the morning of 6 September 1666, no one knew what the future would hold or how London could possibly rise again from the ashes. 'London was, but is no more', wrote John Evelyn. 'I went againe to the ruines, for it was now no longer a Citty.'

ABOVE The Great Fire of 1666 – by an unknown artist of the Dutch School. A view from the south bank opposite the Tower of London. London Bridge survives on the left. St Pauls and the city churches are on fire in the centre. The Tower also survives, easily recognised on the right. In the foreground a mass of homeless Londoners flee from the flames.

6

THE TELESCOPE

NOR LONGER NOW SHALL MAN WITH STRAINING EYE
IN VAIN ATTEMPT TO SEIZE THE STARS. BLEST WITH THIS
THOU SHALT DRAW DOWN THE MOON FROM HEAVEN...
THIS PRYING TUBE TOO SHEWS FAIR VENUS' FORM
CLAD IN THE VESTMENTS OF HER BORROWED LIGHT,
WHILE THE UNWORTHY FRAUD HER CRESCENT HORN BETRAYS...
O MAY THEY CHERISH THEE ABOVE THE BLIND
CONCEITS OF MEN, AND THE WILD SEA OF ERROR
LEARNING THE MARVELS OF THIS MIGHTY TUBE!

Jeremiah Horrocks (1618-41)

WHEN THE TIME CAME to take stock after the Great Fire, it was seen that Gresham
College had managed to survive but the buildings were no longer available for the Royal
Society to hold its meetings. There was no Guildhall in London and there was no
Exchange. Gresham College was seconded for both these functions until such time as
new buildings could be made available.

The members of the Royal Society were not slow to appreciate that the fire presented the best-ever opportunity for town planning in London. The week after the fire, John
Evelyn had already drawn up a plan and he gained an audience with King Charles to
show his ideas for redevelopment:

*Sat at Star Chamber, on the 13, I presented his Majestie with a Survey of the ruines, and a Plot for a new
Citty, with a discourse on it, whereupon, after dinner his Majestie sent for me into the Queenes Bed-chamber, her Majestie and the Duke only present, where they examin'd each particular, and discours'd upon them
for neere a full houre, seeming to be extreamly pleas'd with what I had so early thought on: The Queene was*

In the short time available to him Evelyn had put a lot of thought into his scheme. The new city was to have a rectangular grid of streets with a few diagonal thoroughfares to break the uniformity. At all the major junctions he had put public buildings such as the new cathedral, the Guildhall, and the new Exchange. There were to be more open spaces in the city, pleasant squares and circuses. It was an imaginative plan for a new London. He had designed riverside gardens and he made the River Fleet into a feature of the new design as a waterside walk.

ABOVE Newton's Reflecting telescope. Newton knew that if he could make a telescope with a reflecting mirror then it would eliminate the problem of coloured fringes and would give sharper images than the refracting telescope. He made the telescope with his own hands and presented it to the Royal Society.

Christopher Wren also produced a plan for the redevelopment. At first sight the plans of Evelyn and Wren were very similar but a closer inspection shows that Wren's plan, as might be expected, was the more professional of the two and he had given more attention to the minor details. Wren showed more streets than Evelyn. He made a focal feature out of the entrance to London Bridge with six roads fanning outwards in equally spaced directions from the head of the bridge. It is hard to believe that Wren and Evelyn had not consulted each other in any way as their ideas for the River Fleet were very similar and both planners designed an attractive octagonal road layout around Ludgate Circus.

There was a third plan submitted by another member of the Royal Society. Robert Hooke, who was determined not to be outdone, put forward his own plans for the redevelopment. One of Hooke's many jobs was that of city surveyor and this gave him every right to put forward a scheme. In the event he made a lasting and important contribution to the redevelopment when he designed the Monument to commemorate the Great Fire. There is little doubt that Hooke consulted Wren on the design of the Monument but the detail and the major credit for this moving and enduring memorial of London's greatest ever disaster must go to Robert Hooke. The Monument was not his only venture into architecture for he also designed the Royal College of Physicians and the Bethlehem Hospital in Lambeth. The hospital acquired the synonym 'Bedlam' which was unfortunate for Hooke because the name became associated with chaos and it tended to take people's attention away from the architecture.

It seems ludicrous that such a golden opportunity for the redevelopment of London's central streets, along the lines expounded by Wren and Evelyn, was not carried out. But the problem was not so simple. To put the scheme into operation the legal wranglings over the ownership of the land would take decades to sort out. Two hundred thousand people were homeless; they wanted roofs over their heads and they were not prepared to wait for the lengthy legal procedures to be completed. The priority was to build new houses as quickly as possible. The financing of the rehousing was obviously a serious problem and much of the money to rebuild London was raised through a tax on coal. Streets were widened and gradients were diminished. New building regulations were formulated with two-storey houses in the back lanes and three and four storeys on the main thoroughfares. But all houses were allowed garret rooms and basements so that even the back-street houses could have four floors for living and storage space. The new buildings were of a uniform and attractive red-brick design with smart stone facings. The houses took priority over all other buildings and by 1671 nine thousand had been built. This was a very creditable effort in the space of five years and it went most of the way towards replacing an estimated thirteen thousand inferior houses which had been destroyed by the fire. The rebuilding had been achieved in spite of the wars with the Dutch but, as Brounker and Pepys well knew, the lack of funding for the Navy was the major factor that enabled the Dutch enemy fleet to sail right into the mouth of the Thames in 1667.

Old St Paul's was past redemption. A half-hearted attempt was made to try to build on the fabric of the old building. Wren was in favour of building around the remains of the central tower but his only reason was to do something for the morale of the people and his plan was to pull down the ruins of the tower as soon as the new walls were high enough to hide them. Wren submitted several designs and wooden models for St Paul's Cathedral and he had no serious competition for the design. To the general assent of all concerned the new cathedral on Ludgate Hill would be in the fashionable Renaissance style, rising high above the rest of London. It was designed with two tiers so that, when viewed from a distance, the upper tier would be visible to show the glory of the work even though the lower tier would be hidden by neighbouring buildings. Christopher Wren wanted a dome to rival that of St Peter's in Rome and, on top of the dome, he insisted on building a tower grand enough for any parish church. This created a difficult structural problem because the dome could not support the weight of the tower above it but it was precisely the kind of problem that Wren loved and he was able to use his mathematical skills to solve it. He designed a false inner dome and supported the tower on a conical brick structure built between the inner and outer domes of the cathedral. Construction did not begin until 1674. It had to take third place after the housing developments and the parish churches, otherwise there would have been nowhere for Londoners to live and worship for thirty years.

After the plague and the fire the Royal Society needed a place to meet before it could get back to normal. Dr Pope offered his lodgings at Gresham College for the meetings but the premises were simply not large enough to accommodate all the members. Mr Henry Howard (who later became the Duke of Norfolk) came to the rescue and offered Arundel House in the Strand as a meeting place. The Society was pleased with this new accommodation: they had built up a library of over three thousand printed books and five hundred manuscript volumes and they were sorely in need of the storage space provided by Arundel House. The first meeting at the new premises was held on 9 January 1667.

Arundel House was only on loan, however, and the Royal Society therefore set about

ABOVE St Paul's Cathedral, completed in 1710 and a familiar sight of London ever since. The architect, Sir Christopher Wren, was fortunate to live long enough to see his masterpiece completed.

trying to raise money to build its own premises. Progress was very slow and the members were reluctant to dig into their pockets – after the losses caused by the fire, it was the worst possible time to ask for money. When asked to contribute by Lord Brounker who was his superior at the Navy Office, Samuel Pepys was put in a difficult position but, during the Great Fire, Pepys had fled from London with two thousand pounds in gold so he was wealthy enough to pay:

> *With Lord Brounker to the Royal Society when they had just done: but I was forced to subscribe to the building of a college and did give £40: several others did subscribe, some greater and some less sums; but several I saw hang off; and I [do not] doubt it will spoil the Society, for it breeds faction and ill-will, and becomes burdensome to some that cannot or would not do it.*[2]

Another crisis arose in the summer when the secretary Henry Oldenburg was summoned before the courts for sending information to foreign powers. The Society's charter allowed Oldenburg to correspond with anybody on matters philosophical but, in this case, the charge was that sensitive information which affected national security had been given out. Oldenburg was arrested and unceremoniously thrown into the Tower of London. He was eventually freed but only after serving two-and-a-half months of his sentence. He was not the only member of the Royal Society to be familiar with the Tower from the inside. A few years later Samuel Pepys was accused of being involved with a Popish plot and of selling naval secrets to foreign powers. This was a trumped-up charge concocted by his enemies. Pepys, too, was acquitted but not until he too had spent several weeks inside.

 Henry Oldenburg was the prime mover behind the Royal Society's attempt to establish the priorities of new discoveries, and an item in the minutes describes the formal procedure for registering new ideas and inventions:

> *Mention being made, that a security might be provided for such inventions or notions, as ingenious persons might have, and desired to secure them from usurpation, or from being excluded as having a share in them, if they should be lighted upon by others; it was thought good, if anything of that nature should be brought in, and desired to be lodged with the Society, that, if the authors were not of their body, they should be obliged to shew it first to the President, and then it should be sealed up both by the small seal of the Society, and by the seal of the proposer; but if they were of the Society, then they should not be obliged to shew it first to the President, but only to declare to him the general heads of the matter, and it then should be sealed up as mentioned before.*[3]

The Society had many members outside London and many foreign visitors. One of the country members was Isaac Barrow who held the chair of Lucasian Professor of Mathematics at Cambridge. Barrow was a long-established member who had formerly lectured at Gresham College and he therefore knew many of the members personally. In July 1669 he wrote to his friend John Collins regarding some mathematical problems:

> *… A friend of mine here, that hath a very excellent genius to those things, brought me the other day some papers, wherein he hath sett down methods of calculating the dimensions of magnitudes like that of Mr Mercator concerning the hyperbola, but very generall; as also of resolving aequations; which I suppose will please you; and I shall send them by the next. In the meane time with my best wishes & respects I rest*
> *Your most affectionate friend and obliged Servant*
> *Is Barrow*[4]

A few days later he wrote a second letter enclosing the mathematical papers written by his friend at Cambridge. Then, in August, came a third letter to John Collins wherein we discover the name of the young man in question – he was the second youngest Master of Arts in Barrow's college:

> *I am glad my friends paper giveth you so much satisfaction. His name is Mr Newton; a fellow of our college, & very young (being but the second y[oung]est Master of Arts) but of an extraordinary genius & proficiency in these things. You may impart the papers if you please to my Lord Brounker.*[5]

Collins read through the papers written by this Mr Newton, the protégé of Isaac Barrow, and found them to be exceptionally well written, very clear, and full of new ideas. In November he was writing to his Scottish friend James Gregory at St Andrews University when he included an item of gossip:

> *…Mr Barrow has resigned his Lecturers place to one Mr Newton of Cambridge, whome he mentioned in his Optick Preface as a very ingenious person. One who (before Mercator's* Logarithmeotechnia *was extant) invented the same method and applied it generally to all curves, and diverse wayes to the Circle, which possibly he may send up to be annexed to Mr Barrowes Lectures, not else but that I am Your most affectionate Servitor*
> *John Collins*[6]

The rumour turned out to be true. Isaac Barrow, the Lucasian Professor of Mathematics, had resigned his chair in favour of an unknown man who was only twenty-six years old! Barrow's resignation was partly to further his ambitions for the advancement of his own career. Only a few years previously he had graded Isaac Newton as a second-class student but now he was not only declaring his protégé to be such a genius that he was fit enough to hold the Lucasian chair of mathematics at Cambridge but he was resigning his chair in favour of the younger man.

In the summer of 1668, shortly after receiving his Master of Arts degree, Isaac Newton made his first visit to London. It was two years after the Great Fire so Newton never saw the old London which his contemporaries at the Royal Society had known so well. He saw, instead, a vast chaotic city with no cathedral but with more house-building activity than the world had ever seen before. It would be fascinating to hear what a young new graduate, on his first visit to the capital, thought about the great centre of commerce and industry that he saw before him but he left no first-hand account of his impressions. We do know from his accounts that, when in London, he made several purchases to assist him with his studies into alchemy, a subject that was destined to dominate his researches a few years later.

Newton's first visit to London was the year before the correspondence between Collins and Barrow, and he had no acquaintances to seek out in the London scientific community. The visit was little more than that of a young man eager to get his first sight of his capital city. He returned to Cambridge via Woolsthorpe where his mother reimbursed some of his expenses. He made his second visit to London in November 1669, the month after he was appointed as Lucasian professor. By this time Newton had sent a paper entitled 'De analysi' to John Collins. It contained a brilliant exposition of his methods of infinite series. The paper also included some of the basic ideas of his method of fluxions – no less than the Newtonian form of the differential and integral calculus – and Collins was not slow to appreciate the value of the work. Thus, on his second visit to London, Newton was able to meet John Collins and the latter described the meeting in a letter to his friend James Gregory:

> I never saw Mr Isaac Newton (who is younger then yourselfe) but twice viz somewhat late upon a Saturday night at his Inne, I then proposed to him the adding of a Musicall Progression, the which he promised to consider and send up. I told him I had done something in it, and would send him what Considerations I had about it, but his came up (before I sent him mine) without any Indication of his method. And againe I saw him the next day having invited him to Dinner: in that little discourse we had about Mathematicks, I asked him what he would make the Subject of his first lectures, he said Opticks proceeding where Mr Barrow had left off...[7]

A long and detailed mathematical correspondence followed between Isaac Newton and John Collins. It consisted of fifteen lengthy letters over a period of about eight months. Newton's prodigious mathematical skills became well known to Collins who kept pressing Newton for publication rights on his mathematical papers. At this point Newton was not in contact with anyone in London other than Collins, and it therefore came as a surprise when a telescope arrived at the Royal Society with the compliments of Dr Newton of Cambridge. It was no ordinary telescope. It was only about 12 inches (30 cm) long yet it could magnify forty times and gave a clearer image than a conventional telescope ten times its length. It had been made with a reflecting mirror instead of the lenses employed by normal telescopes of the times. The unusual design gave rise to the problem of where to mount the eyepiece to give minimum disruption to the incoming light. Newton had solved the problem very cleverly by mounting a small 45-degree prism on the axis, thereby reflecting the light to an eyepiece set into the side of the telescope tube. The Society was impressed and delighted with the new acquisition. The use of a curved mirror was not a new idea but it was a concept that

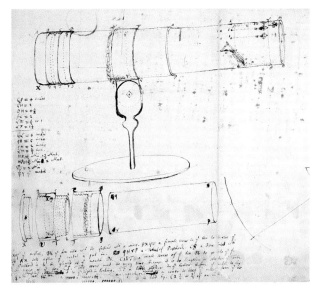

ABOVE A sketch of Newton's first reflecting telescope with his notes on the dimensions and construction. Cambridge University Library Ms Add. 3970 ff 591r–592v

had proved difficult to implement, and craftsmen had been trying for years to perfect the reflecting telescope with very limited success. The telescope was closely examined by the members of the Royal Society, and Henry Oldenburg, the secretary, wrote a generous thank you letter to Isaac Newton. This was the first ever correspondence between Oldenburg and Newton:

> Sr
>
> Your Ingenuity is the occasion of this address by a hand unknowne to you. You have been so generous, as to impart to the Philosophers here, your Invention of contracting Telescopes. It having been considered, and examined here by some of ye most eminent in Opticall Science and practise, and applauded by them, they think it necessary to use some means to secure this Invention from ye Usurpation of forreiners...[8]

Oldenburg's phrase about 'Usurpation of forreiners' has quite an amusing slant considering that he himself was German. One of the 'eminent men in optical science' was the curator of the Royal Society who was not to be outdone by the achievement of an unknown Cambridge don. Robert Hooke announced that, a few years earlier in 1664, he made a 'little tube of about an inch long to put in his fob, which performs more than any telescope of fifty feet long, made after the common manner; but the plague happening which caused his absence, and the fire, whence redounded profitable employments about the city, he neglected to prosecute the same, being unwilling the glass grinders should know anything of the secret'.

The philosophers seem to have been more impressed by Newton having 'contracted' the telescope into a shorter length than by his use of a concave mirror. It was referred to as a 'contracted telescope' rather than as a 'reflecting telescope' and, by doing so, they were missing the main point. In the 1670s the typical astronomical telescope consisted of a large lens mounted on a flagpole, with a system of pulleys to move the lens, and a long stick, rather than a telescope tube, with which to sight the instrument. At night the astronomers wandered round in the dark holding the sighting stick in one hand and the eyepiece to their eye with the other, staring at the lens on the flagpole in the hope of finding the right place for the clearest image. The longer the focal length of the objective lens the greater the magnifying power, and refracting telescopes therefore grew longer and longer and became more and more unwieldy. Thus, Newton's telescope was not judged in terms of magnification but in comparison with the longest telescope it could simulate. It was not a valid comparison for the focal length of the eyepiece was the other factor that determined the magnification. To achieve a magnification of forty in such a small instrument, with such a clear image, free from the coloured fringes seen in the refractors, was thought of as a remarkable achievement.

The story of how Newton came to build the telescope went back several years. Every astronomer had noticed the coloured fringes that appeared at the edges of bright objects seen through a telescope. The fringes were familiar but they were not fully understood. Because of his experiments with the prism, Newton knew that the fringes resulted from the different paths of the different colours through the lens. He prepared a clever experiment in which he took a strip of card and painted half of it red, the other half blue. He took a thread of fine black silk and wound it around the card to give the effect of very fine lines on both a red and a blue background. He then illuminated the card with strong candle light, and he used a telescope lens to create an image of the card on white paper. He discovered exactly what he suspected, that it was impossible to obtain a sharp image of both colours at the same distance from the lens. The blue rays focused an inch-and-a-half (3.8 cm) closer to the lens than the red. He concluded that sharp focus could not be achieved using a glass lens.

Newton also experimented with the use of two refractive media, and he put two thin glass lenses together and filled the space between with water. By using two different refractive media it was possible to minimize the problem but it was a difficult and clumsy way forward and it was not a perfect solution. He knew, however, that all the colours obeyed the same laws of reflection, and that the way to eliminate the aberration was to use a mirror instead of a lens for the telescope objective. Newton was not the first to realize the potential of the reflecting telescope. James Gregory at St Andrews University had been trying for several years to make a reflecting telescope on the same principle, and he had very sensibly employed the best craftsmen he could find but with only limited success. To the surprise of the Royal Society, Newton had fashioned his telescope with his own hands, even to the casting and grinding of the mirror which he made from speculum metal in his own furnace, grinding and polishing the mirror to a fine reflecting finish. The speculum metal was an alloy of copper and tin. Newton had experimented with different proportions and with additives such as antimony and arsenic to improve the surface finish.

His first effort was only 6 inches (15 cm) long; the eye piece was a plano-convex lens with a focal length of one-sixth or one-seventh of an inch (4.2 or 3.6 mm). It had a magnification of about forty. 'I have seen with it Jupiter distinctly round and his satellites, and Venus horned', he wrote to an unknown friend. He was pleased with the image but he was not happy about the reflecting properties of the mirror. The major problem was the tarnishing of the surface of the mirror which required that it had to be removed at regular intervals for repolishing. Newton's drawing of his first telescope survives but the instrument itself does not. The telescope he sent to the Royal Society was his second attempt. It had a larger mirror and it was more robust with an attractive spherical mounting. Newton was delighted and flattered by the reaction of the Royal Society to his telescope. His reply to Henry Oldenburg showed the modesty of his youth:

Sr

At the reading of your letter I was surprised to see so much care taken about securing an invention to mee, of wch I have hitherto had so little value. And therefore the R. Society is pleased to think it worth patronizing, I must acknowledg it deserves much more of them for that, then of mee, who, had not the communication of it been desired, might have let it still remained in private as it hath already done some yeares...[9]

He goes on to supply a few technical details:

The description of ye instrument you sent mee is very well, onely the radius of the concave metall wch you put 14 inches is justly 12 2/3 or 13 inches, & ye radius of ye eye glass wch you put half an inch is the twelft part of it, if not lesse. For ye metall collects ye suns rays at 6 1/3 inches distant, & ye eye glass at less than 1/6th part of an inch from its vertex. By the tooles to wch they were ground I know their dimensions, & particularly measuring the diameter of the hemisphericall concave in wch ye eye glasse was ground I find the 6th part of an inch...

And to this proportion is very consentaneous ye observation of the crowns on the weathercock. For the scheme represents it bigger by 20 times when seen through this, then when through an ordinary perspective. And so supposing that to magnify 13 or 14 times, as by the description it should, this by the experiment proportionably must magnify almost as much as I have assigned it.[10]

A long correspondence followed about the telescope and, in a later letter, Newton was
very honest about the shortcomings of his instrument and the tarnishing of the mirror:

> With the telescope which I have made, I have sometimes seen remote objects, and particularly the
> moon, very distinct, in those parts of it which were neare the sides of the visible angle. And at other
> times, when it hath been otherwise put together, it hath exhibited things not without some confusion;
> which difference I attributed chiefly to some imperfection that might possibly be either in the figures of
> the metalls or eye-glasse; and once I found it caused by a little tarnishing of the metal in four or five
> days of moist weather.[11]

It was on the strength of his telescope that Isaac Newton was proposed as a member of
the Royal Society in December 1671. He was proposed by Seth Ward, the Bishop of
Salisbury, a founder member of the Society whose connections went back to the Oxford
days. Newton ended his letter to Oldenburg by expressing his thanks to Seth Ward. His
election to the Society took place a few days later:

> I am very sensible of the honour done me by ye B[isho]p of Sarum in proposing mee Candidate &
> wch I hope will bee further conferred upon mee by my Election into the Society. And if so, I shall
> endeavour to testify my gratitude by ye promoting your Philosophical designes
> Sr I am
> Your very humble servant
> I Newton[12]

Isaac Newton was thus pleased and flattered that the erudite members of the Royal
Society should make so much of his telescope. He wanted more contact with the
members in London, and he agreed to Oldenburg's suggestion that he should submit a
paper on his theories of light for publication in the *Philosophical Transactions*. The paper
would be read not only by interested parties in England but also by their fellows on
the continent.

    When it arrived, Newton's paper was about five thousand words long. He began by
describing how he had taken a triangular glass prism and passed the light from a hole in
the window shutters to refract the light on to the opposite wall of his room. He went
on to explain how he had measured the dimensions of his spectrum and carefully
calculated the angles through which the rays were refracted. He contemplated whether
or not the rays of light inside the prism were curved:

> Then I began to suspect, whether the rays, after their trajection through the Prisme, did not move in
> curve lines, and according to their more or less curvity tend to divers parts of the wall. And it increase
> my suspition, when I remembred, that I had often seen a Tennis-ball , struck with an oblique Racket,

describe such a curve line. For, a circular
as well as a progressive motion being
communicated to it by that stroak, its
parts on that side, where the motions
conspire, must press and beat the con-
tigous Air more violently than on the
other, and there excite a reluctancy and
reaction of the Air proportionably
greater. And for the same reason, if the
Rays of light should possibly be globular
bodies, and by thier oblique passage our
of one medium into another acquire a
circulating motion, they ought to feel the
greater resistance from the ambient
Either on that side, where the motions
conspire and thence be continually
bowed to the other.[13]

ABOVE Seventeenth century astronomer. The telescope tube
was not seen as a necessity for large telescopes, the mounting
arrangement was very primitive using flagpoles and ropes to
adjust the lens. The cord helped the user to get the eyepiece
the right distance from the objective lens.

He was searching for the nature of
light which he thought might be
transmitted by very small particles.
He wanted to find evidence of
these particles which, if they
existed, should bend their track
like a tennis ball if they could be
made to spin. But he had to admit that he could find no sign whatever of any curvature
– in all his experiments the light always travelled in straight lines. He went on to explain
how he had developed the idea of a reflecting telescope at Cambridge before the time
of the plague, and how his project had been shelved for two years when he spent most
of his time in Woolsthorpe. He had thought about making a microscope with a
reflecting mirror but this project had never become a reality.

He explains that as rays of light differ in their 'refrangibility' so they differ in their
colour. 'To the same degree of refrangibility ever belongs the same colour.' The colour,
once separated, cannot be changed by further refraction or by reflection. He described
the experiments by which he had proved his statements on light. He defined the colours
in the order red, yellow, green, blue, and violet-purple, together with orange and indigo
and 'an indefinite variety of intermediate gradations'. He explained his experiments with
combining colours. Red and yellow light made an impression of orange, this being the
colour lying between them in the spectrum. Similarly orange and green could be

combined to make yellow, and yellow and blue light created an impression of green. By combining all the colours it was possible to create a pure white light again. Newton was quite ecstatic over this effect that he had discovered:

> *But the most surprising and wonderful composition was that of Whiteness. There is no one sort of Rays which alone can exhibit this. 'Tis ever compounded, and to its composition are requisite all the aforesaid primary Colours, mixed in a due proportion. I have often with Admiration beheld, that all the colours of the Prisme being made to converge, and thereby to be again mixed as they were in the light before it was incident upon the Prisme, reproduced light, initirely and perfectly white, and not at all sensibly differing from the Direct light of the Sun, unless when the glasses I used, were not sufficiently clear; for than they would a little incline to their colour.*[14]

Newton's was a brilliant thesis which condensed hundreds of experiments conducted over a period of several years into a paper that was read at one of the Society's meetings. It received a great ovation and it was agreed that Henry Oldenburg should write to the author expressing the thanks of the Society for 'this very ingenious discourse'. Few, if any, appreciated it at the time but Newton's thesis on light was historically very significant in that it was the first ever application of the scientific method. He had made the experiments and noted the results very carefully. He had made measurements. His experiments had led him on to perform more experiments, to formulate a theory, and then to create further experiments to put the theory to the test. He had formulated a theory of light which he knew was not complete, but the experiments were carefully described so that any later researcher could repeat them. The journal book of the Royal Society described the work:

> *…concerning his discovery about the nature of light, refraction and colours, importing that light was not a similar, but a heterogeneous thing, consisting of difform rays, which had essentially different refractions, abstracted from bodies they pass through, and that colours are produced from such and such rays, whereof some in their own nature are disposed to produce red, others green, others blue, others purple, etc., and that whiteness is nothing but a mixture of all sorts of colours, or that 'tis produced by all sorts of colours blended together …*
>
> *[It was] ordered that the Author be solemnly thanked, in the name of the Society, for this very ingenious discourse, and be made acquainted that the Society think very fit, if he consent, to have it forthwith published, as well for the greater conveniency of having it well considered by philosophers, as for securing the considerable notions thereof to the Author, against the arrogations of others.*[15]

The author was once again flattered by the praise that Oldenburg pressed upon him. 'I before thought it was a great favour to have beene made a member of that honourable body', he wrote. 'But I am now more sensible of the advantage. For believe me Sr I doe not onely esteem it a duty to concurre wth them in ye promotion of reall knowledg, but a great deal of privelege that instead of exposing discourses to a prejudic't and censorious multitude (by wch many truths have been bafled and lost) I may wth freedom apply my self to so judicious & impartiall an Assembly.'

When Newton gained his promotion to Lucasian Professor of Mathematics it obviously did a great deal for his confidence, and it is no coincidence that he submitted his telescope and then his paper on light to the Royal Society after he could claim the status of a professor. It was obvious that the understanding of light was a necessary preliminary to the understanding of the universe. All astronomical observations and the great majority of terrestrial experiments were dependent on light for their observation. Newton considered his discovery of the composition of white light to be 'in my judgement the oddest, if not the most considerable detection, which hath hitherto been made in the operations of nature'. His thesis was immediately appreciated as a major work on the subject but one of the main functions of the *Philosophical Transactions* was to invite criticism and discussion on new theories of this kind. Newton's radical ideas generated a great deal of both. Critics of Newton's theory came forward from an international array of scientists. They included Ignatius Pardies, a Jesuit from Paris; the Dutch philosopher Christiaan Huygens who also happened to be resident in Paris; Francis Hall (alias Father Linus) from the Jesuit College at Liège; and Robert Hooke on his home ground at the Royal Society.

Newton's first critic was Father Pardies who was the professor of natural philosophy at the College of Clermont in Paris. Pardies objected to the whole theory being founded on experiments with the prism, and he criticized Newton's *experimentum crucis* as not sufficient to prove his theory of colours. It was a very fair criticism but Pardies had misunderstood the experiment, and Newton went to great lengths to explain his *experimentum crucis* in more detail. Father Pardies generously accepted Newton's careful explanations and, when he understood more fully, he apologized to Newton for the criticism. Newton responded amicably and warmed so much to his critic that he expounded his golden rule of science in a letter to Pardies:

> For the best and safest method of philosophising seems to be, first to enquire diligently into the properties of things, and of establishing those properties by experiments, and then to proceed more slowly to hypotheses for the explanation of them. For hypotheses should be subservient only in explaining the properties of things, but not assumed in determining them; unless so far as they may furnish experiments. For if the possibility of hypotheses is the be the test of the truth and reality of things, I see not how certainty can be obtained in any science; since numerous hypotheses may be devised, which shall seem to overcome new difficulties. Hence it has been here thought necessary to lay aside all hypotheses, as foreign to the purpose, that the force of the objection should be abstractedly considered, and receive a more full and general answer...[16]

Christiaan Huygens (1629–95) was a well-respected researcher in the field of optics. He was impressed by Newton's new theory but he thought it required more proof and that it could stand only as an hypothesis. Newton again went to great lengths to explain his experiments to Huygens and the latter quickly realized that Newton had a very deep and sensitive nature. 'Seeing that he [Newton] maintains his opinions with so much concern, I list not to dispute', wrote Huygens to Oldenburg. Neither Newton nor Huygens wanted to come to blows and they came instead to have a deep mutual respect.

A harsher critic was Francis Hall, an Englishman living in Liège under the name of Line or Linus. He was convinced that Newton's work was wrong and that he had not observed the sun but rather an image of a cloud through the prism. 'And then indeed it was noe marvell, the sayd spectrum should be longer than broad; since the cloud or clouds now enlightened, were in order to those colours like to a great sunne, making a far greater angle of intersection in the sayd hole, then the true rays of the sunne do make; and therefore able to enlighten the whole length of the Prisme, and not only some small part of the thereof …' In trying to repeat Newton's experiment Linus placed his image much too close to the prism and this was the reason why he could not obtain the same results.

No amount of careful explanation by Newton could convince Linus that he had misinterpreted the experiment. After an exchange of carefully worded letters, Newton became exasperated with Linus and he wisely decided to ignore the comments on the grounds that they would die a death when other researchers repeated his experiments. Henry Oldenburg was a very efficient secretary, he loved to prolong the controversy in the *Philosophical Transactions*, and he urged Newton to respond to his critics. The controversy dragged on for more than two years until the death of Father Linus in 1675 from 'a great Epidemicall of Catarre'. This was not the end of the matter. Linus's colleague, John Gascoines of Liège, wrote to defend his deceased friend. He was no experimenter but he did make a good point about the English skies!

'Mr Newton's experiment will hardly stand', wrote Gascoines. 'For as Mr Line was always at home, and in his chamber, and ordinarily kept his Prisme just ready before the hole, also we think it probable he hath tried his experiment thrice for Mr Newton's once, and that in a clearer and more uncloudy sky than ordinarily England doth allow.'[16]

Newton's harshest critic was his own countryman, Robert Hooke, who had already published his theory of light in *Micrographia*, and therefore considered himself to be an expert on the subject. His critique started off well enough. 'I have perused the Excellent Discourse of Mr Newton about colours and Refractions', he wrote. 'And I was not a little pleased with the niceness and the curiosity of his observations.' It was what followed that had the sting in it.

But though I wholy agree with him as to the truth of those he hath alledges, as having by many hundreds of tryalls found them soe, yet as to his Hypothesis of solving the phenomena of Colours thereby I confesse I cannot see any undeniable argument to convince me of the certainty thereof. For all the expts & obss: I have hitherto made, nay and even those very expts which he alledged, doe seem to me to prove that light is nothing but a pulse or motion propagated through an homogeneous uniform and transparent medium…

But how certaine soever I think myself of my hypothesis, wch I did not take up without first trying some hundreds of expts; yet I should be very glad to meet with one Experimentum crucis from Mr Newton, that should Divorce me from it. But it is not that, which he soe calls, will doe the turne; for the same pheomenon will be solved by my hypothesis as well as by his without any manner of difficulty or straining: nay I will undertake to shew That the Ray of Light is as twere split or Rarifyd by Refraction, is most certaine, and that therby a differing pulse is propagated…[17]

In a long letter to Oldenburg, Hooke went on to explain that the colours were transmitted to the light by the prism itself which imparted a compound vibration to the light. He claimed that there were only two primary colours, the red and the blue, and that the colours between were mixtures of red and blue light in differing proportions, a hypothesis which he claimed to have proved by mixing blue and scarlet light to produce white light. His basic argument was that all of Newton's findings could be explained on his own hypothesis of light, and there was no need for more than two primary colours in the spectrum.

Hooke's 'scarlet' and 'blew' light both, in fact, covered quite a wide range of the spectrum outside the red and blue, and this was the reason why he was able to produce a tolerable white light by combining them. But there was a very basic difference between the theories of Newton and Hooke. The scarlet and blue light could be combined to produce a sensation of white light on the retina of the eye but Newton realized that this sensation was a psychological effect produced by the chemicals on the retina. He recognized from his measurements on the spectrum that it was the different refractions of the colours through the prism – a function of the wavelength of the light – that were the physical basis of the different colours. The addition of colours to produce white was no more than an illusion. Hooke went on to criticize Newton for not offering an explanation of how the light rays were propagated. Newton had thought long about this problem but he had been unable to decide on whether light was a wave or a particle motion. He merely presented the facts of his experiment. He did not want to formulate a hypothesis about them. The last thing he wanted was to be drawn into an argument about the nature of light.

7
ALCHEMY

IT IS ONE THING TO SHOW THAT A MAN IS IN ERROR, AND ANOTHER
TO PUT HIM IN POSSESSION OF THE TRUTH.

John Locke(1632-1704)

AMONG THE MANY technical problems that Newton had solved to build his telescope was that of making and polishing the mirror. He had carried out many experiments with the casting of metals before he was able to produce the speculum for the mirror and, even then, he was not satisfied with the metal. He knew he was on the right lines, however, and that, given time, better mirrors were possible. His experiments in smelting metals began in 1669. His accounts for that year show the purchase of 'glasses' and 'furnaces', showing that his interest had been stimulated at the time of his first visit to London:

April 1669	£	s	d
For glasses in Cambridge	0	14	0
For glasses in London	0	15	0
For aquafortis, sublimate, oyle pink, fine silver, antimony, vinegar, spirit of wine, white lead, allome nitre, salt of tartar	2	0	0
A furnace	0	8	0
A tin furnace	0	7	0
Joyner	0	6	0
Theatrum chemicum	1	8	0
...			
Lent Wardell 3s, and his wife 2s	0	5	0[1]

Mixed in with his part-time money-lending activities to the Wardells we find 'glasses' which he purchased to develop his work on the telescope. The chemicals and the furnaces are the clue to his interest in the fledgling science of chemistry but the meaning of the *Theatrum Chemicum* is not very obvious. The purchase is a book with the full title *Theatrum Chemicum Britannicum*. It was a major work published in six volumes, and it was written by Elias Ashmole who became the founder of the Ashmolean Museum in Oxford. At first sight it appears to be a treatise on chemistry but, in fact, it pre-dated chemistry by a thousand years – it was a well-known collection of old British alchemical recipes, much of it written in verse! The book was to help Newton with his investigations into alchemy. He had decided to become involved with the old world search for the philosophers' stone that turned base metals into gold, as well as the search for the elixir of life that promised perpetual youth and eternal life.

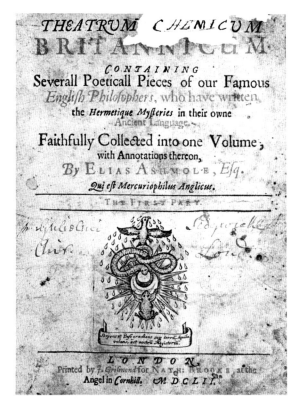

ABOVE Elias Ashmole's *Theatrum Chemicum Britanicum* became a standard work on alchemy. There were many around who believed in the philosopher's stone to turn base metals into gold and in the elixir of life which promised eternal youth.

Elias Ashmole (1617–92) was one of the earliest members of the Royal Society and, in fact, he was admitted in 1661 before the Society received its Royal Charter. He designed a coat of arms for the Royal Society and was given the responsibility of registering it with the College of Arms. He served on a committee 'For collecting all the phenomena of nature hitherto observed, and for all experiments made and recorded' – but for reasons that will soon become apparent his name never appeared in the *Philosophical Transactions*.

Ashmole was one of the old school, and most of his beliefs belonged more to the time of Shakespeare than the time of Newton. He believed in the supernatural. According to John Aubrey Ashmole claimed that, as a boy in Lichfield, he had been entertained by fairies and he knew which houses in the town were built on 'Fayry-ground'. He frequently suffered from an ague, and he treated himself using an old recipe, by hanging three live spiders about his neck, each enclosed in a nutshell. As the spiders died the fever was supposed to die away with it. Ashmole regularly cast horoscopes. The astrologers

Richard Edin, Thomas Streete, and William Lilly were his acquaintances, and they all dedicated publications to him. He collected information for a book on the life of the Elizabethan astrologer and alchemist, Doctor John Dee, but he never actually wrote the biography.

Elias Ashmole's greatest works were on alchemy, and he described the four kinds of philosophers' stone. First, the mineral stone which could convert base metals into gold:

> *fermented with Metalline and Earthy Nature it is wrought up to the degree onely that hath the Power of Transmuting any imperfect earthy matter into its utmost degree of perfection, that is to convert the basest of Metalls into perfect Gold and Silver; Flints into all manner of Precious Stones, [as Rubies, Saphirs, Emeralds, and Diamonds, &c.] and many more Experiments of the like nature...[2]*

Next came the vegetable stone that consisted of a solar, masculine part and a lunar, feminine part. It could cause any plant to grow and produce fruit at any time of the year:

> *[the solar part]...is of so resplendent, transparent Lustre, that the Eye of Man is scarce able to indure it...[and]...if the Lunar part be exposed abroad in a dark Night, Birds will repaire to (and circulate about) it, as a Fly round a Candle, and submit themselves to the Captivity of the Hand...*
>
> *...[it] may be perfectly known the Nature of Man, Beasts, Foules, Fishes, together with all kinds of Trees, Plants, Flowers, &c., and how to produce and make them Grow, flourish & beare Fruit, how to encrease them in Colour and Smell, and when and where we please, and all this not onely at an instant, Experimenti gratia, but Daily, Monethly, Yearly, at any Time, at any Season, yea, in the depth of Winter.[3]*

There was also a magical or prospective stone with which the owner could find any person in the world and which enabled the bearer to understand the languages of birds and animals:

> *...it is possible to discover any Person in what part of the World soever, although never so secretly concealed or hid, in Chambers, Closets, or Cavernes of the Earth. For there it makes a strict Inquisition. In a Word, it fairely presents to your view even the whole World, wherein to behold, heare, or see your Desire. Nay more. It enables Man to understand the Language of the Creatures, as the Chirping of Birds, Lowing of Beasts, &c. To Convey a Spirit into an Image, which by observing the Influence of Heavenly Bodies, shall become a true Oracle; And yet this E[lias] A[shmole] assures you, is not any wayes Necromanticall, or Devilish; but easy, wonderous easy, Naturall and honest.[4]*

Finally, there is the mysterious angelical stone. It had magical powers that enabled the owner to converse with the angels:

…it can neither be seene, felt, or weighed; but Tasted only. The voyce of Man (which bears some proportion to these subtill properties,) comes short in comparison; Nay the Air it selfe is not so penetrable, and yet (Oh mysterious wonder!) A Stone, that will lodge in the Fire to Eternity without being prejudiced. It hath a Divine Power, Celestiall, and Invisible, above the rest; and endowes the possessor with Divine Gifts. It affords the Apparition of Angells, and gives a power of conversing with them, by Dreams and Revelations: nor dare any Evill Spirit approach the Place where it lodgeth.[5]

The alchemists believed that the philosophers' stone could be made from sulphur and mercury. They believed the chemical reactions were living processes with the sulphur as the male element and mercury as the female. The compound produced was called cinnabar. They admitted that it did not always transmute base lead into gold but they claimed that the reason for failure was because the substances were not pure. The 'philosophic' sulphur and 'philosophic' mercury were required for the philosophers' stone and much of the alchemist's time was therefore spent in trying to produce purer samples of these two substances. In the following extract, taken from the medieval alchemist, Geber, silver and gold are created from sulphur and 'Argentvive', the latter element being 'quicksilver' or mercury:

Therefore if clean, fixed, red, and clear Sulphur *fall upon the pure Substance of* Argentvive *(being itself not excelling, but of a small Quantity, and excelled) of it is created pure* Gold. *But if the* Sulphur *be clean, fixed, white and clear, which falls upon the* Substance of Argentvive, *pure silver is made…yet this hath a* Purity *short of the* Purity of Gold, *and a more gross* Inspissation *than* Gold *hath.*[6]

In the seventeenth century a great wealth of literature had been built up on alchemy, and there existed plenty of authentic-sounding stories of the successful transmutation of base metals into gold. A very powerful society of alchemists existed and they combined their philosophy with religious beliefs and guarded their secrets jealously. Newton was running the risk of offending the alchemists by practising their trade, and he also risked offending the university authorities who were very strict about religious practices within their cloistered compounds. He knew, however, that as long as he did not actually publish any controversial works then there was little likelihood of any recriminations. He desperately wanted to get at the truth of nature and the way in which substances combined with heating and chemical reactions – he felt compelled to investigate. The problem with the writings on alchemy was that they were so many. They went right back through the centuries and they came from many different cultures. There was no common nomenclature and this made them very difficult to follow. There was much good and useful material to be found in the writings but there was far more nonsense to be sifted through to get to the facts.

Newton claimed that some of his chemical work was carried out at Woolsthorpe during the plague years but the bulk of it seems to have been done at Trinity College for we know that his room-mate John Wickins acted as Newton's assistant in these early experiments. In the seventeenth century it was not seen as out of place to have a furnace in the living room or the bedroom, and there is a record showing that, in 1673, the chimney of Newton's chamber was rebuilt as an 'Oven mouthed chimney' – presumably to accommodate the experiments in alchemy. John Wickins would help with moving the heavy furnaces to further his room-mate's passion for trying to understanding of the workings of the universe.

In 1674 Newton and Wickins moved to a first-floor room near the gatehouse of Trinity College. Here they were allotted a small garden and, at the end of it, there was a shed that could be used for the experiments with the furnaces. The living accommodation thus became a lot more tolerable and Newton also gained a garden in which to pace up and down with his thoughts. A stone staircase descended from the room to the garden, and the head of the staircase was the place where Newton mounted his telescope to observe the heavens.

The ancient classical theory of matter held that all substances were made from the four elements of earth, water, air, and fire. It was an excellent theory às far as it went, the elements of earth, water, and air representing solids, liquids, and gases. The element fire was something beyond a gas, and it was clear that fire could cause substances to change from solids into liquids and from liquids into gases. Everything, therefore, consisted of these four elements mixed in different proportions. The atomic theory of the Greek philosopher and scientist, Democritus (460–361 BC), was also widely held: this was a simple atomic theory that assumed that all substances were built out of tiny atoms. The atoms were assumed to be simple, small, indivisible particles, perhaps spherical or shaped as regular solids, but they were too small to be seen with the naked eye or even with a microscope.

Subsequently, it turned out to be true that chemical compounds could be broken down into molecules which could be loosely thought of as the same as the atoms of Democritus. The concept of the atom itself being broken down into a nucleus with electrons surrounding it, however, still lay far in the future. In the seventeenth century the atom was much too small to be seen under a microscope so it was little more than a philosophical term. The thickness of a thin film of oil was correctly regarded to approximate to the true size of the atom. This was a quantity that could be measured and Newton, therefore, did have some idea of the tiny dimensions of the atom.

Newton may have been more visionary than others before him but, when it came to speculating on the nature of the atom, he was still very much a prisoner of his times. He surrounded himself with phials, furnaces, retorts, pestles and mortars. He peered into ancient books and manuscripts to try to find a truth and a pattern behind the alchemical reactions. What he sought was not the philosophers' stone, although he did not reject outright the possibility that metals could be transmuted from one to another, but he hoped to find a pattern behind all the reactions and the changing of states and substances in the melting pot. What he was really searching for was the work of the Russian chemist, Dmitri Mendeleyev (1834–1907), nearly two centuries after his time. This was the Periodic Table of the Elements, their scientific classification, their groupings, and the ways in which they combine with one another to form compounds. The laws of physics were hidden by friction and by air resistance but the laws of chemistry lay hidden far deeper – by the molten metals and compounds in the crucible. Newton was able to untangle the laws of physics but, in his time, the laws of chemistry were too obscure for him to unravel, and the truth which he so desperately sought was beyond his reach.

Besides Elias Ashmole, other members of the Royal Society were very interested in alchemy. It was difficult at this stage to differentiate between chemistry and alchemy but, in 1676, Robert Boyle published a paper in which he described how he had made an alloy from mercury and gold. He called his paper 'An experimental Discourse of

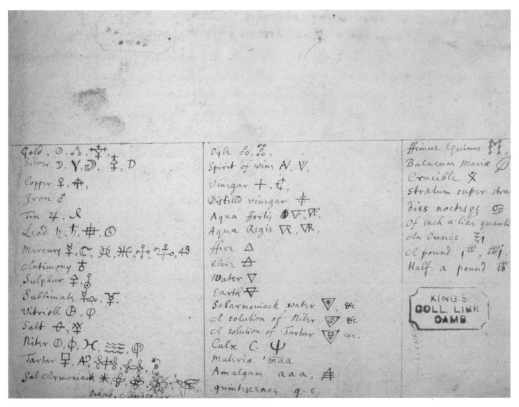

ABOVE Alchemical recipes from Newton's notes, preserved in King's College Library Cambridge.

Quicksilver growing hot with Gold', it seemed that some of the mercury had been transmuted into gold and the experiment therefore attracted a lot of attention from the alchemists. Newton himself was very interested and he wrote privately to Boyle about the experiment. 'I believe the fingers of many will itch to be at the knowledge of the preparation of such a mercury', he wrote, asking Boyle to keep his [own] letter private. He knew, however, that others had discovered the same method, '. . . there being other things besides the transmutation of metals (If those great pretenders brag not) which none but they understand'. He was never wholly convinced that any of his experiments produced a true transmutation from one metal to another but this did not prevent him from continuing the experiments for many years. He wrote copious notes on the subject but his policy was not to publish anything for fear of raising controversy. Newton did eventually publish one short paper on chemistry but it did not appear until late in the 1680s. It was called *De Natura Acidorum* – it was only two pages long and described his speculations on acids and on chemical affinity.

Newton had learnt a lot about the smelting of metals during the making of his reflecting telescope. He carried out many experiments with casting mirrors and he found that an alloy of copper and tin gave the best results for a reflecting surface. When the Royal Society decided to build a reflecting telescope of its own, it was natural that it should consult Isaac Newton about his experience with casting the metal for the mirror. In his letter to Henry Oldenburg, Isaac Newton gives very precise instructions. Here we see Newton as the great sorcerer, peering through the noxious fumes into the crucible, mixing arsenic with the copper and carefully trying not to breathe the poisonous fumes rising from the hot mixture:

> *…I first melted the Copper alone, then put in ye Arsenic, which being melted I stirred then a little together, bewaring in the meane time that I drew not in breath neare the pernicious fumes. After that I put in the Tin, & again, so soon as that was melted, wch was very suddenly, I stirred them well together, & immediately powered them of.*
>
> *I know not whether by letting them stand longer on ye fire after the Tin was melted, a higher degree of fusion would have made the metall porous, but I thought that way I proceeded to bee safest.*[7]

Newton never hesitated to put his own health at risk in his desire to seek out the truth. When he was experimenting on light he wanted to know more about the function of the eye as a receiver for the light. On one occasion he nearly blinded himself by staring at the sunlight to investigate the nature of eye fatigue. His eyes were so fatigued that he suffered a temporary blindness – he could neither read nor write and he had to spend three days in his darkened room before his sight had sufficiently recovered. On another occasion he came even closer to damaging his eyesight. He wanted to investigate the result of distorting the eyeball from its spherical shape and to see what pattern would appear on the retina when the eyeball was pressed out of shape. He used a 'bodkin' – his sketch showed it to be a small knife with a long narrow blade:

I took a bodkine, and put it between my eye and ye bone as neare to the backside of my eye as I could: & pressing my eye wth ye end of it (soe as to make ye curvature in my eye) there appeared sev-erall white, darke, and & coloured circles. Which circles were plainest when I continued to rub my eye with ye point of ye bodkine, but if I held my eye and ye bodkin still though I continued to presse my eye wth it yet ye circles would grow faint & often disappeare untill I renewed ym by moving my eye or ye bodkin.[8]

Newton's investigations into the nature of light were influenced by his tutor Isaac Barrow, the first holder of the Lucasian Chair of Mathematics at Cambridge. In 1669 Barrow published his lectures on light and asked his young protégé, Isaac Newton, to read the lectures and to correct the proofs. The tutor was well pleased with Newton's comments on his work but the strange fact is that, at the time of Barrow's publication, Newton had done most of his own experiments and had formulated his own theory of light which contradicted Barrow's views in several important aspects. Furthermore, as Barrow moved on to higher things, Newton took over the lectures in light and he was soon teaching things that were in contradiction to Barrow's textbook. It seems that Isaac Barrow did not discover Newton's view of light until it was published in the *Philosophical Transactions* about two years later. Only then did Barrow find out that the students had been taught a completely different theory from the one which he had published. Barrow did not take offence. As the first to recognize Newton's genius, it seems probable that he understood the mysterious workings of Newton's mind better than most. He also knew something of Newton's phobia about secrecy. He accepted that his brilliant pupil had been an able assistant to him and he raised no objections to Newton's teachings.

In his capacity as Master of Trinity College, Isaac Barrow tried to persuade the university to build a 'theatre' for graduation purposes, to serve the same function as the Sheldonian at Oxford. The university did not support the idea so Barrow put his efforts into the improvement of his own college instead. He proposed that there should be a magnificent new library at Trinity which would occupy the whole west side of Neville's Court. Barrow did not stay at Cambridge long enough to see his new library started, let alone finished, but Newton saw the laying of the foundations in 1676 and he was still resident in Cambridge in the 1690s when the building was completed. The architect was Christopher Wren. With his heavy commitments in London, it is hard to understand how Wren found time to supervise the building of Trinity College Library. Wren made only the briefest of visits to Cambridge but he and Newton became acquainted, and Newton came greatly to respect Wren as one of the best mathematicians in England.

Newton's quest for truth also included the question of the origin and the creation of the world, and this led him to a study of the scriptures. He was happy enough to accept the biblical account of the Creation but he became convinced that the interpretation of the scriptures had at some point been corrupted. He believed in the Unitarianism tradition which was notorious because it did not accept the doctrine of the Trinity. This was an ironic situation for one so devoted to Trinity College, and Newton had to be very secretive about his beliefs for, if they were discovered, he would certainly have lost his post at the university. He had to take holy orders if he wished to continue at the university. Four times Newton had taken an oath to assert his orthodoxy but, in 1673, the situation reached a climax. His beliefs would not allow him to take the oath a fifth time but the only alternative was to lose his fellowship and consequently his livelihood. He saw a bleak financial future ahead and he wrote to Henry Oldenburg asking to withdraw from the Royal Society on the grounds of the distance from Cambridge to London – he did not state his true reasons:

> ...Sr I desire that you will procure that I may be put out from being any longer fellow of ye R. Society. For though I honour that body, yet since I see I shall neither profit them, nor (by reason of this distance) can partake of the advantage of their Assemblies, I desire to withdraw. If you please to do me this favour you will oblige
> Your humble servant
> I Newton[9]

He included the sum of one pound and six shillings as arrears in his subscription. Oldenburg was very reluctant to lose Newton and offered to 'take from him ye trouble of sending his qterly paymts'. The offer dented Newton's pride. In fact, the Royal Society could hardly afford to lose any members, or their quarterly payments. In 1674 their debts amounted to the considerable sum of £1957, most of which was accounted for by unpaid membership subscriptions.

The affair was soon forgotten and Newton remained a member. Early in 1675 Newton made a special visit to London in an attempt to retain his fellowship without taking the oath of orthodoxy. He needed a special dispensation from the king to retain his post without taking holy orders. The Royal Society and others fully recognized Newton's merits as a scientist and a mathematician, and it seems that Charles II also knew of his work. The king was not fully conversant with Newton's heretical beliefs but he was willing 'to give all just encouragement to learned men who are & shall be elected to ye said [Lucasian] Professorship'. It set a new precedent and it says much for the open-mindedness of the king and of the times that Newton was able to retain his chair without taking the oath.

It was during this visit to London that Newton made his first appearance at a meeting of the Royal Society on 18 February 1675. He was still in London during

March, and he attended two more meetings when he hoped to see Robert Hooke perform the *Experimentum Crucis* to demonstrate his theory of light before the Society. He was disappointed when Hooke decided instead to read a paper of his own on diffraction and interference. Newton and Hooke met face to face for the first time at these meetings of the Royal Society. There is a feeling that, after the exchange of letters about the theory of light, the meeting was not the total disaster that might have been predicted as a result of earlier and subsequent events. The two did not renew their correspondence immediately but, about a year later, Hooke decided to write to Newton at Cambridge. It was a polite and well-worded letter that amounted to an olive branch and an apology for their differences in times past. Hooke suspected that Oldenburg had exaggerated his criticism of Newton's discourse on the hypothesis of light and he wanted to clarify this with Newton:

Sr

The Hearing of a letter of yours read last week in the meeting of ye Royall Society made me suspect yt you might have been some way or other misinformed concerning me and this suspicion was the more prevalent with me, when I called to mind the experience I have formerly had of the like sinister practices. I have therefore taken the freedom wch I hope I may be allowed in philosophicall matters to acquaint you of myself, first that I do noeways approve of contention or fending and proving in print, and shall be very unwillingly drawn to such kind of warr. Next that I have a mind very desirous of and very ready to imbrace any truth that shall be discovered though it may much thwart and contradict any opinions or notions I have formerly imbraced as such. Thirdly that I doe justly value your excellent Disquisitions and am extremely well pleased to see those notions promoted and improved which I long since began, but had not time to compleat.

Having made a handsome apology for what had passed, Hooke went on to praise Newton's work and to flatter him for having carried his ideas further than his own. He made all the right noises about the search for the truth and the need to work together for a common end:

That I judge you have gone farther in that affair much than I did, and that as I judge you cannot meet with any subject more worthy your contemplation, so I believe the subject cannot meet with a fitter and more able person to inquire into it than yourself, who are every way accomplished to compleat, rectify and reform what were the sentiments of my younger studies, which I designed to have done somewhat at myself, if my other more troublesome employments would have permitted, though I am sufficiently sensible it would have been with abilities much inferior to yours. Your Designes and myne I suppose aim both at the same thing wch is the Discovery of truth and I suppose we can both endure to hear objections, so as they come not in a manner of open hostility, and have minds equally inclined to yield to the plainest: deductions of reason from experiment. If therefore you will please to correspond

about such matters by private letter I shall very gladly imbrace it and when I shall have the happiness
to peruse your excellent discourse (which I can as yet understand nothing more of by hearing it cursori-
ly read) I shall if it be not ungrateful to you send you freely my objections, if I have any, or my con-
currences, if I am convinced, which is the more likely. This way of contending I believe to be the more
philosophicall of the two, for though I confess the collision of two hard-to-yield contenders may produce
light yet if they be put together by the ears of other's hands and incentives, it will produce rather ill
concomitant heat which serves for no other use but [to] kindle cole. Sr I hope you will pardon this
plainness of your very affectionate humble servt
Robert Hooke[10]

Newton accepted the apology and wrote back a few days later. His letter was worded in a conciliatory fashion, and it was in this reply to Hooke that he went so far as to make his famous remark about standing on the shoulders of giants:

Sr

At ye reading of your letter I was exceedingly well pleased & satisfied wth our generous freedom, &
think you have done what becomes a true Philosophical spirit. There is nothing wch I desire to avoyde
in matters of Philosophy more then contention, nor any kind of contention more then one inprint: &
therefore I gladly embrace your proposal of a private correspondence. What's done before many witnesses
is seldome wthout some further concern then that for truth: but what passes between friends in private
usually deserves ye name of consultation rather then contest, & so I hope it will prove between you &
me. Your animadversions will be therefore very welcome to me: for though I was formerly tired wth this
subject, & have not yet nor I beleive ever shall recover so much love for it as to delight in spending
time about it; yet to have at once in short ye strongest or most pertinent Objections that may be made,
I could really desire, & know no man better able to furnish me wth them then your self. In this you
will oblige me. And if there be any thing els in my papers in wch you apprehend I have assumed too
much, or not done you right, if you please to reserve your sentiments of it for a private letter, I hope
you will find also that I am not so much in love wth philosophical productions but yt I can make
them yeild to equity & friendship. But, in ye meane time you defer too much to my ability for search-
ing into this subject. What Des-Cartes did was a good step. You have added much several ways, &
especially in taking ye colours of thin plates into philosophical consideration. If I have seen further it is
by standing on ye sholders of Giants…

Newton went on to make reference to two of Hooke's experiments and he even offered to make an astronomical observation for him. We discover that, when in London, he had even gone as far as to call at Hooke's lodgings to see him:

But I make no question but you have divers very considerable experiments besides those you have published,
& some it's very probable the same wth some of those in my late papers. Two at least there are wch I know

you have observed, ye dilatation of ye coloured rings by ye obliquation of ye eye, & ye apparition of a black spot at ye contact of two convex glasses & at ye top of a water bubble; and it's probable there may be more, besides others wch I have not made: so yt I have reason to defer as much, or more, in this respect to you as you would do to me, especially considering how much you have been diverted by buisiness. But not to insist on this: your Letter gives me occasion to inquire concerning an observation you were propounding to me to make here of ye transit of a star near ye Zenith. I came out of London some days sooner then I told you of, it falling out so that I was to meet a friend then at Newmarket, & so missed of your intended directions. Yet I called at your lodgings a day or two before I came away, but missed of you. If therefore you continue in ye mind to have it observed, you may by sending your directions command your humble Servant,

Is. Newton[11]

The subservient forms of address, the 'affectionate' and 'humble' servants, were of course no more than the polite formality of the times. But Hooke addressed Newton as 'my much esteemed friend' and Newton responded with 'his honoured friend'. They did not correspond again for over a year but there was a friendly exchange of six short letters between December 1677 and June 1678 when Newton signed off as 'your real friend and humble servant' and Hooke returned with 'your very affectionate humble servant'. Newton's letters were addressed 'For his ever honoured friend, Mr Robert Hooke'. 'If this come to your hands before you leave Lincolnshire', wrote Hooke to Newton, 'pray inquire what plaines there are in that country fit for measuring any considerable Length in a straight line... ' A few days later Newton replied to his 'ever honoured friend' that 'Ye longest Level, out of ye fens, that I can hear of, is upon Lincoln heath from Lincoln to Summerby, neare Grantham, which is recconned twenty mile & lies in a line north and south...' Hooke offered no reason for his proposed surveying trip but perhaps he had ideas for measuring the curvature of the Earth.

The correspondence serves to show another great dilemma in Newton's character. His relationship with Hooke improved to the point where they certainly professed great friendship in their correspondence even though their courtesy was greatly exaggerated. During this same period, however, Isaac Newton became less and less sociable and he became increasingly irritable in the correspondence between himself and other researchers. For a decade or more he tried to decrease his acquaintance and to retreat more and more into his ivory tower at Trinity College. The first sign of his problem came very early in his correspondence with the Royal Society. John Collins had furthered Newton's acquaintance by introducing him to Michael Dary, the author of a mathematical textbook published in 1669, and he had also involved Newton with an annuity problem that he thought would be of interest to other parties. For the best of reasons, John Collins wanted to involve Newton more and more with the mathematical and scientific community but Newton wrote to John Collins expressing his reservations.

Sr

Two days since I received yours & Mr Dary's letter with a book for wch I thank Mr Dary, & have here inclosed sent him my thoughts of what hee desired. That solution of the annuity Probleme if it will bee of any use you have my leave to insert it into the Philosophical Transactions *soe it bee without my name to it. For I see not what there is desireable in publick esteeme, were I able to acquire & maintaine it. It would perhaps increase my acquaintance, ye thing which I chiefly study to decline...*[12]

To push forward the frontiers of knowledge, to voyage on strange seas of thought alone, took a great toll. John Wickins and Humphrey Newton, both of whom lived with Isaac Newton at different times, told of how he became totally engrossed in his thoughts. Meals, appointments, and even sleep were all forgotten when a new problem took over his mind. Letters and outside disturbances were seen as annoying interruptions to his thoughts and meditations.

The character of the absent-minded professor was born at Cambridge with Isaac Newton. When he applied his mind to an abstract problem, nothing was allowed to distract him, and the enquiries of outsiders, however well meaning, were seen as intrusion s on his privacy. When the controversy over his theory of light rose its head yet again, he was engrossed in new fields of thought and it was too much for him to have to defend his earlier work. He regretted ever having published his ideas in the first place, and he resented having to find the time and effort to defend himself against the critics. At the Jesuit college in Liège, Father Linus was succeeded by Anthony Lucas who, in 1676, decided to contact Newton yet again about the experiment with the spectrum and thereby to reopen old wounds. Newton answered the enquiry from Lucas generously enough. He replied with a very long and detailed letter, carefully trying to avoid the confusions that Linus had encountered. His painstaking efforts were of no use. Lucas continued the correspondence and wrote a second and then a third letter to Newton, showing that he had not understood Newton's careful explanations. Eventually Newton could take no more and he vented his frustration in an angry reply:

....Pray trouble your self no further to reconcile me with truth but let us know your own mistakes...You endeavor to oblige into a new dispute with you by calling me a Demurrer... And my prefer to answer one or two of your objections which you should recommend for ye best you despise as if it was Illegal (as you term it) if I answer not all. Do men use to press one another into Disputes? Or am I bound to satisfy you? It seems you thought it not enough to propound Objections unless you might insult over me for my inability to answer them all, or durst not trust your own judgement in choosing ye best. But how know you yt I did not think them too weak to require an answer & only to gratify your importunity [complied] to answer one or two of ye best? How know you but yt other prudential reasons might make me averse from contending with you ? But I forbeare to explain these things further for I do not think

this a fit Subject to dispute about, & therefore have given these hints only in a private Letter, of which kind you are also to esteem my former answer to your second. I hope you will consider how little I desire to explain your proceedings in public & make this use of it to deal candidly wth me for ye future.[13]

The rebuke did not deter Anthony Lucas. He wrote back yet again but this time Newton simply ignored his correspondence.

At Cambridge Newton continued to deliver his lectures to an ever-shrinking class of students, and he made no effort to water down his lectures to the point where the students could understand them. When nobody at all turned up, he would dutifully wait fifteen minutes before leaving the lecture room to get back to his researches.

Alchemy was not his only major interest during this period. His thoughts turned to how the world had been created and he began to wonder about the age of the Earth and the time scales involved. He was unable to attribute the creation of the world to anything other than God, and he was happy to accept the account in Genesis as being near to the truth. Archbishop Ussher's (1581–1656) chronology of the Bible was published in 1654 when he estimated that the date of the creation was in 4004 BC. His dates were based on the biblical genealogies and the number of generations since Adam and Eve. Newton was not convinced by Ussher's chronology and he was very disturbed when he calculated that a sphere the size of the Earth, at the temperature of red-hot iron, would take 50,000 years to cool down to the Earth's current temperature. This calculation did not cause him to reject the scriptures, and he looked for other factors to explain the discrepancy. He wisely chose not to publish any of his theological ideas. He knew that the angry reaction experienced in an earlier age by Copernicus and Galileo was bound to follow.

He decided that the two most reliable histories of humankind were the Bible and the works of the Greek historian Herodotus (c. 484–424 BC). With his usual thoroughness, he spent much of his time studying the scriptures and, though his Hebrew was far from fluent, he studied them in the original language wherever possible. Seventeenth-century theology was teeming with new sects and philosophies and, as we have seen, the one which Newton thought closest to the truth was the Unitarian creed which was orthodox except in one very important particular – it rejected the doctrine of the Trinity. The roots of Unitarianism went back to the fourth century when the Trinity was condemned by the Greek theologian, Arius, at the Council of Nicaea in AD 325. As with so many other religious sects, the Unitarians themselves were divided and they had formed at least three separate groups by the seventeenth century. The Arians claimed that Jesus was begot by God but that he existed before time began, that he should be worshipped, and that through him God created all things. The Socinians, also Unitarians, saw Christ as an object of prayer but denied that he existed before his appearance on Earth. Thirdly, there were the Humanitarians who saw Christ merely as an exceptional man but not as a god, and he was therefore undeserving of worship. Of these three interpretations, it was the first, the Arian creed, that Isaac Newton espoused.

To get to the source of the scriptures it was necessary to study the chronology which, in this context, meant the dating of the main events in the history of the world. Newton knew that, where Archbishop Ussher's chronology related solely to the Bible, there were other reliable sources that could help him with the dating. One such source was the in work of Herodotus who related the story of Jason and the Golden Fleece. Newton evidently believed everything in Herodotus to be true, and he put a lot of effort into dating the voyage of Jason and the Argonauts which he claimed to have been a real event that happened in 957 BC. He knew that an astronomer named Chiron had prepared a celestial sphere for the voyage of the Argonauts to help them with their navigation, and Newton also knew the positions of the stars where Chiron had placed the equinoctial and solstitial points on his celestial sphere. The ancient astronomer had located these points many degrees away from their positions in Newton's century. Isaac Newton knew that, because of the precession of the equinoxes, these equinoctial points progressed around a small circle in the sky by about 50 seconds of arc every year. They had progressed a total of nearly 37 degrees from the time of the Argonauts to the time of Newton, and he calculated that 2646 years were required for this amount of progression. His method was very scientific but, with the advantage of hindsight, it seems obvious that he was putting far too much trust in his source data.

The estimate is valuable in that it probably indicates the time when the story of the Argonauts was first told. But the fact that Jason's voyage was a mythical event meant that the calculation was of limited value. Newton was perfectly correct, however, to apply astronomical principles to the dating of historical events. Today, the most reliable chronologies have been corrected by reference to observations of eclipses of the Sun, or to known comets that enable the astronomer to fix an accurate date and sometimes even a time of day. A good example is the eclipse of the Sun predicted by Thales of Miletus in 585 BC.

Throughout the 1670s, Newton retreated more and more into his ivory tower but he made the occasional visit to London and he managed to visit his mother at Woolsthorpe nearly every year. In the summer of 1679 he heard that his mother was seriously ill. Her son Benjamin Smith, Newton's stepbrother, had been taken ill by a 'malignant' fever which, in the seventeenth century, probably meant a 'contagious' fever. Hannah travelled to Stamford to nurse her son and, as a result, she caught the fever herself. When Isaac discovered the situation, he in turn travelled to Stamford to nurse his mother. He found Hannah very ill. It was a moving deathbed scene, and he sat up all night with her giving her his own medical concoctions:

...sate up whole nights with her, gave her all her Physic himself, dressed all her blisters with his own hands & made use of that manual dexterity for wch he was so remarkable to lessen the pain wch

always attends the dressing and torturing remedy usually applied in that distemper with as much readiness as he ever had employed it in the most delightfull experiments.[14]

Benjamin Smith recovered from the fever and Isaac Newton did not contract it himself but Newton's vast store of knowledge and learning was of no avail to his mother and, at the beginning of June, Hannah Ayscough Newton Smith died. Hannah lived long enough to see her son become a professor at Cambridge University – this alone would have been a source of great pride for her – but she did not live long enough to see the full flowering of his genius and the recognition he received from society. Her body was taken from Stamford back to Colsterworth where the parish register records her burial on 4 June 1679.

Isaac Newton remained some months at Woolsthorpe to sort out his mother's estate. The manor of Woolsthorpe was his by birthright and he was his mother's main beneficiary. His stepbrother Benjamin Smith and stepsisters Mary and Hannah Smith received a smaller share of the estate but they had no cause for complaint. They had inherited from their father, Barnabas Smith, more than thirty years before. Hannah's death was the occasion for a family reunion but there is no correspondence from this time to throw any light on the relationships between Isaac Newton and his half siblings. Hannah Smith junior was married to the Reverend Robert Barton who held a living in Northamptonshire. It is of interest to note in passing that their third child, Catherine, was born in the year that her grandmother, Hannah Smith senior, died. Catherine Barton was destined to play a major part in her uncle Isaac's old age.

It took Isaac Newton until November to sort out the estate. The illness and the death of his mother cast a great cloud over him and he achieved relatively little in the year 1679. He had written to Robert Boyle in the previous February but he had no other communication with the scientific world until he returned to Cambridge on 27 November.

There was a letter waiting from his old adversary Robert Hooke.

8

THE FREEZE

ONE CANNOT CONCEIVE ANYTHING SO STRANGE AND SO
IMPLAUSIBLE THAT IT HAS NOT ALREADY BEEN SAID BY ONE
PHILOSOPHER OR ANOTHER.

René Descartes (1596-1650)

'FINDING BY OUR REGISTERS that you were pleasd to correspond wth Mr Oldenburg and having also had the happinesse of Receiving some Letters from you my self, make me presume to trouble you wth this present scribble...', wrote Hooke to Newton. 'I hope therefore that you will please to continue your former favours to the Society by communicating what shall occur to you that is philosophicall, and in returne I shall be sure to acquaint you wth what we shall Receive considerable from other parts or find out new here . . .' He went on to reassure Newton that whatever ideas he may choose to send would not be taken any further without his consent. 'And you may be assured that whatever shall be soe communicated shall be noe otherwise farther imparted or disposed of then you yourself shall prescribe.'

He went on to describe the mensuration work done by the Frenchman Picard who had calculated the size of the Earth by measuring the length of a degree of latitude. He mentioned the astronomical work of Cassini and Römer at the Paris Observatory. At Greenwich John Flamsteed, the Astronomer Royal, had made a new estimate of the solar parallax which gave a more accurate figure for the distance to the Sun. Hooke then described a problem of celestial mechanics which he had been working on. 'And particularly if you will let me know your thoughts of that of compounding the celestiall motions of the planetts of a direct motion by the tangent & an attractive motion towards the centrall body', added Hooke. He was working on the problem of planetary motion and he wanted a mathematical proof of some of his ideas.

ABOVE *The Great freeze* by A D Hondius. Old London Bridge severely restricted the flow of water through its narrow arches and in a severe winter the Thames could freeze over above the bridge. The artist shows some very dangerous sports and pastimes. Nonsuch House can be identified as the tallest house, with the cupolas, near the centre of the bridge.

Newton admitted to being out of touch with the latest news and he thanked Hooke very generously. He addressed his letter to his 'Ever honoured friend' and excelled himself by signing off as 'yr humble servant to command'. In his letter he suggested an experiment to prove the rotational motion of the Earth by a direct measurement. In principle the experiment was very simple. The idea was to drop a body from a point high above the Earth's surface, to note the point where it struck the ground, and to determine whether this point was east or west of the release point. Newton got carried away with the idea and went on to design the details of the experiment in his usual thorough manner:

Suppose then in a very calm day a Pistol Bullet were let down by a silk line from the top of a high Building or Well, the line going through a small hole made in a plate of Brass or Tinn fastened to ye top of ye Building or Well & yt ye bullet when let down almost to ye bottom were setled in water so as to cease from swinging & then let down further on an edge of steel lying north & south to try if ye bullet in setling thereon will almost stand in equilibrio but yet with some small propensity (the smaller ye better) decline to ye west side of ye steel as often as it is so let down thereon. The steel being so placed underneath, suppose the bullet be then drawn up to ye top & let fall by cutting clipping or

burning the line of silk, & if it fall constantly on ye east side of ye steel it will argue ye diurnall
motion of ye earth. But what ye event will be I know not having never attempted to try it. If any
body may think this worth their triall the best way in my opinion would be to try it in a high church
or wide steeple the windows being first well stopt. For in a narrow well ye bullet possibly may be apt
to receive a ply from ye straitned Air neare ye sides of ye Well, if in its fall it come nearer to one side
then to another. It would be convenient also that ye water into wch ye bullet falls be a yard or two
deep or more partly that ye bullet may fall more gently on ye steel, partly that ye motion wch it has
from west to east at its entring into ye water by meanes of ye longer time of descent through ye water
carry it on further eastward & so make ye experiment more manifest.[1]

Hooke's reply came a few days later, after a regular meeting of the Royal Society. 'Let this therefore assure you that I very much Value the great favor & kindness of your Letter and more Especially for communicateing your Notion about the Descent of heavy Bodys', he wrote. ''Tis certainly right & true soe far as concerns the falling of the body Let fall from a great hight to the Eastwards of the perpendicular and not to the westward of it as most have hitherto Imagined.' He reported that the notion had been discussed at the Royal Society. 'And in this opinion concurred Sir Christopher Wren, Sir John Hoskins, Mr Henshaw, and most of those that were present at our meeting on Thursday Last to whom I read soe much of your letter (and not more) as conserned Monsieur Mallement and this Experiment.' The latter news was not welcome to Isaac Newton when he found that his request for anonymity had been broken. What followed hurt him even more. Hooke went on to point out that Newton's assumptions about the fall of the body were wrong!

'But as to the curve Line which you seem to suppose it to Desend by (though that was not then at all Discoursed of) Viz a kind of spirall which after sume few revolutions Leave it in the Center of the Earth my theory of circular motion makes me suppose it would be very differing and nothing att all akin to a spirall but rather a kind elleptueid.' Hooke went on to imagine the whole Earth split into two hemispheres a yard (almost a metre) apart, with the projectile descending into the chasm between. He had calculated that the projectile would fall not to the east, as declared by Newton, but rather to the south-east, and in the latitude of London it would tend more to the south than the east.

For several years Newton's thoughts had been engrossed in alchemy and theology. He was still grieving from the death of his mother and he had not put sufficient thought into the problem of the trajectory. He realized that he had made an error and he wrote back to Hooke admitting the mistake. The letter was dated 14 December 1679. Newton still formally claimed to be a 'very humble servant' but Hooke had broken faith with him and was no longer addressed as an 'ever honoured friend'.

Hooke replied on 6 January. He reported that he had made the experiment and he was pleased to find that in three trials the ball fell to the south-east as the theory predicted. But the results showed a lack of accuracy: the horizontal distance moved by the ball varied greatly from only a quarter-of-an-inch (6.35 mm) to a much greater amount which he did not specify. His letter included other items of gossip. In May of the previous year the astronomer, Edmund Halley (1656–1742), had returned from a two-year visit to the island of St Helena in the South Atlantic where he had been busy cataloguing the stars of the southern constellations. Astronomically it had been a very successful expedition. Halley had mapped 341 stars which were not visible from Europe, he had observed eclipses of the Sun and the Moon, and he had watched a transit of the planet Mercury across the face of the Sun.

But this was not all. While at St Helena, Halley had been able to show that the force of gravity varied with height above sea level. This was the effect which Hooke had unsuccessfully tried to measure, with his weights and pack thread, several years before in Westminster Abbey. Halley discovered the effect almost by accident. He possessed a very sensitive instrument which was not available to Hooke in the 1660s. It was a pendulum clock.

Galileo was the first to observe that the swing of a pendulum was asynchronous, that is, the period of a pendulum was independent of the amplitude of the swing. He had timed the swing of the chandeliers in the cathedral of Pisa by using his pulse as a timekeeper. A pendulum was therefore the ideal mechanism with which to regulate a clock, and Galileo went on to design a pendulum clock but he did not actually make one. It was not until 1657 that Christiaan Huygens produced a practical design for such a clock and, with the assistance of a local clock-maker, he made the first working model. The English were quick to follow. Ahasuerus Fromanteel saw Huygens's clock and he produced the first English pendulum clock in the following year. Robert Hooke was very interested. He had many ideas for clock-making, including a clock regulated by a sprung balance wheel which he hoped would keep good time at sea. His most enduring contribution to clock-making was the anchor escapement, a mechanism that improved the accuracy of the timepiece by allowing the clock to have a long pendulum with a short arc of swing. In 1671 a London clock-maker, William Clement, produced the first successful clock incorporating Hooke's anchor escapement, and it soon became the clock-maker's standard. The next few decades were the formative years of the London clock-making industry, centred on Fleet Street, when the artisans produced many accurate and beautiful long-case clocks with exquisite metal-working and furniture-making skills. Soon the main provincial centres were also producing accurate timepieces, and the English long-case clock became an item for every household wealthy enough to afford one. By the time Halley made his voyage to St Helena, he was able to take a clock that was accurate to within a few seconds a week.

At St Helena, Edmund Halley set up his clock at the top of Mount Actaeon, at a height of about 800 metres above sea-level. He discovered that it ran measurably slower than on low ground. He correctly concluded that the reason was that the force of gravity decreased with distance from the centre of the Earth. He also noticed another unexpected effect. Even at sea-level his pendulum clock ran slower than it did in England and he had to shorten the pendulum to make the clock keep good time. It appeared that gravity not only decreased with height above the Earth's surface but it also seemed to decrease in the tropical latitudes. When he was back in England Halley published his findings in the *Philosophical Transactions*. The variation of gravity with height was easy to prove and could be demonstrated without leaving England but, unfortunately, Halley had not taken sufficiently accurate readings to prove his assertion about the variation of gravity with latitude:

> *In all parts of the Surface of the Earth, or rather in all Points equidistant from its Center, the force of Gravity is nearly Equal; so that the length of the Pendulum vibrating Seconds of time, is found in all parts of the World to be very near the same. 'Tis true at S. Helena in the Latitude of 16 Degrees South, I found that the Pendulum of my Clock which vibrated Seconds, needed to be made shorter than it had been in England by a very sensible space, (but which at that time I neglected to observe accurately) before it would keep time; and since, the like Observations has been made by the French Observers near the Equinoctial: Yet I dare not affirm, that in mine it proceeded from any other Cause, than the great height of my place of Observation above the Surface of the Sea, whereby the Gravity being diminished, the length of the Pendulum, vibrating seconds, is proportionably shortned.*[2]

The variation with latitude was the effect of the flattening of the Earth at the poles but neither Halley nor Hooke knew about the flattening. Newton was very interested in the observation, he took note for future reference but he was too busy with other matters to pay any more attention to it at the time. Hooke's letter went on to discuss gravity and the force between the Sun and the planets, and he put forward his own theory of gravity: 'My supposition is that the Attraction always is in a duplicate proportion to the Distance from the Center Reciprocall, and Consequently the Velocity will be in a subduplicate proportion to the Attraction and Consequently as Kepler supposes Reciprocal to the distance.'

What Hooke described was in fact his wording for the inverse square law of gravity. It was the key to the motions of the planets but his wording is very confused and his statement about the velocity is a long way off the mark. At first sight it looks like an earth-shattering statement with Hooke pre-empting all the ideas attributed to Newton. In fact, Hooke was merely repeating the ideas of several other people before him. Many had speculated that gravity obeyed an inverse square law. Newton himself had wondered about the inverse square law when he compared the Moon's gravity to that of the apple at Woolsthorpe in the 1660s. It was easy enough to state the law; the problem was how to prove it by showing that it predicted the motions of the planets as demonstrated by

Kepler's laws. This was a simple calculation for a planet with a constant speed in a circular orbit – but the orbits of the planets were not circles, they were ellipses – and this made the problem a whole order of magnitude more difficult. Hooke wrote a second letter to Newton specifically asking him to calculate the trajectory of a body moving under the central force he had suggested. 'I have no doubt but by your excellent method you will easily find out what the curve must be', he wrote. By the 'excellent method' he was referring to Newton's work on the fluxions.

Isaac Newton did not reply.

The new decade was marked by a magnificent new comet, first seen in the November sky of 1680 and heading towards the Sun. The next month a second very bright comet was observed, this time heading away from the Sun. The two comets generated a lot of excitement in the astronomical world, and it is worthy of note that the December comet was observed across the Atlantic in Maryland by none other than Arthur Storer, the school

ABOVE John Flamsteed by an unknown artist. Flamsteed became the first Astronomer Royal and one of his tasks was to complete the mapping of the skies. He was greatly hindered by lack of funds and he had to purchase his own instruments.

bully from Newton's schooldays. Storer wrote to his uncle Humphrey Babington with a request to pass the information on to Isaac Newton. Newton and John Flamsteed, the Astronomer Royal, both made observations and corresponded with each other about these new objects in the night sky. The appearance of two such bright comets so close together was quite a coincidence, and the Astronomer Royal became convinced that they were actually the same comet. Newton did not agree. Comets were thought to be random, 'one-off' appearances. The idea that a comet could be subject to the same law of gravity as the planets did not occur to either of them and, at the time, no one believed that a comet could return to the Sun in a captive orbit in the same way as the planets returned at regular intervals. Flamsteed erroneously thought the comet had passed between the Earth and the Sun. Newton felt that this was impossible but, a few years later, when he began to consider that comets could be attracted by the Sun, he came to accept Flamsteed's suggestion that the two observations could indeed be the same comet.

In 1682 another comet appeared in the sky. It was the regular visit of Halley's comet which reached its closest approach to the Sun on 14 September – but the comet had yet to be named after Edmund Halley because neither he nor anyone else knew that the comet had been seen from the Earth many times before. It was years later, and after the publication of Newton's *Principia*, that Halley began to suspect that the comet of 1682 could be following a closed orbit around the Sun. He searched the records for previous comet sightings and eventually he was able to show that it had been sighted at regular intervals of seventy-six years. Therefore, he was able to predict when it would return again, even after his death.

The pieces of the puzzle of the universe were beginning to come together but in London and elsewhere life had to carry on as normal. The November of 1683 was exceptionally cold and, throughout December, the weather became still colder. At Oxford Anthony à Wood described how his bottle of ink froze by the fireside:

> *Dec 15, Sat [1683] a great deal of snow fell: a child of two going to Wheatly starv'd to death at the bottom of Shotover. Frost followed: and continued extreem cold. Innocents day, Friday, Dec 28, a very cold day. Wednesday night, 2 Jan. [1684] my bottle of ink frose at the fier side; Thursday night, the like; Friday night, Jan 4, the like. Weather so cold, as not the like knowne by man...*[3]

In London there was a minor epidemic of smallpox. It was a bleak, cold Christmas and the smoke from the coal fires left a great smog over the shivering city. The sluggish waters of the River Thames cooled towards freezing as the sharp frosts of an exceptionally hard winter set in. The narrow arches of London Bridge restricted the river water on its passage to the sea. Ice formed on the Thames above London Bridge and soon it became hard enough to support the weight of a man. On 1 January enterprising traders were setting up stalls on the ice, and Evelyn described the severe weather in his diary: 'The weather continuing intollerably severe, so as streetes of Boothes were set up upon the Thames etc: and the aire so very cold and thick, as of many yeares there had not been the like: The small pox being very mortal, many feared a worse Contagion to follow etc;'[4]

A few days later the river was frozen from bank to bank, and the foolhardy were boasting about crossing the ice to the other side. On 9 January John Evelyn himself crossed on the ice. By this time, Londoners felt so safe on the frozen surface of their river that a coach and horses could cross and whole new streets were appearing on the ice:

> *I went crosse the Thames upon the Ice (which was now become so incredibly thick, as to beare not onely whole streetes of boothes in which the roasted meate, and had divers shops of wares, quites crosse as in a Towne, but Coaches and carts and horses passed over): So I went from Westminster stayers to Lambeth and dined with my L. Archbishop, where I met my Lord Bruce, Sir Geo. Wheeler, Coll: Coock and severall Divines, after dinner, and discourse with his Grace 'til Evening prayer, Sir Geo: and I returnd, walking over the Ice from Lambeth stayres to the Horse Ferry, and thence walked on foote to our Lodgings:*[5]

Two weeks later there had been no let-up in the cold weather and the ice was even more solid than before. The Thames had become a fairground with bull baiting, horse racing, sledding, and skating. Enterprising printers had set up shop on the ice to print ballad sheets and souvenirs. The wherrymen lamented the loss of their livelihood as coaches plied not only across the river but also along the great frozen ribbon of ice, using it as a spacious new highway to Westminster and beyond. The ice supported a whole new town:

[24 January] The frost still continuing more and more severe, the Thames before London was planted with bothes in formal streetes, as in a Citty, or Continual faire, all sorts of Trades and shops furnished, and full of Commodities, even to a Printing presse, where the People and Lady's tooke a fansy to have their names Printed and the day and yeare set downe, when printed on the Thames: This humour tooke so universaly, that 'twas estimated the Printer gained five pound a day, for printing a line onely, at six-pence a Name, besides what he gott by Ballads etc: Coaches now plied from Westminster to the Temple, and from several other stiars too and froo, as in the steetes; also on sleds, sliding with skeetes; There was likewise Bull-baiting, Horse and Coach races, Pupet plays and interludes, Cookes and Tipling, and lewder places; so as it seem'd to be a bacchanalia, Triumph or Carnoval on the Water, whilst it was a severe Judgement upon the land: the trees not onely splitting as if ligtning-strock, but Men and Cattel perishing in divers places, and the very seas so locked up with yce, that no vessels could stirr out, or come in: The fowl Fish and birds, and all our exotique Plants and Greenes universaly perish-ing; many Parks of deere destroied, and all sorts of fuell so deare that there were great Contributions to preserve the poore alive; nor was this severe weather much lesse intense in other parts of Europe even as far as Spaine, and the most southern tracts...[6]

There were, of course, many drawbacks to the bitter weather. The sewage problem was even worse than usual, water pipes froze and there was a serious problem of water supply, but the most obvious and pressing difficulty was that of keeping warm. Evelyn claimed that the cold air did not allow the smoke from the coal fires to rise and, consequently, London became enveloped in a thick smog:

London, by reason of the excessive coldnesse of the aire, hindring the ascent of the smoke, was so filled with the fuliginous streame of the Sea-Coale, that hardly could one see cross the streete, and this filling the lungs with its grosse particles exceedingly obstructed the breast, so as one could scarce breath: There was no water to be had from the Pipes and Engines, nor could the Brewers, and divers other Tradesmen work, and every moment was full of disastrous accidents etc:[7]

By the 'Sea-Coale' Evelyn was referring to the produce of the North Sea coal trade; Londoners had long since exhausted their local supply of timber for heating their houses and coal was imported by sea from the mines at Tyneside and elsewhere. Despite the severe weather, the Royal Society still managed to hold its regular meetings, albeit poorly attended. The problem of gravitation was a topic very much under discussion,

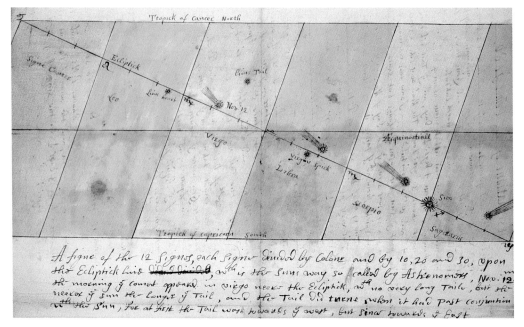

ABOVE An observation of the comet of 1680 by Thomas Hill of Canterbury. Showing the motion of the comet through the zodiac from Virgo to Sagittarius. Cambridge University Library Ms. Add. 3965, f 564v

PREVIOUS PAGE *The Frost Fair* 1683/4 by Abraham Daniel Hondius. The great freeze of 1684 was remembered for many years afterwards as the most severe winter in living memory. A whole street of booths was laid on the ice and a coach and horses could drive across. Some idea of the amount of rebuilding in the 17 years since the fire can be seen in the background.

and Christiaan Huygens had recently published a formula for what he called the 'centrifugal force' – the outward thrust experienced by a body such as a planet moving uniformly around a circle. This formula, they knew, was one of the key factors required to solve the problem of the planetary orbits.

After the meeting, Edmund Halley, Christopher Wren, and Robert Hooke retired to a coffee house to discuss the problem of gravitation and how it related to the system of the world. At this time, Wren was turned fifty and Hooke was in his late forties – both were survivors from the Oxford days. Halley was the junior member and was only twenty-six. All three of them had come to the conclusion that the law of gravity was an inverse square law. All three knew that the law could not be raised from the status of a hypothesis unless Kepler's laws of planetary motion, which by now were accepted as established fact, could be proved from it. But the required proof was a very intricate and taxing mathematical problem. Christopher Wren had tried to solve the problem and had to admit failure. Edmund Halley had proved himself a very able mathematician but he also admitted that his attempt had failed. Perhaps it was a problem that would never be solved. Robert Hooke was not a man to admit failure – he coyly announced that he had solved the problem but that he would keep his solution to himself so that others trying the same problem would know the value of his work. Christopher Wren knew Hooke of old and he offered a book to the value of forty shillings to anyone who could solve the problem. Edmund Halley described the meeting in his own words:

> Mr Hook affirmed that upon that principle all the Laws of the celestiall motions were to be demonstrated, and that he himself had done it; I declared the ill success of my attempts; and Sr Christopher to encourage the Inquiry sd, that he would give Mr Hook or me 2 months time to bring him a convincing demonstration therof, and besides the honour, he of us that did it, should have from him a present of a book of 40s. Mr Hook then said that he had it, but that he would conceale it for some time that others triing and failing, might know how to value it, when he should make it publick; however I remember Sr Christopher was little satisfied that he could do it, and tho Mr Hook then promised to show it him, I do not yet find that in that particular he has been as good as his word.[8]

A few weeks later it became clear to Wren and Halley that Hooke's demonstration was not forthcoming. If the problem could be solved there was but one person in the whole of England with the mathematical skills to do it, and they all knew that he resided at Trinity College in Cambridge. Someone must travel to Cambridge and confront Isaac Newton with the problem.

Robert Hooke was definitely the wrong man to make the visit. Newton had taken offence when Hooke had exposed his error in front of the Royal Society, and Hooke's credibility with Newton was at rock bottom. Christopher Wren was the obvious man to go: Newton thought very highly of Wren's skill as a mathematician, and Wren the architect could witness the progress on his library at Trinity College. But Wren was far too busy rebuilding London to spare any time to solve the problems of the universe. It was the younger man, Edmund Halley, who must make the momentous visit to Cambridge and gain an audience with the Lucasian Professor of Mathematics.

Halley had not yet met Isaac Newton but he knew of his awesome reputation, he knew of his desire for privacy, and he knew that Newton did not suffer fools gladly. Halley was in no hurry to go to Cambridge but he did not forget his mission. By the time he made the journey in August 1684 the hard winter was history. In the English countryside the corn stood high in the fields and was being reaped with sickle and scythe as every available hand laboured to bring home the harvest. Halley had no problem finding the Lucasian Professor. He was greeted by the sharp nose, the prematurely grey but full head of hair, and the slightly protruding and deeply penetrating eyes of Isaac Newton. He had little idea how Newton would respond to his request, and he must have been pleased with his reception when Newton turned out to be friendly and co-operative. After a little small talk and few formalities, Doctor Halley came to the point of his visit and asked the all-important question:

> *In 1684 Dr Halley came to visit him at Cambridge, after they had been some time together, the Dr*
> *asked him what he thought the Curve would be that would be described by the Planets supposing the*
> *force of attraction towards the Sun to be reciprocal to the square of their distance from it. Sr Isaac*
> *replied immediately that it would be an Ellipsis, the Doctor struck with joy & amazement asked him*
> *how he knew it, why saith he I have calculated it, whereupon Dr Halley asked him for his calculation*
> *without any farther delay, Sr Isaac looked among his papers but could not find it, but he promised him*
> *to renew it, & then to send it to him...*[9]

In the midst of his joy Halley did not doubt for a moment that the man before him was telling the truth. Isaac Newton had already solved the key problem at the heart of the theory of gravitation! Torn between elation and dismay, Halley watched in trepidation as Newton searched among his many papers but was unable to find the written version of his solution. Before him was the absent-minded professor of mathematics who carried the secret of the universe in his head! It was small wonder that Halley's next act was to ask Newton to rework his calculation.

It says much for Halley's tact and diplomacy that he returned from Cambridge with a promise from Newton to renew the necessary calculation and to supply Halley with a copy. It leaves a few questions unanswered. Was Newton's study a totally disorganized chaos of papers and half-completed experiments or was it as neatly ordered as his notebooks and his mind? Perhaps Newton knew exactly where his calculation was but wanted time to think about it before showing it to Halley. Why was Newton, who was always complaining about the demands on his time, so co-operative with Edmund Halley? Newton was well aware of Halley's astronomical work in the Southern Hemisphere and, at their meeting, the two must have discussed many topics of common interest. Halley must have told Newton about his findings in St Helena when the pendulum clock ran slow. Newton would have read the account already in the *Philosophical Transactions* but there was no substitute for talking to the author face to face. Perhaps Newton expounded his ideas on the Comet of 1680/81 and set Halley thinking about the motion of comets. The outcome was that, when Halley left Cambridge, he became more and more convinced that Newton's ideas must be written up and published for the world to see and read. He knew that the Royal Society was by far the best body to handle the publication.

In some ways Halley was very fortunate. His timing was perfect. He arrived at Cambridge at a time when Newton's researches on alchemy were getting nowhere and his academic life was coming to a dead end. The latest discoveries on gravitation had given Newton some new ideas to work on, and he had the vision to realize that a golden opportunity had arrived and that the time was right to make his researches known to the world. He came to the realization that it was his calling to write up and publish these ideas for posterity. He knew that his ideas would generate controversy in the world of natural philosophy but, for once, he was prepared to publish and to face the consequences.

Isaac Newton was as good as his word. It is probable that he did find his original calculation for it survives among his papers. In any case, however, he must have had a good notion of how he had arrived at the solution. He decided to rework it, perhaps with a view to finding a more elegant proof but, in his haste, he sketched a badly drawn diagram where he confused the axes of the ellipse with a pair of conjugate diameters. It was a human error but, once he had spotted his mistake, he extracted the correct solution very quickly. He sent it to London in the care of his friend Edward Paget and, by November it was with Edmund Halley.

ABOVE Edmund Halley by Thomas Murray. Halley played a very valuable role in the publication of Newton's *Principia*. He persuaded Newton to write the book and paid for much of the publication from his own pocket.

The treatise which Halley received was even more than he had hoped for. It was entitled *Du motum corporum in gyrum* [On the motion of bodies in orbit]. On 10 December Halley reported the communication to the Royal Society and his findings were recorded in the minutes:

> *Mr Halley gave an account, that he had lately seen Mr Newton at Cambridge, who had shewed him a curious treatise,* De Motu; *which, upon Mr Halley's desire, was, he said, promised to be sent to the Society to be entered upon their register.*
>
> *Mr Halley was desired to put Mr Newton in mind of his promise for the securing his invention to himself till such time as he could be at leisure to publish it. Mr Paget was desired to join with Mr Halley.*[10]

There was a murmuring and an atmosphere of excitement at the Society. Edmund Halley knew that something very special was about to be made known to the world, and his enthusiasm rubbed off on the rest of the members.

9
PROBLEMS

THE TRUTH IS, THE SCIENCE OF NATURE HAS BEEN ALREADY TOO
LONG MADE ONLY A WORK OF THE BRAIN AND THE FANCY: IT IS NOW
HIGH TIME THAT IT SHOULD RETURN TO THE PLAINNESS AND SOUND-
NESS OF OBSERVATIONS OF MATERIAL AND OBVIOUS THINGS.

Robert Hooke (1635-1703)

ALL CAMBRIDGE KNEW that the Lucasian Professor of Mathematics was a great recluse, an absent-minded fellow who wandered around the college in a trance, his thoughts always totally concentrated on pondering his latest philosophical question.

He had minimal contact with the other Fellows at Trinity College but sometimes, when he felt like it, he would choose to communicate with them. There is an anecdote that one day he came into the hall of Trinity College and announced that the English had lost a great sea battle with the Dutch. Naturally, the Fellows asked him how he came by this information. He announced that 'he heard the report of a great firing of cannon, such as could only be between two great fleets, and that as the noise grew louder and louder he concluded that they drew nearer to our coasts and consequently we had the worst of it'. Newton had heard the guns of the naval battle of Southwold Bay, off the coast of Norfolk, on 28 May 1672, and his colleagues must have been impressed when news subsequently arrived at Cambridge to show that he was correct in his conclusions. It suggests that his hearing must have been quite exceptional to enable him to hear the cannon-fire at such a distance from the coast but, in fact, other reports indicate that the noise of the battle was heard by people who were 'out at work in the fields to the very centre of England'. It was not Newton's hearing that was particularly remarkable but rather the atmospheric conditions and the silence that was usual in the pre-industrial countryside of the seventeenth century.

The one man who knew more than anyone else about Isaac Newton at this time was

John Wickins with whom Newton shared his lodgings. The first meeting between Isaac Newton and John Wickins has been described in an earlier chapter from a letter written by Wickins's son Nicholas. The rest of the letter adds a few more details:

He was turning grey, I think, at thirty, and when my father observed that to him that as the effect of his deep attention of mind, he would jest with the experiments he made so often with quicksilver, as if from hence he took so soon that colour.

He sometimes suspected himself to be inclining to a consumption, and the medicine he made use of was the Leucatello's Balsam, which, when he had composed himself, he would now and then melt in quantity about a quarter of a pint, and so drink it.[1]

ABOVE   René Descartes (1596-1650). *Cogito, ergo sum.* (I think, therefore I am.) The Frenchman Descartes was a great philosopher and mathematician. He developed what we now call Cartesian geometry which brought together classical geometry and algebra.

Isaac Newton was a great amateur physician and he gave out his medical knowledge very freely. He thought that Leucatello's Balsam could cure all kinds of ailments. In one of his papers he recommends it for measles, plague, and smallpox 'a half an ounce in a little broth; take it warm, and sweat after it. And against poison and the biting of a mad dog; for the last you must dip lint and lay it upon the wound, besides taking it internally. There are other virtues of it; for wind, cholic, anoint the stomach and so for bruises.' We are hearing echoes of the advice given to customers in the apothecary's shop in Grantham High Street.

When Edmund Halley made his famous visit to Cambridge in 1684 the Lucasian Professor was aged forty-one, and there is little doubt that he was quite grey. A decade later his hair was white but he did have the good fortune to retain a full head of hair throughout his life. Shortly before Halley's visit, Newton had lost the companionship of his closest friend when John Wickins left Cambridge to take up a living at Stoke Edith in Monmouthshire. Having reached his early forties, Newton might well have preferred to live on his own for a time. He seems to have done so for about a year but he needed somebody to replace Wickins as a copyist or amanuensis, a suitable person to help with

ABOVE Neville's Court, Trinity College. Newton might have been seen at one time in Neville's court clapping his hands. He was able to synchronise the sound of the clap with the echo from the wall and he used the result to estimate the speed of sound.

his voluminous researches and his correspondence.

In 1685 Newton acquired a young man as an amanuensis who also served him in the capacity of a sizar. He was Humphrey Newton and was from Newton's old school at Grantham. The two had much in common but, although they had the same surname and came from the same area, they were not related as far as they could tell. Humphrey Newton remained at Cambridge for about five years. In addition to his duties as a sizar he was required to copy out Newton's masterpiece, the *Principia*.

We discover from Humphrey Newton that Isaac was always very close to his studies. He had very few visitors but did sometimes entertain the masters of the colleges. Among the few who called on him at his lodgings were a Mr Ellis, John Laughton the Trinity College librarian for whom Newton must have been a regular customer, and John Vigani with whom he loved to talk chemistry. For a time he took 'much delight and pleasure' in the company of Vigani but the chemist made a terrible *faux pas* when he told Newton a dubious joke about a nun. The joke must have been in very bad taste and Isaac Newton, greatly to his credit, wanted nothing more to do with Mr Vigani after this episode.

Newton took little or no recreation or exercise, and he was sometimes confined to his room for weeks on end when he was intent at his studies. He carried out his duties as a lecturer but the teaching did not seem to interest him and he made no effort to simplify his subject so that the students could understand him. In term time he was obliged to give his lectures 'where so few went to hear him and, fewer understood him that oftimes he did in a manner, for want of hearers, read to the walls'. Humphrey Newton described his eating and sleeping habits:

So intent, so serious upon his studies that he ate very sparingly, nay, ofttimes he has forgot to eat at all, so that, going into his chamber, I have found his mess untouched, of which, when I have reminded him, he would reply – 'Have I?' and then making to the table, would eat a bit or two standing, for I cannot say that I ever saw him sit at the table by himself. At some seldom entertainments, the Masters of Colleges were chiefly his guests…

I cannot say I ever saw him drink either wine, ale, or beer, excepting at meals, and then but very
sparingly. He very rarely went to dine in the hall, except on some public days, and then if he has not
been minded, would go very carelessly, with shoes down at heels, stockings untied, surplice on, and his
head scarcely combed.[2]

The researches into alchemy were pushed aside for the writing of the *Principia* but they
were not totally abandoned. At one stage it appears that they served as some kind of
recreational sideline for the occasions when the author needed a break from thinking
about mathematics and astronomy. Humphrey Newton gives plenty of detail:

About 6 weeks at spring, and 6 at the fall, the fire in the elaboratory scarcely went out, which was well
furnished with chemical materials as bodies, receivers, heads, crucibles, etc., which was made very little
use of, the crucibles excepted, in which he fused his metals he would sometimes, tho' very seldom, look
into an old mouldy book which lay in his elaboratory, I think it was titled Agricola de Mattalis, *the*
transmuting of metals being his chief design for which purpose antimony was a great ingredient.[3]

Thus, if we are to believe the testimony of his amanuensis, Isaac Newton believed that
the transmutation of metals was a possibility. In another passage we get a tantalizing
glimpse of a great mind probing for some secret which, in his century, was 'beyond the
reach of human art and industry' but which would be discovered by a far-distant posterity. He badly wanted to know the patterns and the laws of science behind the chemical
reactions:

He rarely went to bed till two or three of the clock, sometimes not until five or six, lying about four or
five hours, especially at spring or fall of the leaf, in which times he used to employ about six weeks in
his elaboratory, the fire scarcely going out either night or day; he sitting up one night and I another, till
he had finished his chemical experiments, in the performance of which he was the most accurate, strict,
exact.

  What his aim might be I was not able to penetrate into but his pains, his diligence at these set
times made me think he aimed at something beyond the reach of human art and industry.[4]

When Newton was held up by a mathematical problem or a form of words to explain
his ideas, the routine of the furnace and the molten metals in the crucible enabled his
subconscious to work on the dilemma. Sometimes he would pace up and down the small
garden with his thoughts. He was not a regular attendant at the college chapel but, on
Sunday mornings, he was frequently to be seen at the university church of St Mary's in
Cambridge. His health was generally good at this time except for one occasion when he
suffered from a stomach complaint and he was confined to his bed for a few days.
According to Humphrey Newton, Isaac took his illness very philosophically and was

indifferent as to whether he lived or died. 'For if I die', said Isaac to his amanuensis, 'I shall leave you an estate.' It is rare to discover a sizar who thought so highly of the one for whom he performed his menial tasks, and even rarer for a Fellow to think so highly of his sizar. Humphrey Newton described Isaac Newton as 'very meek, sedate, and humble, never seemingly angry, of profound thought, his countenance mild, pleasant, and comely', a description that has conveniently been ignored by Newton's detractors but accepted as gospel by Newton's early biographer, David Brewster. Humphrey became such an ardent admirer of Isaac Newton that he named his son after him. In another passage he tells us more about the distracted character of his namesake:

> *Near his elaboratory was his garden, which was kept in order by a gardener. I scarcely ever saw him do anything as pruning, etc., at it himself. When he has sometimes taken a turn or two, has made a sudden stand, turn'd himself about, run up the stairs like another Archimedes, with an 'eureka' fall to write on his desk standing without giving himself the leisure to drew [sic] a chair to sit down on. At some seldom times when he designed to dine in the hall, would turn to the left hand and go out into the street, when making a stop when he found his mistake, would hastily turn back, and then sometimes instead of going into the hall, would return, to his chamber again.[5]*

It would be misleading to say that Humphrey Newton knew nothing of what he copied. He must have been fully aware of the amazing results that were developed in the text of the *Principia*. It is true to say, however, that he understood little or nothing of the mathematical demonstrations which were essential for a full understanding of the work.

What then were the contents of the *Principia*? It took some time for them to become known because very few people were in a position to master the book completely. Firstly, it required a knowledge of Latin. This was not a serious problem in an age when most people with a grammar-school education would be conversant with the language of the Romans – in fact, entry to university could not be gained without some proof of proficiency in Latin. The second requirement of the *Principia* was much more severe. An exceptionally high level of mathematics was required and Newton admitted that he had made no attempt to water down this aspect of his book because he wanted to 'avoid being baited by little smatterers in mathematics'. He did make one concession, however, in that he did not introduce the method of fluxions into his demonstrations. He had used the fluxions to arrive at many of his conclusions but, because his methods had never been published, he was forced to rework the problems in the methods of classical geometry so that others would more readily accept his findings. This meant that, in many cases, he had to appeal to limiting cases to arrive at his results from first principles. After his death, the mathematical methods he used were superseded by the differential and integral calculus so that the proofs and demonstrations in the *Principia* became a monument to the ultimate achievements in classical mathematics. They stood in a time capsule, in a lonely grandeur of their own, astonishing techniques of classical geometry never matched before or since.

The *Philosophiae Naturalis Principia Mathematica*, to give the book its full title, began with a number of basic definitions. One of the most difficult concepts to define was mass, which the author described as 'the quantity of matter in a body' – an obvious tautology. Mass was impossible to define from first principles but Newton had to start somewhere. Time was also impossible to define from first principles and he merely stated that it flowed uniformly. He had to differentiate between the inertial mass of a body and its weight in a gravitational field. He defined the inertia of a body moving with uniform speed, and from this he was able to define the concept of the force that changed its motion. He went on to describe circular motion and what he called the centripetal force which he differentiated subtly from Huygens's centrifugal force. Space and time were absolute, and motion was presented by reference to an absolute datum.

He then defined his three famous laws of motion:

1   Every body continues in its state of rest, or of uniform motion in a right line, unless it is compelled to change that state by forces impressed upon it.
2   The change of motion is proportional to the motive force impressed; and is made in the direction of the right line in which the force is impressed.
3   To every action there is always opposed an equal reaction.

The first of these laws had been anticipated by Descartes and, before him, by Galileo. The second law was based on Galileo's experiments with rolling balls on inclined planes but Newton had taken the law much further. The concepts of force and acceleration had to be rigorously defined. Unlike most of his predecessors, Newton knew the importance of direction: a body falling vertically downwards under gravity was a very simple case of force and acceleration but, in general, the forces were vectors, that is, they had a direction that need not be the same as that of the motion. The third law seemed deceptively simple but Newton had been studying the action of billiard balls. He knew that when two balls collided they experienced an equal and opposite reaction which determined their subsequent motion, and he also knew that this was part of a more general rule. The laws and the scholia were no more than necessary preliminaries to the books themselves. They were followed by Book One which applied the laws of motion as Newton defined them to particular cases of bodies moving in straight lines. A second section dealt with motion in a circle, and the ideas were developed to prove Kepler's areal law for planetary motion, i.e. that the planet's radius vector sweeps out equal areas in equal times. He posed the problem of a body moving around a conic section in obedience to Kepler's law, and he showed that in all cases the force varied inversely as the square of the distance. He claimed that the converse was also true but, by some oversight, he omitted to go on and prove it. He *did have* the proof of the converse – that an inverse square law implies an orbit which is a conic section – for this was the very problem that Halley had asked of him on their famous first meeting. It was also the problem which Hooke had requested from him in writing, the proof of which he had supplied to Halley after his historic visit to Cambridge.

This much alone would have been sufficient to secure Newton's claim to a place in scientific history. He had been working on these problems for many years, however, and the fact that he had suspected an inverse law twenty years previously meant that, by the time he came to write up his ideas, he had solved a great many secondary problems relating to gravitation. This was one of the major reasons why the *Principia* made such an impact on the

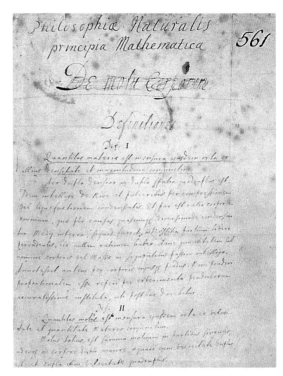

ABOVE A early draft of Newton's *Principia* showing some of his definitions.

scientific world: it was not simply a statement of the law of gravitation, it was a highly polished thesis with ideas and proofs enough to keep the astronomers and mathematicians at work for more than a century.

He knew that the centre of gravity of a closed system always remained at the same position in space or, if it was not at rest, then it moved at a constant velocity. He was able to show that, for a sun with a single planet orbiting around it, both bodies actually moved in an ellipse around their common centre of gravity. He solved the difficult problem of the gravitational attraction of the Earth on the apple, showing that the gravitational attraction of a sphere acts as though all the mass was concentrated at its centre. He went on to study a few cases where the attracting body was not a sphere: for example, the Earth which he modelled as a sphere flattened at the poles.

The second book of the *Principia* was concerned with fluid motion and with bodies moving in resisting mediums. At first sight, the motion of fluids seems out of place in a book that deals with planets moving in a vacuum but Newton had good reasons for considering fluids. He wanted to study the effects of a resisting medium on motion but his main reason was that he was anxious to disprove the prevailing theory of the times – that the planets were carried around the Sun by vortices in an ethereal fluid which occupied the whole of space. The vortex theory had been put forward by René Descartes and it was accepted by all his followers.

Descartes is remembered today for his system of Cartesian geometry, where every curve has an algebraic equation and the problems of geometry can be reduced to problems of algebra. His was a brilliant system, and the introduction of the calculus made it into an even more powerful mathematical tool than the original ideas of Descartes' geometry. It was Descartes who first suggested that celestial and terrestrial bodies were subject to the same laws, and that there was no radical distinction between motions in the heavens and on the Earth. When the Frenchman came to explaining the system of the universe however, Newton did not agree with his findings and it was necessary for him to overthrow the theory of the vortices before he could put forward his own theory for the system of the world.

One of Newton's greatest strengths was that he took the doctrine of Francis Bacon to its limits, and he firmly believed in experimentation and measurement. He performed a lot of experimental work on spheres falling in a resisting medium. He considered the cases where the resistance was proportional to the velocity, to the square of the velocity, and as a combination of both factors. He presented the general principles of hydrostatics on the assumption that 'a fluid be composed of particles fleeing from each other' and that under compression the fluid obeyed a form of Boyle's law. He dealt at length with the results of fourteen experiments on wax and lead globes falling in water-filled vessels, and he experimented with globes of air and mercury dropped from the top of St Paul's Cathedral. The time taken for these globes to descend agreed with Newton's theoretical predictions and he was able to formulate the law known as Newton's law of fluid friction. It seems that, for these experiments, he must have had the co-operation of Christopher Wren and that part of the interior of the new cathedral must have been sufficiently complete for him to try out the experiments. Wren was President of the Royal Society at this time but, at the end of June 1686, he was succeeded in this post by the diarist Samuel Pepys.

Newton investigated the question of wave motion in a fluid. As usual, he had experimental data to support his findings. He calculated the speed of sound by measuring the echoes in Neville's Court at Trinity College and, as well as determining the velocity, he was also able to calculate the wavelength of the sound waves. He knew that the speed of sound varied with atmospheric conditions and he concluded that light did not obey the same laws as sound. He assumed, therefore, that light could not be propagated as a wave. He did experimental work on the damping of a pendulum in a resisting medium, and he used an impressive pendulum over 12 feet (3.7 m) long to get his results. In one experiment he tried to use his long pendulum to detect the existence of the ether but the result was negative. This experiment added more support to his theory that light could not be a wave motion.

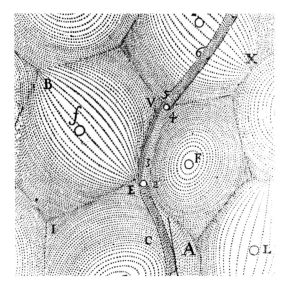

ABOVE The French philosopher Descartes suggested that the planets were carried around the sun by a set of vortices in a fluid. Newton spent a lot of effort proving that such a system was not possible within the laws of fluid dynamics

It was in the final part of Book Two that Newton launched his attack against the Cartesian theory of vortices. He argued that the vortices required a constant supply of energy to remain in existence and it was therefore impossible for the planets to be circulating in a fluid medium as Descartes had hypothesized. There was another objection. He showed that the vortex motion was not consistent with Kepler's third law relating the periodic times of the planets to the mean radii of their orbits.

And so the books took shape and eventually Newton came to work on Book Three which he called the *System of the World*. The idea was to show that the universal law of gravitation could explain the motion of every body in the universe, both in the heavens and on the Earth. Edmund Halley read the proofs of Books One and Two, and with his great diplomacy he continued to guide the publication through the press and the Royal Society. He knew that there was a third book to follow but he knew little about its contents.

Then came a problem. The Royal Society very much wanted to be associated with the *Principia*, and they were in complete agreement with Halley regarding the importance of the work. The negative side was that the Society had no money to pay for the publication. Considering the problems of the times and the fact that the Royal Society staggered on from year to year in near bankruptcy, it was a minor miracle that it was still in existence. Many of the members were, as usual, far behind in paying their subscriptions but the Society had recently agreed to publish a book called *Historia Piscum* written by a deceased member, Francis Willoughby. *This History of Fishes* was an expensive book and lavishly illustrated. The Royal Society could not extricate itself from the expense of publishing and, consequently, there was no money left to publish Newton's *Principia*. The Society was very happy to vote for publication to go ahead but their decision did not commit them to any financial support — what this amounted to in practice was that Edmund Halley was obliged to finance the rest of the publication with his own money! The society did offer Halley some of their assets, namely fifty copies of Willoughby's *History of Fishes* but, although Halley may have been happy to receive a single copy, he could not pay his printer's bill in books. His only options seemed to be start up a publication fund, to find the money himself, or to forget the *Principia* altogether.

Halley had his own family to support and he was not in affluent circumstances at the time. Even so, he readily went ahead with the expense. He did not try to raise the money by subscription through the members of the Society, neither did he approach Newton for the money even though Newton could probably afford it better than he. Halley knew that he had to treat the great man at Cambridge with kid gloves for fear of him refusing to publish his work. Halley's father had recently died; he had been a wealthy soap boiler and consequently Edmund's finances were adequate for the publication. Thus, Edmund Halley effectively became the publisher and owner of the *Principia*. He believed that the book would become a great success and he was prepared to proceed with publication at his own expense. Halley informed Newton of what had happened at the latest meeting of the Royal Society:

> *Your Incomparable treatise intituled* Philosophic Naturalis Principia Mathematica, *was by Dr Vincent presented to the R. Society, on the 28th past, and they were so very sensible of the Great Honour you do them by your Dedication, that they immediately ordered you their most hearty thanks, and that a Councell should be summoned to consider about the printing thereof; but by reason of the Presidents attendance upon the King, and the absence of our Vice-Presidents, whom the good weather had drawn out of Town, there has not since been any Authentick Councell to resolve what to do in the matter: so that on Wednesday last the Society in their meeting, judging that so excellent a work ought not to have its publication any longer delayd, resolved to print it at their own charge, in a large Quarto, of a fair letter; and that this their resolution should be signified to you and your opinion therin be desired, that so it might be gone about with all speed.*
>
> *I am intrusted to look after the printing it, and will take care that it shall be performed as well as possible, only I would first have your directions in what you shall think necessary for the embellishing therof, and particularly whether you think it not better, that the Schemes should be enlarged, which is the opinion of some here; but what you signifie as your desire shall be punctually observed.*[6]

Halley then came to the delicate part of his letter. There was a big problem. There were others, and one in particular, who had pretensions to the theory of gravitation:

> *There is one thing more that I ought to informe you of, viz, that Mr Hook has some pretensions upon the invention of ye rule of the decrease of Gravity, being reciprocally as the squares of the distances from the Center. He sais you had the notion from him, though he owns the Demonstration of the Curves generated therby to be wholly your own; how much of this is so, you know best, as likewise what you have to do in this matter, only Mr Hook seems to expect you should make some mention of him, in the preface, which, it is possible, you may see reason to prefix. I must beg your pardon that it is I, that send you this account, but I thought it my duty to let you know it, that so you may act accordingly; being in myself fully satisfied, that nothing but the greatest Candour imaginable, is to be expected from a person, who of all men has the least need to borrow reputation. When I shall have received your directions, the printing*

shall be pushed on with all expedition, which therfore I entreat you to send me, as soon as may be[7]

Newton's first reaction was mild. 'I thank you for what you write concerning Mr Hook', he replied to Halley. 'For I desire that a good understanding may be kept between us.' He went on to say that there was no proposition to which Hooke could lay any pretensions and that he had made a mention of him among other researchers in the third book. He referred to his written communications with Hooke a few years earlier about measuring the Earth's rotation. As to the inverse square law, he remembered discussing the problem with Sir Christopher Wren two years before the correspondence with Hooke. 'You are acquainted with Sir Christopher Wren', he wrote, and he suggested that Halley checked out the facts of the case with Wren.

Edmund Halley breathed a sigh of relief. He replied a few days later in a brief letter, saying that the second book of the *Principia* was ready for the press. He had finished the proofreading and he was very pleased with it. But Halley's relief was premature and the crisis had not passed. Newton had been stewing on Hooke's claim and all his past resentment built up to an explosive outburst. Two weeks later Halley received a second letter from Newton bitterly criticizing Hooke's claim to have discovered the inverse square law of gravitation.

That what he told me of ye duplicate proportion was erroneous, namely that it reacht down from hence to ye center of ye earth. That it is not candid to require me now to confess my self in print then ignorant of ye duplicate proportion in ye heavens for no other reason but because he had told it me in the case of projectiles & so upon mistaken grounds accused me of that ignorance. That in my answer to his first letter I refused his correspondence, told him I had laid Philosophy aside, sent him only ye experimt of Projectiles (rather shortly hinted then carefully described) in complement to sweeten my Answer, expected to heare no further from him, could scarce perswade my self to answer his second letter, did not answer his third, was upon other things, thought no further of philosophical matters then his letters put me upon it, & therefore may be allowed not to have had my thoughts of that kind about me so well at that time.[8]

This was bad enough but worse was to follow:

Since my writing this letter I am told by one who had it from another lately present at one of your meetings, how that Mr Hook should there make a great stir pretending I had all from him & desiring they would see that he had justice done him. This carriage towards me is very strange & undeserved so that I cannot forbeare in stating yt point of justice to tell you further, that he has published Borell's Hypothesis in his own name & the asserting of this to himself & completing it as his own, seems to me the ground of all ye stir he makes. Borel did something in it & wrote modestly, he has done nothing & yet written in such a way as if he knew & had sufficiently hinted all but what remained to be determined by ye drudgery of calculations & observations, excusing himself from that labour by reason of his other business: whereas he should rather have excused himself by reason of his inability. For tis plain

by his words he knew not how to go about it. Now is not this very fine? Mathematicians that find
out, settle & do all the business must content themselves with being nothing but dry calculators &
drudges & another that does nothing but pretend & grasp at all things must carry away all the inven-
tion as well of those that were to follow him as of those that went before.9

Newton's letter continued in the same vein, his resentment against Hooke spilling over
as he brought forward more and more incidents to show that Hooke was by no means
the first to suggest that the orbits of the planets implied an inverse square law. He was
prepared to concede that some of Hooke's letters had caused him to study the problem
in more detail but the suggestion that Hooke should be given the credit for discovering
the law of gravitation was too much for him to stomach.

It was true that Hooke had been working for several years on the problem of gravitation but, when it came to solving the mathematics of the key problems, he ground to a
complete halt. This was why he wrote to Newton for a solution and why he brought up
the subject in the coffee house with Halley and Wren. In his capacity as Curator of the
Royal Society, Hooke was able to pick up all the gossip and ideas of every active member
as well as the ideas of other philosophers outside England. Many of his ideas were certainly
original but the great majority had been taken from others, modified but then put forward as a Hooke original. He certainly deserved a little credit for his contribution to the
Principia but his claim was to take the credit for the plum prize, the inverse square law of
gravitation, the main crux of years of work by Newton. It was hardly surprising that
Newton was incensed by this man who laid claim to everything to be his own.

On 20 June 1686 Newton wrote to Halley. His letter began well enough but there
was a terrible sting in the tail:

The Proof you sent me I like very well. I designed ye whole to consist of three books, the second was
finished last summer being short & only wants transcribing & drawing the cuts fairly. Some new
Propositions I have since thought on wch I can as well let alone. The third wants ye Theory of Comets.
In Autumn last I spent two months in calculations to no purpose for want of a good method, wch made
me afterwards return to ye first Book & enlarge it wth divers Propositions some relating to Comets oth-
ers to other things found out last Winter. The third I now designe to suppress. Philosophy is such an
impertinently litigious Lady that a man had as good be engaged in Law suits as have to do with her. I
*found it so formerly & now I no sooner come near her again but she gives me warning...*10

All Halley's work and diplomacy were to no avail. Newton's resentment ran so high that
he had decided to withdraw the third book of the *Principia*. Without Book Three the
work would still be a major contribution to human knowledge but Halley knew that the
final book, *The System of the World*, was the crowning achievement which would make it
stand out to posterity as a landmark.

10

THE *PRINCIPIA*

I SAW ETERNITY THE OTHER NIGHT
LIKE A GREAT RING OF PURE AND ENDLESS LIGHT
ALL CALM, AS IT WAS BRIGHT;
AND ROUND BENEATH IT, TIME IN HOURS, DAYS, YEARS,
DRIV'N BY THE SPHERES
LIKE A VAST SHADOW MOV'D; IN WHICH THE WORLD,
AND ALL HER TRAIN WERE HURL'D

Henry Vaughan (1622-1695)

IN ONE OF HIS CUTLERIAN LECTURES at Gresham College Robert Hooke had given three rules for a system of the world which show a lot of similarity to those given by Newton:

> *First. That all Coelestial Bodies whatsoever, have an attraction or gravitating power towards their own Centers, whereby they attract not only their own parts, and keep them from flying from them, as we may observe the earth to do, but that they do also attract all the other Coelestial Bodies that are within the sphere of their activity… The second supposition is this, That all bodies whatsoever that are put into a direct and simple motion, will so continue to move forward in a streight line, till they are by some other effectual powers deflected and bent into a Motion, describing a Circle, Ellipsis, or some other more compounded Curve Line. The third supposition is, That these attractive powers are so much the more powerful in operating, by how much nearer the body wrought upon is to their own Centres.* [1]

At first sight, Hooke appears to be putting forward the idea of universal gravitation, the suggestion that every body in the heavens attracted every other body, but he falls down by suggesting that the attraction is 'within the sphere of their activity'. In 1666 Newton had postulated that the force on the apple was of the same nature as the force on the

Moon but, again, both these objects were in the sphere of activity of the Earth. The idea that the planets were attracted to bodies outside their 'sphere of activity', that is, other planets, was suspected before the time of Hooke and Newton by Kepler and also by the English astronomer, Jeremiah Horrocks. As early as 1639, Horrocks had noticed that the giant planets Jupiter and Saturn were not in the positions predicted by Kepler's laws. They seemed to have some effect on each other which pulled them out of their predicted orbits.

Hooke's second supposition was very close to Newton's first law of motion but this, too, had already been postulated by Galileo and Descartes. His third proposition was certainly correct but it was not precisely formulated and, when he tried to define it more specifically, he could not back it up with the necessary mathematics.

Hooke certainly had his support-

PHILOSOPHIÆ

NATURALIS

Adams. 5.68.3

PRINCIPIA

MATHEMATICA.

Autore *JS. NEWTON*, *Trin. Coll. Cantab. Soc.* Mathefeos Profeffore *Lucafiano*, & Societatis Regalis Sodali.

IMPRIMATUR·

S. PEPYS, *Reg. Soc.* PRÆSES.

Julii 5. 1686.

LONDINI,

Juffu *Societatis Regiæ* ac Typis *Jofephi Streater*. Proftat apud plures Bibliopolas. *Anno* MDCLXXXVII.

ABOVE The title page of Newton's *Principia*. The name of Samuel Pepys appears as president of the Royal Society. This copy probably belonged to Richard Towneley of Towneley Hall in Lancashire whose name is written below that of Pepys. Cambridge University Library Adams 5.68.3

ers at the Royal Society. One of these was John Aubrey who will always be remembered for his invaluable little book, *Brief Lives*, which gives potted biographies of prominent people of his times including many members of the Royal Society. Aubrey was a great friend of Hooke and he was one of the first people to appreciate his talents. He gives us Hooke's version of the events in a letter to Anthony à Wood at Oxford. It cannot be considered an unbiased account of the events but it is useful in stating Hooke's grievance:

About nine or ten years ago, Mr Hooke wrote to Mr Isaac Newton of Trinity College, Cambridge, to make a demonstration of this theory (of gravity), not telling him, at first, the proportion of the gravity to the distance, nor what was the curved line that was thereby made. Mr Newton, in his answer to this letter, did express that he had not known it; and in his first attempt about it, he calculated the curve by supposing the attraction to be the same at all distances: upon which, Mr Hooke sent, in his next letter the whole of his hypothesis, that is, that the gravitation was reciprocal to the square of the distance…which is the whole celestial theory, concerning which Mr Newton has a demonstration, not at all allowing he received the first intimation of it from Mr Hooke. Likewise Mr Newton has in the same book printed some other theories and experiments of Mr Hook's, as that about the oval figure of the earth and sea: without acknowledging from whom he had them.

Aubrey, prompted by Hooke, then launches into superlatives regarding the merit of the discovery:

Mr Wood! This is the greatest discovery that ever was since the world's creation. It never was so much as hinted by any man before. I know you will do him right. I hope you may read his hand. I wish he had written plainer and afforded a little more paper.
Yours John Aubrey.[2]

This was not the first but the fourth time that Hooke had crossed Newton. When Newton first sent his reflecting telescope to the Royal Society, it was Robert Hooke who claimed that he had made a smaller telescope, with greater magnification, several years before him. When Newton decided to publish his theory of light, it was Hooke who was one of the main critics and who turned out to be the biggest thorn in his flesh. After an amicable exchange of letters over the experiment to detect the Earth's motion, Hooke had exposed a fault in Newton's analysis in front of the Royal Society, despite the fact that Newton had supplied Hooke with the information on the understanding that it remained confidential. There were other episodes of claims by Hooke which did not involve Newton. In 1672, for example, when Leibniz showed his mechanical calculator to the Royal Society, Hooke claimed he could make a better and simpler calculator but he never went on to produce the promised machine. In 1674, when Christiaan Huygens constructed a watch governed by a spiral spring attached to a balance wheel, Hooke cried foul and claimed that Huygens had stolen his invention. Wren and Halley had both witnessed Hooke's claim that he could solve the problem of a planetary orbit under an inverse square law, and no one was more aware than these two that Hooke was unable to solve it. Newton claimed that Hooke published Borell's hypothesis as his own work, and he also knew that many astronomers and mathematicians before Hooke had suggested that the action of the Sun on the planets obeyed an inverse square law.

Edmund Halley was fully sympathetic to Newton's feelings. His main concern was that he had to persuade Newton not to give up on the publication of his third book. Halley still did not know the full contents of Book Three but he did know that the *Principia* would be incomplete without it. In his reply to Newton, Halley defends the 'litigious lady' of natural philosophy whom Newton wished to disown. Other members of the Royal Society were in agreement with Halley and they, too, offered Newton their support:

I am heartily sorry, that in this matter, wherein all mankind ought to acknowledge their obligations to you, you should meet with anything that should give you disquiet, or that any disgust should make you think of desisting in your pretensions to the Lady, whose favours you have so much reason to boast of. Tis not shee but your Rivalls enviing your happiness that endeavour to disturb your quiet enjoyment, which when you consider, I hope you will see cause to alter your former Resolution of suppressing your third Book, there being nothing which you can have compiled therein, which the learned world will not be concerned to have concealed; These Gentlemen of the Society to whom I have communicate it, are very much troubled at it, and that this unlucky business should have hapned to give you trouble, having a just sentiment of the Author therof.[3]

In his next paragraph Halley mentions the famous meeting, in the cold winter of 1684, between Wren, Hooke, and himself. He explained how he had arrived at the conclusion of an inverse square law of gravity from consideration of Kepler's law relating the period of a planet to its mean distance from the Sun. He told the story of Hooke's claim to have solved the problem and how Christopher Wren and himself asked Hooke to produce the proof of his pretensions. Halley then gave his own account of what actually happened, as he saw it, at the meeting of the Royal Society when Hooke had put forward his claim. It appears that Sir John Hoskins, a friend of Hooke's, was acting as President, and the discussion centred around Newton's book and Halley's involvement with it. The contents of the *Principia* were eagerly anticipated by the Society. Newton's work was highly praised but Hooke was disturbed to find that his own contributions received no mention from Sir John Hoskins. Hooke took offence to such an extent that he and Hoskins 'who till then were the most inseparable cronies, have since scarce seen one another, and are utterly fallen out'. After the breaking up of the meeting, several members adjourned to the coffee house as usual. It was there in the informal atmosphere that the smouldering Robert Hooke pressed his claim to his colleagues, not just as the discoverer of the theory of gravitation but as the inventor of celestial mechanics as well. It was a false claim in as much as his system of mechanics contained several invalid assumptions and would never have stood up to scrutiny.

Edmund Halley knew that Newton had little to fear from Hooke's claim for priority. At this point, he may not have known much about the contents of Book Three of the *Principia*, but he knew from the groundwork set up by the first two books that it would contain knowledge that was new to humankind. One of these new contributions to knowledge, which closely affected Halley, was Newton's theory of comets. He realized that, although Newton's mathematical demonstrations were essential to the system of the world, the great majority of philosophers would have great difficulty in understanding them. He also knew, however, that they would be able to accept more readily the physical results that were developed in Book Three. He urged the author once more not to deprive the world of the climax to his thesis:

> *Sr I must now again beg you, not to let your resentments run so high, as to deprive us of your third book, wherin the application of your Mathematicall doctrine to the Theory of Comets, and severall curious Experiments, which, as I guess by what you write, ought to compose it, will undoubtedly render it acceptable to those that will call themselves philosophers without Mathematicks, which are by much the greater number.*[4]

Halley's letter was written at the end of June 1686. The next month he received two letters from Newton, one concerning his [Halley's] observations on the pendulum on the island of St Helena and the other referring to some work of Huygens. In the first of these letters Newton added that he accepted Halley's account of what had happened at the Royal Society, and he showed remorse at his hasty outburst against Hooke. 'I understand he was misrepresented to me and I wish I had spared ye postscript in my last letter', wrote Newton regretfully. He then went on to admit that it was a letter from Hooke that prompted him to solve the problem of the elliptical orbit. He also admitted that the notion of a body falling from a great height to the south-east was an idea that had been prompted by Hooke and that it was Hooke's suggestions which had caused him to work on the problem in the first place. He implied that, even though he was not prepared to give Hooke any acknowledgement for the inverse square law, he was prepared to mention Hooke's work in one of the later scholia. It was a fair and generous letter and deserves to be quoted at length. It shows that, although Newton was quick to flare up into a temper, he was a sensitive man and he regretted his outburst. His anger was the natural result of pent-up emotion against Hooke's continual claims for priority:

> *…I am very sensible of ye great kindness of ye Gentlemen of your Society to me, far beyond wt I could ever expect or deserve & know how to distinguish between their favour & anothers humour. Now I understand he was in some respects misrepresented to me I wish I had spared ye Postscript in my last. This is true, that his Letters occasioned my finding the method of determining Figures, wch when I had tried in ye Ellipsis, I threw the calculation by being upon other studies & so it rested for about 5 yeares till upon your request I sought for yt paper, & not finding it did it again & reduced it into ye Propositions shewed you by Mr Paget but for ye duplicate proportion I can affirm yt I gathered it from Keplers Theorem about 20 yeares ago. And so Sr Christopher Wren's examining ye Ellipsis over against ye Focus shews yt he knew it many yeares ago before he left of his enquiry after ye figure by an imprest motion & a descent compounded together. There was another thing in Mr Hooks letters wch he will think I had from him. He told me yt my proposed expt about ye descent of falling bodies was not ye only way to prove ye motion of ye earth & so added ye expt of your Pendulum Clock at St Hellena as an argumt of gravities being lessened at ye equator by ye diurnal motion. The expt was new to me but*

not ye notion. For in yt very paper wch I told you was writ some time above 15 yeares ago & to ye best of my memory was writ 18 or 19 years ago I calculated ye force of ascent at ye Equator arising from ye earth's diurnal motion in order to know what would be ye diminution of gravity thereby. But yet to do this business right is a thing of far greater difficulty then I was aware of. A third thing there was in his letters, wch was new to me & I shall acknowledge it if I make use of it. Twas ye deflexion of falling bodies to ye south east in our Latitude. And now having sincerely told you ye case between Mr Hook & me I hope I shall be free for ye future from ye prejudice of his Letters. I have considered how best to compose ye present dispute & I think it may be done by ye inclosed Scholium to ye fourth Proposition. In turning over some old papers I met with another demonstration of that Proposition, wch I have added at ye end of this Scholium. Which is all at present from

Your affectionate Friend & humble Servant

Is. Newton.[5]

Halley was relieved and pleased that Newton regretted his outburst. He was still left in doubt, however, about Book Three of the *Principia*. There was no further communication between the two men until October when Halley wrote a routine letter with details of the progress on Books One and Two. Newton replied on the 18 October but still made no mention of Book Three and *The System of the World*. Newton had also been corresponding with the Astronomer Royal, John Flamsteed (1646–1719). In Paris, the Italian-born French astronomer, Giovanni Cassini (1625–1712), claimed to have seen two 'planets' orbiting Saturn but Flamsteed had observed only one. Flamsteed provided the information Newton wanted, which showed that the moons of Jupiter obeyed Kepler's laws in their orbits about the planet. He was also able to establish that the planet Jupiter was not a perfect sphere but an oblate spheroid like the Earth, that is, a sphere flattened at the poles because of its rotational motion. Newton hoped to obtain similar information for Saturn but the more distant planet was harder to observe, and Flamsteed was unable to oblige him. Fortunately, Newton had the data he wanted for Jupiter, and Saturn was therefore of secondary importance.

It was not until the next year, at end of February, that Halley wrote again to Newton. By this time Halley was in a terrible quandary regarding the third book of the *Principia*. He still had no idea whether Newton intended to publish his third book or to carry out his threat to suppress it. Time was getting short, Books One and Two were at the printers, and Book One was almost completed. The suspense was weighing on him, and he could wait no longer for Newton to make up his mind. In March he decided to make a direct approach and, with great tact, he asked about Book Three, *The System of the World*:

Honoured Sr

I received yours, and according to it, your Second Book, which this week I will putt to the press, having agreed with one that promises me to get it done in 7 weeks, it making much about 20 sheets; The first

Book will be about 30, which will be finished much about the same time; This week you shall have the 18th sheet according to your direction:

You mention in this second, your third Book de Systemate mundi, *which from such firm principles, as in the preceding you have laid down, cannot chuse but give universal satisfaction: if this be likewise ready, and not too long to be got printed by the same time, and you think fit to send it; I will endeavour by a third hand to get it all done together, being resolved to engage upon no other business till such time as all is done: desiring hereby to clear myself from all imputations of negligence, in a business, wherein I am much rejoyced to be any wais concerned in handling to the world that that all future ages will admire: and as being*

Sr

Your most obedient servant

Edm Halley[6]

It was nearly a month before Halley got a reply. He would have been more than happy to receive an acknowledgement from Newton and confirmation that the author had resumed work on the system of the world. The reply, when it came, exceeded Halley's wildest expectations. On 4 April Halley received not just a reassurance that Newton was going ahead but the actual manuscript for the final book of the *Principia* As he read eager-

ABOVE The Paris Observatory. Three different telescopes can be identified, the observations seem to be of Saturn, Jupiter and Mars.

ly through the text he was absolutely amazed and delighted with the demonstrations that unfolded before him. It was no exaggeration to say that the book contained the secrets of the universe. The orbits of the planets and their moons were described; the motions of the comets; the action of the Moon and the Sun to produce the tides; and the reason for the precession of the equinoxes. It was a complete system to explain the workings of the world and of the heavens. Six months earlier Halley referred to the *Principia* as 'your incomparable treatise'. It had now reached immortal status. 'I received not the last part of your divine treatise until yesterday', he wrote to Newton. In the heat of the moment Edmund Halley forgot that he was an atheist.

The reason why Newton had been corresponding with the Astronomer Royal became apparent. As the moons of Jupiter orbited the giant planet, they obeyed the same laws as the planets orbiting the Sun. There was something, however, that perturbed the orbits and drew them away from an ellipse: it was the effect of the Sun's gravity that caused the perturbation. The effect was also true of the Earth's moon – a moon which was so large compared to the Earth that the two could be called a binary planet system. Newton was able to formulate a theory for the motion of the Moon but he knew his theory was not exact. The problem of the motion of the Moon involved the gravitational forces between three bodies, a problem so difficult that it did not admit to a general solution.

At some point in the writing of Book Three, the light which had been glimmering for a long time dawned on Isaac Newton. The planets traced their ovals around the Sun. The Moon traced its curved path around the Earth but the Moon's ellipse was changing all the time. The moons of Jupiter showed a similar effect. The giant planets of Jupiter and Saturn exerted a mysterious effect on each other when they came into conjunction. The reason had been suspected for a long time but Newton was the first to be able to formulate it mathematically. The truth was that Jupiter and Saturn attracted each other, and their moons were drawn by the Sun as well as by the planets to which they belonged. All the effects could be explained in one very simple principle. The basic principle of gravitation was that every particle of matter in the universe attracted every other particle of matter. Gravitational attraction was a basic property of all matter.

Flamsteed confirmed that the planet Jupiter was flattened at the poles. Newton was able to explain the flattening effect in terms of the rotation of the planet. He deduced that all planets had solidified from a gaseous or liquid form and that the Earth should show a flattening at the poles similar to that of Jupiter. The flattening would cause the Earth to nutate (nod) slowly as it rotated on its axis – that is, over a long period of time, the Earth's axis would not point fixedly at the pole star but it would move around a small cone in the sky. This nutation was known as the precession of the equinoxes, an effect which had been known since ancient times but which could not be explained on any previous theory of the world.

He demonstrated that the slowing down of Halley's clock on the island of St Helena had two causes. One was the diurnal rotation of the Earth: this meant that every object on the surface was carried around in a circle each day, an effect that was greater at the Equator than in northern latitudes because the equatorial objects moved in a larger circle. The second effect was the flattened shape of the Earth which meant that the North and South Poles were about 17 miles (27 km) nearer to the centre than points on the Equator. Both these effects combined to reduce the force of gravity in the tropical latitudes.

The ancients knew that the tides were governed by the motion of the Moon. Newton's *Principia* showed mathematically how the combined gravitational effect of the Moon and the Sun caused the tides. The influence of the Moon on the oceans was one of the great arguments in favour of astrology – the purpose of the Moon seemed to be to govern the motion of the seas. It was obvious that the Sun governed the night and the day, and its movement through the Zodiac governed the seasons of the year. Having explained the function of the Sun and the Moon, astrologers thought it reasonable to assume that the planets and other heavenly bodies also served some pre-ordained purpose in the scheme of the universe, and they had no difficulty in assigning influences to the different planets. When Newton was able to show that the tides could be explained in terms of the gravitational attraction of the Moon on the oceans, this did not shake the faith of the astrologers but it made the rational scientists think again about astrology. The gravitational influence of the Sun also had an effect on the tides; it was a much smaller effect than that of the Moon but it did explain the exceptionally high and low tides which occurred when the Sun lay in certain directions. Every other body in the universe also affected the tides but, after the Moon and the Sun, the influences of the planets were far too small to be measured. It could be argued that the idea of the force of gravity – all matter attracting all other matter through empty space – was just as fanciful as any of those propounded by astrologers. The difference, however, was that the idea of gravity was a simple one that explained many phenomena. In Book Three of the *Principia* Newton had demonstrated the effects of gravity with awesome mathematical precision.

Newton included a section on the motion of comets, just as Edmund Halley had hoped he would. It was obvious to astronomers that the starry messengers with their long tails were something quite apart from the planets, and the idea that comets could be governed by the same laws as the other bodies in the Universe had never occurred to the astronomers before Newton. He reasoned that, if the comets contained matter, then they must be subject to the same gravitational forces as the planets, and he set about trying to calculate the orbit of the comet of 1680, a comet for which he had many reliable observations. It was a very arduous task. The planets moved more or less in a single plane, the plane of the ecliptic, and the calculation of their orbits was a two-dimensional problem involving only the geometry of the plane. In general, a comet cared nothing for the ecliptic, and its orbit could lie in any plane. This made the calculation extremely difficult but,

ABOVE Jupiter from Voyager 1, showing the bands and the great red spot. A sight which the seventeenth century astronomers would love to have seen.

by means of an iterative process – by making a guess at the orbit and assuming that its path was parabola – Isaac Newton was able to calculate an approximate path and use the error between theory and observation to correct his guess. By this means he was able to calculate the orbit of the 1680 comet and to show that it moved around the far side of the Sun, passing very close at its closest approach. It was obvious to Edmund Halley that, if Newton was right about comets, then it was possible for one or more of these myste-rious wanderers to be moving around the Sun in a closed orbit, an orbit that would cause to approach the Earth again after a fixed period of time:

Your method of determining the Orb of a Comet deserves to be practised upon more of them, as far as

may ascertain whether any of those that have passed in former times, may have returned again: for their
Nodes and Perihelia being fixed will prove it sufficiently, and by their Periods the transverse diameters
will be given, which possibly may render the problem more Easy. If you can remove the fault in the
Comets Latitudes 'twill do better, but as it is, the Numbers you have laid down, do make out the veri-
ty of your Hypothesis past dispute. I do not find that you have touched that notable appearance of
Comets tayles, and their opposition to the Sunn; which seems rather to argue an efflux from the Sunn
than a gravitation towards him. I doubt not but this may follow from your principles with the like ease
as all the other phenomena; but a proposition or two concerning these will add much to the beauty and
perfection of your Theory of Comets.[7]

The idea set many thoughts in motion for Edmund Halley. Newton thought the comet
of 1680 followed a trajectory very close to a parabola. This meant that it would never
again return to the Sun, but it was obvious that some of the other comets could be in
elliptical orbits about the Sun – orbits very like those of the planets but greatly elongat-
ed. There was, therefore, a possibility that a comet could return. It took Edmund Halley
many years to prove his point but he began to search historical records for the appearances of comets. He discovered reliable records of thirty-six comets seen between 837
and 1698. He plotted the years and looked for regular time intervals between the observations. But he did not know which comets were periodic and he did not know the
lengths of their periods. He made calculations on twenty-four of the comets. He then
repeated the calculations on the 1680 and the 1682 comets. He became convinced that
the comet observed in 1531 and the comet of 1607 were the same as that of 1682. It
seemed that the period of the 1682 comet could be about seventy-six years but it could
be longer or shorter if the comet happened to pass close to one of the giant planets.
Eventually, he discovered that the comet which heralded the Battle of Hastings in 1066
– the comet woven into English history on the Bayeux Tapestry – could be the same
comet a mere eight revolutions ago. If his theory was correct, then it was clear that the
comet would return: he predicted that it would appear in about 1758. His problem then
was to try to predict the return exactly. This was not easy because the comet was drawn
off its course by the gravity of the outer planets making its period irregular. Edmond
Halley knew that he would have to live to be over a hundred if he were to see his 1682
comet again.

Newton took due notice of Halley's comments about the nature of comets. In his final
draft he speculated about the nature of the comet's tail and the atmosphere around it. In
Book Three of the *Principia* Newton included acknowledgements to Wren and Halley,
among others, as well as to Robert Hooke as he had promised. He included a general
scholium in which he speculated about the ether, the nature of gravity, and God.

Newton regretted that he was unable to extend *The System of the World* from the
macroscopic world to the microscopic. His experiments with chemistry had convinced

him that some substances had an affinity for each other, and that they combined very readily as though they were attracted by a force of some kind, whereas other substances seemed to repel each other. He thought that the tendency for a gas to expand implied that there existed a repulsive force between the atoms. In the seventeenth century, magnetism and electrostatics were hardly understood at all but it was obvious that, in both phenomena, the forces involved were repulsive as well as attractive:

> ...to derive the rest of the phenomena of Nature by the same kind of reasoning from mechanical principles, for I...suspect that they may all depend upon certain forces by which particles of bodies, by some causes hitherto unknown, are either mutually impelled towards one another, and to cohere in regular figures, or are repelled and recede from one another, These forces being unknown, philosophers have hitherto attempted the search of Nature in vain; but I hope the principles here laid down will afford some light either to this or some truer method of philosophy.[8]

He did realize that he had not explained how the force of gravity could operate at a distance through a vacuum. What was the physical difference between a volume of space containing a gravitational field and a volume of space containing no gravity? He was not prepared to get involved with this question:

> Tis unconceivable that inanimate brute matter should (without ye mediation of something else wch is not material) operate upon & affect other matter without mutual contact...That gravity should...act...at a distance through a vacuum without the mediation of anything else . . . is to me so great an absurdity that I believe no man who has in philosophical matters any competent faculty of thinking can ever fall into. Gravity must be caused by an agent acting constantly according to certain laws, but whether this agent be material or immaterial is a question I have left to ye consideration of my readers.[9]

Newton acknowledged his debt to Halley in the handsomest of terms. 'In the publication of this work the most acute and universally learned Mr Edmund Halley not only assisted me in correcting the errors of the press and preparing the geometrical figures', he declared. 'But it was through his solicitations that it came to be published.' Samuel Pepys knew very little of the mathematics in the *Principia* but, in his capacity as President of the Royal Society, he was particularly honoured. He received a special mention as 'Imprimatur' on the frontispiece of the book.

Edmund Halley was determined to make sure that the book received some acknowledgement outside the scientific world and he had a special copy produced for the king. It was unfortunate that Charles II died the year before the *Principia* was published – his interest in science and his support to the Royal Society would have made him the ideal monarch to receive a copy of Newton's masterpiece. It was James II who had followed

Charles as the King of England. The king could not to be expected to understand the *Principia*, but Halley pointed out to him the theory of the tides and its value to navigation. Halley's superbly polite and diplomatic letter is a model example of how to approach royalty:

ABOVE James II by Godfrey Kneller. Edmund Halley made sure that King James received a copy of Newton's *Principia*. It was unfortunate that Charles II died in the year before the publication, he was far more interested in science and he would have been able to appreciate the book far better than James.

May it please Your most Excellt. Maty.
I could not have presumed to approach Your
Maties. Royall presence with a Book of this
Nature, had I not been assured, that when
the weighty affaires of Your Governmt. per-
mit it; Your Maty. has frequently shown Your
selfenclined to favour Mechanicall and
Philosophicall discoveries: And I may be bold
to say, that if ever Book was so worthy the
favourable acceptance of a Prince, this, where-
in so many and so great discoveries concern-
ing the constitution of the Visible World are
made out, and put past dispute, must needs
be gratefull to Your Matie; Being especially,
the labours of a worthy subject of your own,
and a member of that Royall Society found-
ed by Your late Royall Brother for the
advancement of Naturall knowledge, and
which now florishes under your Majesties most Gracious Protection.

But being sencible of the little leisure wch. care of the Publick leaves to Princes, I believed it necessary
to present with the Book a short Extract of the matters conteined, together with a Specimen thereof, in
the genuine Solution of the Cause of the Tides in the Ocean. A thing frequently attempted But till now
without success. Whereby Your Matie. may Judge of the rest of the Performances of the Author....

If by reason of the difficulty of the matter there be anything herein not sufficiently Explained, or if
there be any materiall thing observable in the Tides that I have omitted wherein Your. Matie. shall
desire to be satisfied, I doubt not but that if Your Majesty shall please to suffer me to be admitted to
the honour of Your Presence, I may be able to give such an account thereof as may be to Your Majesties
full content:
I am Great Sr. Your Maties. most Dutifull & obedient Subject
Edmond Halley[10]

Isaac Newton gave birth to the *Principia* but Edmund Halley was its midwife. It was fitting that Edmund Halley should write the review of the *Principia* in the *Philosophical Transactions*, for he knew far more about the book than anyone except the author:

> *This incomparable Author having at length been prevailed upon to appear in publick, has in this Treatise given a most notable instance of the extent of the powers of the Mind; and has at once shewn what are the Principles of Natural Philosophy, and so far derived from them their consequences, that he seems to have exhausted his Arguments, and left little to be done by those that shall succeed him.*[11]

The book was not without its critics. The continental mathematicians were not at all convinced that Newton had disposed of the theory of vortices. Both Huygens and Leibniz, for example, continued to subscribe to some form of vortex theory throughout the rest of their lives. Writing in 1688 after he had read *Principia*, Huygens noted that 'Vortices [are] necessary; [without them] the earth would run away from the sun; but very distant the one from the other, and not, like those of M.Des Cartes, touching each other'. Leibniz, also post-*Principia*, in his Tentamen (1689) spoke of planets being carried through the heavens by the motion of a fluid ether. Despite the critics, however, the French greatly admired the work. The great mathematician the Marquis de l'Hopital was first shown the *Principia* by an Englishman, Dr John Arbuthnot. L'Hopital's reaction is one of the best testimonies to the fund of knowledge in the *Principia* and also an indication of Newton's character. Arbuthnot described l'Hopital's reaction when he had read the book:

> *...he cried out with admiration good God what a fund of knowledge there is in that book! He then asked the Dr every particular about Sr I. even to the colour of his hair said does he eat & drink & sleep. is he like other men? And was surprized when the Dr told him he conversed chearfully with all his friends assumed nothing & put himself upon a level with all mankind.*[12]

The Frenchman was correct with some of his deductions. We know from Humphrey Newton's evidence that, during the creative process of writing the *Principia*, Isaac Newton did not in fact 'eat & drink & sleep' like other men. When the full impact of *The System of the World* was felt, even astronomers were writing poetry about it:

> *Here ponder too the laws which God,*
> *Framing the universe, set not aside*
> *But made the fixed foundations of his work*
> Edmund Halley

II

GREENWICH

IT IS THE VERY ERROR OF THE MOON
SHE COMES MORE NEAR THE EARTH THAN SHE WAS WONT

William Shakespeare (1564-1616)

JOHN FLAMSTEED WAS BORN IN 1646 at Denby in Derbyshire and, like many scientific men of his generation, he was the son of a clergyman. In common with his contemporary Robert Hooke, Flamsteed was a sickly child and, at the age of about fourteen, he had an attack of what seems to have been rheumatic fever. He was taken to Ireland in 1665 to be touched by Vincent Greatrakes, the seventh son of a seventh son who was supposed to possess miraculous healing powers. The miracle did not seem to work for Flamsteed's illness but he developed his talents at mathematics and astronomy, and he made such a good name for himself that he became the first Astronomer Royal.

King Charles decided to found an observatory for 'the most exact care and diligence to rectifying the tables of the Motions of the Heavens, and the Places of the fixed stars, so as to find out the much desired Longitude at Sea, for perfecting the art of Navigation'. The king needed a good astronomer to run his observatory, a man who had proved himself to be a competent observer of the stars. On the recommendation of Sir Jonas Moore, the Master of Ordnance at the Tower of London, the king appointed John Flamsteed as his astronomical observer. His duties were defined as:

> ...forthwith to apply himself with the most exact care and diligence to the rectifying of the tables of the motions of the heavens, and the places of the fixed stars so as to find out the so much-desired longitude of places for perfecting the art of navigation.[1]

The decision to build an astronomical observatory was made in 1675, and the site chosen was in the Royal Park at Greenwich. This was the obvious place for the new observatory. It was far enough out of London not to be troubled by the smoke of the city; it was right at the heart of the shipping; and on the banks of the Thames. There was a small hill, which Christopher Wren thought was the ideal site, where in the distant past there had once stood a castle. On 22 June 1675, a royal warrant addressed to the Master General of the Ordnance described the plans for the new observatory:

Whereas, in order to the finding out of the longitude of places for perfecting navigation and astronomy, we have resolved to build a small observatory within our park at Greenwich, upon the highest ground, at or near the place where the castle stood, with lodging rooms for our astronomical observator and assistant, Our Will and Pleasure is that according to such plot and design as shall be given you by our trusty and well-beloved Sir Christopher Wren, Knight, our sur-

ABOVE Flamsteed's large sextant with telescope sightings and mountings on the roof of the Greenwich Observatory. An engraving from *Historia Coelestis Brittanica* (1725).

veyor-general of the place and scite of the said observatory, you cause the same to be built and finished with all convenient speed, by such artificers and workmen as you shall appoint thereto, and that you give order unto our Treasurer of the Ordnance for the paying of such materials and workmen as shall be used and employed therein, out of such monies as shall come to your hands for old and decayed powder, which hath or shall be sold by our order on the 1st of January last, provided that the whole sum to be expended or paid, shall not exceed five hundred pounds; and our pleasure is, that all our officers and servants belonging to our said park be assisting to those that you shall appoint for the doing thereof, and for so doing, this shall be to you, and to all others whom it may concern, a sufficient warrant.[2]

John Flamsteed was promoted from Royal Observer to Astronomer Royal. He held the post for a remarkably long time, from his appointment in 1675 until his death in 1719, when he was succeeded by Edmund Halley. It is a curious fact that Halley, a young man who was still an undergraduate at the time the observatory was founded, was involved with the Royal Greenwich Observatory from the very beginning but he had to wait forty-five years before he obtained the post of Astronomer Royal for himself. In June 1675, he and Flamsteed met with Robert Hooke at the Tower of London to discuss the design of a mural quadrant for the new observatory and, on 2 July, Halley was present with Wren and Hooke when they viewed the proposed site in Greenwich Park.

Greenwich was the site of a Tudor royal palace which had been badly damaged during the time of Oliver Cromwell. Charles was prepared to rebuild the palace, with Christopher Wren as his architect, but, by this time, Greenwich was rapidly expanding and it was no longer considered a suitable place for a royal residence. Consequently, the refurnished palace ended up as a hospital for sailors. The other fine building at Greenwich was the Queen's House designed by Inigo Jones, and it was from there that Flamsteed made his first observations until such time as the new observatory was available.

The financing of the observatory was a rather piecemeal affair. A gatehouse was demolished from the Tower of London and this provided some of the timber. A fort was pulled down at Tilbury and supplied some of the lead and iron needed in the construction. The sum of £520 was raised from the sale of spoilt gunpowder and a supply of bricks was purchased with the proceeds. Christopher Wren, a man uniquely qualified as both astronomer and architect, was the ideal person to design the observatory. Wren claimed that he designed his observatory 'for the Observator's habitation and a little for pompe' but observatories were much rarer buildings than houses and churches, and there

ABOVE Royal Greenwich Observatory. The decision to build an observatory at Greenwich was made in 1675. John Flamsteed, the first Astronomer Royal, took up residence in June 1676. The design of the building was by Christopher Wren who had himself been professor of astronomy at Oxford, it was the first time that a building had been designed specifically as an observatory.

was little precedent for Wren to go on. His building was certainly an architectural gem and much in keeping with his other work at Greenwich. Robert Hooke, always at the thick of things and well in with Christopher Wren, supervised much of the actual building work.

Flamsteed's apartment was ready on 10 July 1676, and he began to observe from the Octagon Room of the new observatory on 19 September. Sir Jonas Moore provided two superbly accurate and very tall pendulum clocks made by the royal clock-maker, Thomas Tompion, each with a long pendulum of 13 feet (3.96 m) so that the beat was two seconds. The observatory had no less than seven clocks in all. Two of them were of a special design intended to reduce the angle of swing of the pendulum. One of the clocks was adjusted to sidereal time – rather than the solar hours, it displayed the time in degrees of the Earth's rotation relative to the stars. Jonas Moore also provided the first astronomical instruments, consisting of a micrometer, a sextant, and a mural arc. The mural arc, designed by Robert Hooke, proved to be unsatisfactory and, when Flamsteed found that he could not use it, he uncharitably thought that Hooke had made it so deliberately to obstruct him. As a result of this difficulty, Hooke and Flamsteed were never on the best of terms. The Astronomer Royal then had a wooden arc made by a local carpenter. This was also unsatisfactory but he did use it successfully to take meridional altitudes. In the early years he had to depend largely on his sextant for his observations. Flamsteed had several other instruments, including telescopes with focal lengths of 8, 16, 27, and even 60 feet (2.4, 4.9, 8.2, and 18 m). He had two small quadrants, and a third quadrant which was on loan from the Royal Society.

The Astronomer Royal's salary was a hundred pounds per annum; it was an adequate income for the times but not generous. At first, John Flamsteed had no skilled assistants to help with the observations but he mentions a 'silly surley labourer' to help with the general maintenance and the manual work of moving equipment. He had to take in pupils for private lessons in mathematics and astronomy to eke out his subsistence. In 1684 he became the incumbent of the Parish of Burstow near Reigate. This necessitated a 20-mile journey into the depths of Surrey to perform his duties. It was extra work for him but it probably doubled his salary. When his father died in the 1680s he found himself better off and he was able to purchase a large mural quadrant at his own expense. The brass quadrant was made by his new and competent assistant, Abraham Sharp. It had an angle of 40 degrees and was mounted in place during the summer of 1689. The radius of the new brass arc was 6 feet 7 inches (2 m), and it had a sighting telescope 7 feet (2.1 m) long. It cost him £120: this was more than his annual salary as Astronomer Royal but he considered the money well spent, and his new instrument did a lot to improve the quality of his observations. Abraham Sharp proved to be a faithful assistant who remained at Greenwich for more than forty years until Flamsteed's death in 1719.

At this time John Flamsteed was the only professional observer in England. Chairs of

ABOVE Octagon Room, Royal Greenwich Observatory. The astronomer on the right is using a refracting telescope, the one on the left is measuring angles with a quadrant. A third man sits at a table writing down the observations. Built into the wall are clocks by Thomas Tompion. The portraits on the wall are of Charles II and his brother the Duke of York who became James II.

astronomy existed at the universities of Oxford and Cambridge, and also at Gresham College, but they tended to be held by theoreticians, in contrast to John Flamsteed who was employed primarily to make observations. The lot of the astronomer was a long, lonely vigil in the cold winter nights at Greenwich, painfully measuring the altitudes of the stars as they passed the meridian and noting the transit time for each one. On a clear night he lost no opportunity of plotting the position of the Moon so that his observations could be used to determine the equations of its motion. Over the years it is estimated that Flamsteed made about 20,000 observations from Greenwich. In one of his letters he describes the dawn breaking over the marshes after a long night of observation: 'The sun rose then over ye Thames & adjacent Marshes, set over a drie hill on ye west end of London. It was a misty morning and a great fogg over ye Meadows.'[3]

From the 1660s, England's maritime trade developed very rapidly. The taking of New Amsterdam (renamed New York by the British) from the Dutch stimulated the growth of the American Colonies, and transatlantic trade grew steadily. Ships returning from America were advised to sail along a line of latitude to make a landfall on the English coast but skilled navigators were few and cloudy skies were common – it was not unusual for English ships to stray so far off their latitude that they sighted the coast of Ireland or Brittany before seeing the coast of England. Even the latitude could not be guaranteed in bad weather so the likelihood of knowing the longitude after an Atlantic crossing was reduced to guesswork. Charles II was well aware that the unsatisfactory state of navigation contributed to the detriment of the maritime trade of his country.

A good navigator with the right instruments could find the latitude with relative ease: so long as he could see the sky it was simply a matter of measuring the angular height of the Pole Star above the horizon and making a simple calculation. The stars revolved around the pole, the altitude of the Pole Star was constant for a specific latitude, and the observation could therefore be made at any time of the night. Latitude could even be measured during the day. If the date was known, then the height of the noon sun above the horizon was the only measurement needed. Finding the longitude was a far more difficult problem but the *Ballad of Gresham Colledge* made light of the matter:

> *The Colledge will the whole world measure;*
> *Which most impossible conclude,*
> *And Navigation make a pleasure*
> *By finding out the Longitude.*
> *Every Tarpaulin shall then with ease*
> *Sayle any ship to the Antipodes*
> Joseph Glanville[4]

Finding the longitude was a problem of such complexity that for centuries it seemed insuperable. In 1598 Philip III of Spain offered a prize of a hundred thousand crowns to anyone who could come up with a solution. Holland, the next great maritime nation after Spain, offered a prize of thirty thousand florins. The English eventually offered twenty thousand pounds. When it came to offering a reward, the English were well over a century behind the Spanish but, with the growth of the American colonies and the great expansion of maritime trade, they too had become obsessed with the problem of finding a ship's position at sea.

In principle, all that was required was a clock that could give the time at sea accurately. The local shipboard time could be found from the noonday sun and, if a set of tables was available to correct for the latitude and seasonal changes, the time could also be found at sunset and sunrise. The shipboard time had to be compared to the time at the zero meridian as indicated on the ship's chronometer. The latter had to be set to the correct time when the ship left its home port.

For the English, zero meridian was at Greenwich. The longitude could be calculated easily from the difference between shipboard time and Greenwich time. Thus, a time difference of 1 hour implied a twenty-fourth part of a circle, or 15 degrees of longitude. There is a confusion between the angular minute, one-sixtieth part of a degree, and the temporal minute, one-sixtieth of an hour. Thus, to measure the longitude to within 15 minutes of arc, which was 15 nautical miles on a great circle, required knowing the time to within 1 minute (of time). If the sailors were to be able to chart their position to within a few nautical miles on the surface of the Earth, then the clock had to be accurate enough to give the Greenwich time to less than 1 minute.

Candles and water clocks could measure hours but this measure was far too crude for a ship at sea. The pendulum clock was a very accurate timepiece – some of them were easily capable of keeping time to within a few seconds a day – and, by the 1660s, clocks were commercially available to give very accurate time on land. Pendulum clocks had been designed for maritime use but, in heavy weather, the pendulum swing could not survive the pitch and roll of the ship so some other method of regulating the clock had to be devised. One possibility was to build a clock with a sprung balance wheel instead of a pendulum. The method was sound but it was far ahead of its time. The accuracy of the seventeenth-century balance-wheel clock was not as good as that of the pendulum clocks, and this idea had to be abandoned for nearly a century.

There was another, much cheaper, alternative to the mechanical clock. Astronomers claimed that there was already a clock in the sky that could be used to calculate a universal time at any place on the Earth. The clock face was the planet Jupiter and its moons were the moving fingers. When Galileo had first trained his telescope on Jupiter, he was amazed to find four points of light in the vicinity of the planet. When he further discovered that the points of light changed position over a short period of time, he realized that he had discovered four moons orbiting the planet – they became known as the Galilean satellites of Jupiter.

The Paris Observatory was founded in the year of London's Great Fire by the Sun King, Louis XIV (1638–1715) of France. It possessed telescopes far more powerful than those used by Galileo – French astronomers could see the satellites of Jupiter so clearly that they could observe them moving behind the planet to become eclipsed by the shadow. The times of these eclipses could be measured very accurately, and there were a thousand such eclipses every year. It followed that, if tables could be compiled showing the times of the eclipses, then an observer anywhere on the Earth could use the moons of Jupiter to determine the time.

It was a marvellous and very simple idea but it suffered from two setbacks. When the Danish astronomer, Christensen Römer (1644–1710), came to study the moons of Jupiter, he found that the eclipses were occurring behind schedule and that the astronomical clock in the sky seemed to be losing time. The effect seemed to be entirely out of keeping with the laws of the heavens but, in his attempt to explain the phenomenon, Römer realized that he had accidentally stumbled on an amazing scientific discovery. He knew that Jupiter had moved to a more distant point in its orbit and he concluded that the few minutes of error represented the extra time taken by the light to travel from

ABOVE Octagon Room, Royal Greenwich Observatory. A more modern view of the picture on page 188. The astronomers are long gone but the clocks and the portraits remain unchanged since the observatory was built.

Jupiter to the Earth. He was able to make the very first estimate of the speed of light and, had he known the scale of the universe with greater accuracy, his estimate would have been very close to the true figure. [Römer's estimate was that light travelled at a speed of 225,000 kilometres an hour (140,000 miles/second) whereas the modern value is 299,792 km/s (186,291 mi./s).]

This first difficulty with the Jupiter method could easily be overcome by using Romer's correction but there was a second problem which was much more serious. With its long, static telescopes and modern equipment, the Paris Observatory could see the Galilean satellites easily and measure the times of the eclipses but, on a swaying ship at sea, it was virtually impossible to get a sighting of Jupiter's moons, let alone to watch patiently for the occurrence of an eclipse. The method was simply impracticable even in the calmest of weather. The French persevered with their method, however, and it was used very successfully to establish the longitude of islands and places on *terra firma* but not for ships at sea.

In 1674 the Duchess of Portsmouth introduced a French gentleman called le Sieur de St Pierre to the Court of Charles II. St Pierre assured the king that he had 'found out the true knowledge of the longitude, and desires to be put on tryall thereof'. There was another clock in the sky, he claimed, one that was much easier to observe than Jupiter.

ABOVE To solve the problem of finding the longitude at sea the position of the Moon in the sky had to be predicted with great accuracy. This proved to be a major problem. Flamsteed made many observations of the position of the moon.

This clock was the Moon, which travelled across the starry background faster than any other object in the heavens. The Moon seemed to have been put there by God for the purpose of telling the time at sea. The king was sufficiently convinced to appoint a committee of learned men from the Royal Society to investigate the claim of le Sieur de St Pierre. The committee included Lord Brounker, Seth Ward, Christopher Wren, and (naturally) Robert Hooke. As a test of his claim, they were to provide St Pierre with astronomical data so that he might try to determine where the observations had been made. They would then try to establish whether or not the method would be practical and useful to shipping, and they would report their findings back to the king. The committee asked John Flamsteed to assist them: at this time he was already well known to be a skilful observer, and he had recently arrived in the capital as a guest of Sir Jonas Moore at the Tower of London. Flamsteed was sceptical about the Frenchman's claim but he agreed to co-operate, and he produced the test data that St Pierre wanted. It transpired that the Frenchman failed to convince the committee with his claim but it was clear that his method might be made to work if lunar motion could be better defined and if the positions of the fixed stars were known more accurately.

The sphere of the fixed stars rotated once a day about the Pole and, in every rotation, the Moon moved about 12 degrees against the stars. If the position of the Moon could be measured to within 1 minute of arc, then it should be possible to tell the time to within 2 minutes. There were basically four requirements for the lunar method of finding longitude. Firstly, a set of tables was needed to show the exact positions of the fixed stars near the Moon's path. A second set of tables was required to give the predicted position of the Moon at any time of the year. Thirdly, an instrument was needed to measure the angles from the nearest point on the Moon's disc to the star of the Moon to the fixed stars. A set of instructions was also needed to help the navigator determine the longitude from the measurements and the tables.

The first requirement seemed simple enough but the best tables available were those of the Danish astronomer of aristocratic descent, Tycho Brahe (1546–1601). The tables had been meticulously compiled with the naked eye and were already over a hundred years old. Tycho's tables were simply not accurate enough for the job in hand. The sky needed to be surveyed anew with telescopic sightings, and a more accurate star catalogue had to be made. The second requirement, to predict the position of the Moon in the sky, was sterner stuff and far more difficult than anyone imagined at the time. The Moon was very regular and predictable in its phases: the mistress of the night sky followed very nearly the same laws as the planets but she continually wandered off course, and no theory existed that was capable of predicting her future position with the necessary accuracy. The third requirement, to measure the distance from the limb of the Moon to the fixed stars, was solved by the marine sextant which was accurate enough to take the angular measurements. The instructions for navigators could not be completed without the tables of the Moon's position.

After the publication of Newton's *Principia* it seemed obvious that the universal theory of gravitation could be used to formulate a precise theory for the motion of the Moon, leading to the final solution of the problem of longitude. Newton was prepared to tackle the problem but he needed observational data from Flamsteed to prove his theory and to calculate the constants of lunar motion. At first, Flamsteed and Newton enjoyed very good relations: they had exchanged data on the comet of 1680/81 and there is a tradition that the Astronomer Royal and Isaac Newton sometimes enjoyed a game of backgammon together. As time progressed, each party became increasingly frustrated with the other. Newton needed the lunar observations to test his theory but, as Flamsteed's health declined, the astronomer became reluctant to release his data. The problem was aggravated by the fact that they held opposite views about Flamsteed's work. Newton saw Flamsteed as a paid servant of the Crown, and felt that the Greenwich observations belonged to his country and to anyone who might have need of them. In contrast, Flamsteed, who had spent large sums of money purchasing his own equipment, felt that the data belonged to him and that he could choose when and where to publish and to whom he could supply information.

To solve the motion of the Moon required a solution of the three-body problem which Newton had tried to solve in the *Principia* with only limited success. In this case, the three bodies were the Sun, the Earth, and the Moon, and each exerted a gravitational attraction on the other two. It is a curious fact that, when Newton and Flamsteed were searching the literature for theories of lunar motion, the best they could find had been put forward before they were born by one of their own countrymen working almost in total isolation. A lunar theory had been proposed early in the century by Jeremiah Horrocks, a brilliant young astronomer who had died in 1641 at the age of twenty-one.

Jeremiah Horrocks was born in 1618 at Toxteth just outside Liverpool. In 1632 he was admitted as a sizar to Emmanuel College, Cambridge. In November 1639, Horrocks became the first person to observe a transit of the planet Venus across the face of the Sun. He made the observation when he was living at Hoole, a village on the Lancashire coast about 18 miles north of Liverpool. Horrocks was an unfortunate astronomer, mainly because he died before reaching his prime but also because the English Civil War held up the publication of his works until long after his death. It is generally thought that some of his papers were lost during the Civil War and that others were destroyed in 1666 by the Great Fire of London. What remains of his work, however, shows him to be an extraordinary genius. His treatise of the transit, *Venus in sole visa*, was first published in 1662 by Johannes Hevelius at Danzig – this was somewhat to the embarrassment of the English scientific community who felt that they themselves should have made the publication. Horrocks' manuscript arrived at Danzig by a circuitous route. Hevelius obtained a copy through Huygens in Holland; Huygens, in turn, had been given a copy by one of the English astronomers. For ten years Hevelius's publication was the only work by Horrocks that was readily available to English astronomers but it provided the stimulus for the Royal Society to publish the remaining works of their fellow countryman. The task was put into the very capable hands of John Wallis, and the works were eventually published through the Royal Society under the title *Opera Posthuma* in 1672. It was only then that Flamsteed and Newton became fully aware of some of the astronomical work that had been achieved in their own country before they were born.

The achievements of Jeremiah Horrocks in his short life, working with very primitive instruments so early in the seventeenth century, amazed the members of the Royal Society, and both Newton and Flamsteed quickly came to recognize that Horrocks was a genius of the first rank. Jeremiah Horrocks was only nineteen years old when he formulated his theory of the Moon's motion yet, forty years later, it offered a model that was closer to the truth than any subsequent theory! It was found necessary to add refinements to the model which Horrocks had proposed but all parties were in agreement that the Horrocian theory of lunar motion was basically correct.

From his careful observations of the Moon, Horrocks deduced that it moved in an ellipse around the Earth with the Earth at one focus. So far so good. The Moon behaved in the same way towards the Earth as the planets behaved towards the Sun. He was able to show, however, that after a full revolution the Moon did not return to the same point in its orbit. To correct this error he added two new terms to the motion: one term was a precession of the orbit, and the second was a change in the eccentricity of the ellipse.

There were other discoveries in the posthumous work of Horrocks. He had found that the major planets, Jupiter and Saturn, were not in the positions predicted by Kepler's laws, and he was puzzled by the fact that they exerted some unseen attraction on each other that pulled them out of their orbits. Isaac Newton knew that the cause of this attraction was the gravitational force between them.

ABOVE *The Founder of English Astronomy* by Eyre Crowe. The picture shows Jeremiah Horrocks who died in 1641, a generation before the existence of the Royal Society and the Royal Greenwich Observatory. He lived to be only 22, but his theory of the lunar motion was a work of genius, it was still in use a hundred years after his death.

Both Newton and Halley were interested in Horrocks' account of the transit of Venus. This astronomical observation entailed a great deal more than the drawing of a round spot on the image of the Sun. From his measurements of Venus, combined with those of a transit of Mercury which was observed by Gassendi in 1631, Jeremiah Horrocks was able to calculate the parallax of the Sun, a small angle relating to the distance from Earth to the Sun. He obtained a value that put the Sun at a distance of about seventy million miles, a figure that was smaller than the true value by about 15 per cent but which was a major advance on Kepler's estimate of twenty million miles. It was actually a better estimate than the figure used by Newton many years later. Edmund Halley showed how the transit of Venus could be used to obtain a much more accurate figure for the solar parallax. It was ironic that the next transit of Venus was not until the 1760s, even later than the return of Halley's comet. Halley could not live to see his comet return, nor could he hope to observe a transit of Venus to implement his method of solar parallax. It was left to the British naval explorer, James Cook (1728–79), and his astronomer, Charles Green, to take the measurements for Halley's method at Tahiti on the voyage of the *Endeavour* in 1768.[5]

With his long hours of observation, his parish duties, and his erratic schedules, it was not surprising to find that John Flamsteed was always complaining of his health. He was forced to make the majority of his own observations; there was no heating in the observatory, his health was delicate, and the winter nights on the exposed hilltop at Greenwich could be bitterly cold.

'…I was ill now of ye headache not being able to calculate', he wrote as a postscript in one of his letters. 'My work of ye fixed stars was also interrupted by my distemper.' A month later he complained of being ill again and 'much troubled by paines in my head'. He found that 'sweating modratly has given me some relief for my Headache' and that 'by waters and excersice my Malady is something abated'. Flamsteed was something of a hypochondriac: one day, after all the grumbling about the sweating and the headaches, he rode nearly forty miles on horseback, probably on a return journey to visit his parish at Burstow near Reigate. He found that the riding helped him so much that he resolved to ride every day of the week.

John Flamsteed was well aware of the fact that Newton had a need for his work, and he showed Newton fifty observations of the Moon and promised to send him another hundred. The Astronomer Royal was as good as his word but, like Newton, he was very possessive of his work and he insisted that it should go no further. When Flamsteed complained of the amount of clerical work and calculation required to refine his lunar data, Newton unwisely hurt his pride by offering to pay for an assistant. When the offended Flamsteed replied to Newton, he launched into a bitter attack on somebody whom he cannot even bring himself to mention by name – he simply used the term 'that character':

> But I am displeased Wth you not a little for offering to gratifie me for my paines either you know me
> not so well as I hoped you did or you have suffered your selfe to be possest with that Character which
> ye malice & envy of a person from whom I have deserved much better things has endeavord to fix on
> me & which I have disguised because I knew he used me no other ways then he has done the best men
> of ye Ancients nay our Savior his Apostles….[6]

By 'that character' Flamsteed was referring to Edmund Halley. He was particularly neurotic about Halley getting hold of his work, and it was common knowledge that, after the publication of the *Principia*, Newton and Halley were quite close friends. Flamsteed hardly lost an opportunity to run down Halley in his correspondence. The origins of their friction is difficult to find but it was almost certainly a result of Halley's carefree attitude towards religion. He was a well-known and outspoken atheist referred to in some circles as 'the infidel mathematician'. Poor Flamsteed was so upset by Halley's blasphemies that hardly a letter passed without some reference to him. In a confused letter he claimed to know Halley better than did Newton:

> *I find you understand him not so well as I doe. I have had some years experience of him &: very fresh*
> *instances of his ingenuity with which I shall not trouble you tis enough that I suffer by him I would*
> *not that my freinds should & therefore shall say no more but that there needs nothing but that he shew*
> *himselfe an honest man to make him & me perfect freinds & that if he were candid there is no body*
> *liveing in whose acquaintance I could take more pleasure: but his conversation is such yt no modest*
> *man can beare it no good man but will shun it.*[7]

He was concerned that Halley might be blackening his character: '...your last letter yt
mentions another sort of recompense but I considered that you might be possest with ye
Charecter which a malitious false friend has spread of me', he wrote to Newton.
On another occasion he actually mentioned Halley by name but it was no more than a
scribbled note in the margin, referring to a position for which Halley had applied at
Christ's Hospital School: 'Mr Halley has got himselfe recommended by Mr Pepys, who
understands little of ye business, but his ill moralls & abuseing religion has been
objected to yt he injures himselfe...'

There was certainly a lot of jealousy surrounding the scientific claims and discoveries
of the times, and it sometimes seemed that no one was free of the problem. It is difficult
to understand why there was so much friction among men who clearly had common
interests and a lot to gain by helping one another. The Royal Society and the Greenwich
Observatory were always struggling for finance, and the stresses certainly told on men like
Hooke and Flamsteed. Hooke was always capable of controversy, and he never failed to
put in a claim for priority. When he discovered his law relating tension and extension, he
first published it as an anagram so that he could stake his claim when he was ready to tell
the world. Flamsteed was so self-righteous that he lectured Newton, of all people, on
pride and humility. Newton did not suffer fools gladly, and he was neurotic about
publishing any of his work for fear of becoming involved in controversy – a policy that
eventually backfired on him. Edmund Halley, in his dealings with Newton, seems to have
been the perfect diplomat, yet he seems almost to have gone out of his way to upset
Flamsteed by his outspoken atheism and for no very obvious reason.

It must be admitted that the seekers of truth and knowledge all had their human
failings. Somehow, in spite of everything, the path of knowledge was still opening up to
their enquires.

12

METAMORPHOSIS

A LITTLE PHILOSOPHY INCLINETH A MAN'S MIND TO ATHEISM, BUT
DEPTH IN PHILOSOPHY BRINGETH MEN'S MINDS ABOUT TO RELIGION.

Francis Bacon (1561–1626)

AT THE TIME WHEN NEWTON was immersed in writing the *Principia*, England, as usual for the times, was in turmoil. Charles II died in February 1685. The 'Merry Monarch' may not have been the most serious king of the century but he will always be remembered by the scientific community for his charter to the Royal Society and for the founding of the Royal Greenwich Observatory. King Charles may not have been a very active member of the Royal Society but he had had something in common with Isaac Newton. Not only did he have his own chemical laboratory, but he was experimenting with mercury in the month of his death. For Charles, however, the 'litigious lady' of natural philosophy did not have the same charms as the ladies of the Court. He had a wife, he had mistresses, and he had children but he had no legitimate heir to the throne of England. Consequently, he was succeeded by his brother, James II.

James quickly managed to make himself very unpopular, mainly because he wanted England to return to the Roman Catholic faith. In the summer of 1685, the Duke of Monmouth, an illegitimate son of Charles II, landed at Lyme Regis in Dorset to make a claim for the English throne. Monmouth's army consisted largely of a hurriedly recruited body of West Country peasants armed with little more than billhooks and scythes. They were easily defeated by James's professional soldiers at the Battle of Sedgemoor, the last pitched battle ever to be fought on English soil. The aftermath of Monmouth's rebellion was a retribution so terrible that it became known as the 'Bloody Assizes'. The infamous Judge Jeffreys was responsible for the assizes and he sentenced 320 men to die on the gibbets in the western counties and another 850 to be transported to a life of slave labour on the plantations in the American Colonies. Their only crime was that they had been pressed into service by the Duke of Monmouth's henchmen. The total lack of mercy shown by Jeffreys did nothing to improve the popularity of James II.

The effects of the new regime were first felt at Cambridge early in 1687, just as Newton was finishing off his third book of the *Principia*. The king wanted to admit a Benedictine monk called Alban Francis to the degree of MA without him taking the oath of allegiance to the Church of England. The oath was a constitutional requirement – others before Father Alban had been awarded the degree without taking the oath but these were mostly visitors from non-Christian countries. A very notable exception was Isaac Newton himself. As we saw in an earlier chapter, the Lucasian Professor of Mathematics had been given a special dispensation by Charles II to continue in his post without having to take the oath. In 1687 the situation was more serious than in former years. It was obvious that James wanted to set a precedent, and the Alban affair was seen as a threat to introduce Catholics into senior positions within the university.

ABOVE John Wallis by Gerard Soest. John Wallis was at college with Jeremiah Horrocks, but unlike his friend he lived until his eighties. Wallis was a respected founder member of the Royal Society, he urged Newton to publish his ideas on the calculus.

Newton became very involved with the issue and, when the Cambridge Senate met on 11 March, he was chosen as one of two representatives to advise the vice-chancellor, John Peachell, on the legalities of the case. Peachell was made distinctive by his unfortunate nose which gains a mention in Pepys's diary: 'My old acquaintance, Mr Peachell, whose red nose makes me ashamed to be seen with him, though otherwise a good-natured man'.

This development seems quite out of character for Newton. For more than two decades he had been a reclusive researcher, caring for nothing except alchemy, theology, and natural philosophy, and he did not seem the natural choice to defend the university against a political threat of this nature. But Newton was nothing if not thorough. He studied the constitution and he wrote no less than five drafts for the defence. On 21 April 1687 we find Isaac Newton standing with his vice-chancellor and his Cambridge colleagues before the notorious Judge Jeffreys at the Court of Ecclesiastical Commission in

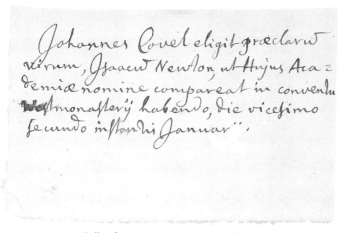

ABOVE Ballot for Isaac Newton A ballot slip casting a vote for Isaac Newton at the 1689 election. Cambridge University Archives, o.III.8/2

London. With his ferocious, bullying style, Jeffreys had no problem in making poor Peachell's nose redder than ever and in reducing him to a complete state of ridicule. As a result, the vice-chancellor was removed from his office, and the case for the university seemed lost. The drama was not over, however: Peachell was a weak man but the other delegates knew that their case was perfectly legal. Without their vice-chancellor, the depleted Cambridge delegation stood up to Jeffreys and they argued their case much more effectively. Jeffreys was frustrated and incensed by the resistance, so he fell back to his 'Bloody Assizes' role and roared at them to 'go your way, and sin no more, lest a worse thing come unto you'. The threat was very clear, careers and even lives were at stake, but the university had done enough to stave off the threat and to persuade the king to abandon his campaign. Within two years, the king's popularity had fallen so low that the threat of Catholic infiltration had disappeared completely. James II had fled into exile and the notorious Judge Jeffreys was a prisoner in the Tower of London.

The House of Lords passed a new resolution banning any person of the Roman Catholic faith from becoming sovereign of the country and also banning the sovereign from marriage to anyone of that faith. The sequel was the cliff-hanging but bloodless revolution when William of Orange and his wife Mary were invited to become the king and queen of England. In December 1688, the wars and differences with the Dutch were forgotten when William and Mary made their triumphant entry into London.

The service rendered by Isaac Newton over the Alban affair was fully recognized by his peers at the university and, in January 1689, when William III called the Convention Parliament to settle the succession problem, the Senate of Cambridge University met to select their candidates for the election. Isaac Newton was nominated, along with two others, as a Parliamentary candidate for the University of Cambridge. His role in the Alban Francis controversy must have increased his standing in the University and the result of the 1689 election was:

Sir Robert Sawyer   125 votes

Mr Newton   125 votes
Mr Finch   117 votes

The tie was not the great drama which it might at first appear: the university returned two members to Parliament. Sir Robert Sawyer and Mr Isaac Newton were declared as duly elected as members for Cambridge University.

There is no evidence that Newton ever spoke in debate in the House of Commons but there is an anecdote that he once asked an usher to close a window. Whether he spoke or not, Newton did take his seat in the Commons and he had a very clear understanding of what was going on in Parliament. He left a fairly full account of the proceedings, as they affected Cambridge, in a series of letters sent to John Covel who was the new vice-chancellor and successor to John Peachell.

It would seem that the last thing Isaac Newton might want to do after his years of seclusion at Cambridge would be to mix with the overconfident and highly opinionated group of social climbers which was the House of Commons. Yet he had to go somewhere and do something after giving the *Principia* to the world. The publication of his work had freed him of a certain responsibility to science and had caused him to change his attitudes to society. He was no longer seeking to 'reduce his acquaintance'; in fact, his attitude was quite the contrary and he began to yearn for an active life in London society as opposed to the reclusive life of Cambridge. The publication of the *Principia* had made him into a public figure. It had done much for his confidence and he could command respect in levels of society to which he could not aspire before. The number of his acquaintances grew considerably and he made many new friends.

The Convention Parliament included an old friend from Cambridge. His name was Charles Montague. He had been a student under Newton and, at the time, the two had made an abortive attempt to start up a Philosophical Society. Montague was an ambitious man – so ambitious that he married a woman in her sixties who was about thirty-five years his senior! His wife's main attraction seems to have been that she was the widow of the third Earl of Manchester, and consequently she had been left a very wealthy woman with an income of about £1500 per annum. Montague made his first impression on society when he wrote a popular satire called *The Town Mouse and the Country Mouse* which was published at almost the same time as the *Principia*. It was politics, however, which was his real ambition. He became a prominent member of the Whig party and he rose to become Chancellor of the Exchequer, a post which he held from 1694 to 1699. At the same time he retained his interest in philosophy, and he became president of the Royal Society for almost the same period, from 1695 to 1699. Newton and Montague served together in the Convention Parliament but, in the early 1690s, as Charles Montague's political career progressed, Newton saw less and less of him. Early in the eighteenth century, when Newton had moved to London and Charles Montague had become Lord

Halifax, they saw much more of each other but, as we shall see, it was not Isaac who was the main attraction in Newton's household.

One of the most prominent of Newton's new acquaintances was the philosopher John Locke (1632–1704). Locke was about ten years older than Newton and had been educated at Oxford as a physician. As a result of his controversial political beliefs, Locke went into exile in Holland for six years, and it was there that he came to know Christiaan Huygens very well. He read the *Principia*, studying the text and all the diagrams, but he understood nothing of the mathematics. With the help of Huygens, however, he came to recognize the great merits of Newton's work. After the revolution of 1688 he took the opportunity to return to England. In his essay, 'Concerning Human Understanding', Locke was modest about his own work but praised Newton highly. 'It is ambitious enough in an age which produces . . . the incomparable Mr Newton', he wrote, '. . . to be employed as an under-labourer in clearing the ground a little, and removing some of the rubbish which lies in the way of knowledge.' Locke and Newton found that they had much in common, including their interest in chemistry as well as their unorthodox theological beliefs. Their relationship was very free and relaxed. In a letter dated 3 May 1692, Newton began by inviting Locke to make the journey from Sussex to Cambridge to visit him:

> *Now the churlish weather is almost over I was thinking within a Post or two to put you in mind of my desire to see you here where you shall be as welcome as I can make you, I am glad you have pre-ventd me because I hope now to see you ye sooner. You may lodge conveniently either at ye Rose Tavern or Queen's Arms Inn.*[1]

The change from Newton the recluse to Newton the sociable was very obvious from his informal and friendly tone. Another sign of the esteem in which he held Locke was his willingness to visit him at his home, Masham House in Sussex. Newton spent most of his life at two places of work, Cambridge and London. He made a visit to Oxford late in his life and he made many visits to his home at Woolsthorpe but, for him, a visit to Sussex was new ground and a long journey. He chose to visit Locke's home in January 1691 and again in the autumn of 1702.

At about the same time as his friendship with John Locke was developing, Newton befriended a much younger man named Nicholas Fatio de Duillier, usually referred to simply as Fatio. Again, it was the *Principia* that caused Fatio to seek out Isaac Newton and, like Locke, he acted as an intermediary between Newton and Huygens. Fatio was the son of a wealthy Swiss landowner. He was well travelled for his age and he had moved around Europe to meet all the leading scientists of the time. He first met Newton in 1689 at a meeting of the Royal Society and they quickly became good friends. Newton enjoyed the company of the younger man and seems to have been quite amused by his youthful enthusiasm. David Gregory confided that 'Mr Newton and Mr Halley laugh at Mr Fatio's manner of explaining gravity'. Fatio had other talents besides his mathematics: he was fluent in French and he was useful to Newton in translating French scientific papers. A close relationship developed between the two men and Fatio, like Locke, was invited to visit the Lucasian Professor of Mathematics at Trinity College in Cambridge. In 1692, after one of his visits to see Newton, Fatio caught a cold and felt so ill that he thought he was going to die. He wrote dramatically to Newton in despair:

> *I have Sir allmost no hopes of seeing you again. With coming from Cambridge I got a grievous cold, which is fallen upon my lungs. Yesterday I had such a sudden sense as might probably have been caused upon my midriff/diaphragm by a breaking of an ulcer, or vomica, in the undermost part of the left lobe of my lungs . . . My pulse was good this morning; it is now feaverish an hath been so most part of the day. I thank God my soul is extreamly quiet, in which you have had the chief hand . . . Were I in a lesser fever I should tell You Sir many things. If I am to depart this life I could wish my eldest brother, a man of extraordinary integrity, could succeed me in your friendship.[2]*

Fatio de Duillier thought he was on his deathbed, and Newton was very alarmed at the prospect of losing his friend. He replied straight away suggesting that Fatio sought the best medical treatment, and he offered his own money if Fatio needed it.

> *Sr*
> *. . . last night received your letter wth wch how much I was affected I cannot express. Pray procure ye advice & assistance of Physitians before it be too late & if you want any money I will supply you. I rely upon ye character of your elder brother & if I find yt my acquaintance may be to his advantage I intend he shall have it . . . Sr wth my prayers for your recovery I rest*
> *Your most affectionate*
> *And faithful servant to serve you*
> *Is Newton[3]*

Newton need not have been so concerned. His friend Fatio soon recovered and lived for another sixty years. Newton invited Fatio to return and stay with him again in Cambridge, at least until such time as he had made a full recovery, and he blamed the London air for the length of time Fatio needed to return to health. Fatio was a compulsive traveller, however, and he frequently disappeared to the Continent for long spells. In the meantime, though he complained of the air in London, Isaac Newton found himself spending more and more time in the capital.

It might be thought that, because of Newton's entry into society and the way in which his life and circle of friends and acquaintances was opening up, he was entering what should have been a very satisfying part of his life. Yet, in 1693, at the age of fifty, we find that he suffered from a nervous breakdown. Some have attributed the breakdown to the strain of writing the *Principia*, and there is no doubt that his diet, his sleep, and therefore his health were all seriously effected by the effort of getting his masterpiece into print. But the nervous breakdown was six years later than the publication of the *Principia*. There are several factors that may have caused the breakdown but they are all merely speculative. Newton himself attributed his problem to sleeping too often by a coal fire – at one point he claimed that he suffered from insomnia and that he was unable to sleep for five consecutive nights. Others have suggested that the cause may have been mercury poisoning following his frequent sojourns over the furnace. It is true that the experiments with mercury did not come to an end after the publication of the *Principia* but he did not seem to exhibit any other symptoms of mercury poisoning. News of his breakdown eventually reached Europe and then returned to England in a garbled and amplified form. Soon, Huygens was informing Leibniz that Newton's friends had been forced to lock him up. Another highly elaborate version of the story was that he had lost many of his papers in a fire started by his dog Diamond – in fact, there is no evidence that Newton ever gave house room to dogs or cats.

In September 1693, he wrote a confused letter to Samuel Pepys which shows that he was in a state of depression. He implies that he had tried to obtain a favour from Pepys but that he regretted his actions and felt he must withdraw from the acquaintance:

> *Sir,*
> *Some time after Mr Millington had delivered your message, he pressed me to see you the next time I went to London. I was averse; but upon his pressing consented, before I considered what I did, for I am extremely troubled at the embroilment I am in, and have neither ate nor slept well this twelve month, nor have my former consistency of mind. I never designed to get anything by your interest, nor by King James' favour, but am now sensible that I must withdraw from our acquaintance, and see neither you nor the rest of my friends any more, if I may but leave them quietly. I beg your pardon for saying I would see you again, and rest your most humble and obedient servant,*
> *Is Newton*[4]

Another letter, written three days later to John Locke, survives. It confirms that he was indeed in a very depressed state of mind:

> *Sr*
> *Being of the opinion that you endeavoured to embroil me with woemen & by other means I was so much affected with it as that when one told me you were sickly & would not live I answered twere better if you were dead. I desire you to forgive me this uncharitableness. For I am now satisfied that what you have done is just & I beg your pardon for my having hard thoughts of you for it & for representing that you stuck at ye root of morality in a principle you laid down in your book of Ideas &*

designed to persue in another book & that I took you for a Hobbist. I beg your pardon also for saying
or thinking that there was a designe to sell me an office, or to embroile me. I am
Your humble & most
Unfortunate Servant
Is Newton[5]

It is impossible to imagine why Newton should think that his friend Locke would 'embroil him with woemen' – Newton was always respectful to women but his life shows only minimal evidence of any sexual feelings towards them, and Locke more than anyone would be fully aware of this. In August he received a letter from his half-sister, Hannah Barton, writing from Brigstock in Northamptonshire. It shows that Isaac's illness was not the only medical problem in the family at this time. Hannah's husband was very ill, and she wrote a confused letter to her brother about her finances:

Dear Brother
My dear Husband ever since his return to Brigstock has been very ill, he has Dr Wright with him or
Mr Fowller Most days. I find noe hopes of Cure but that hee lossis his flesh and strength very fast.
My Daughters and his portions are soe settled that I am to pay them £8 a year Apeece for intrest soe
that as I aprehend it I am to Loose all Taxis, or other hassards, this I wish to advise in but know not
with whom, besides I am overwhelmed in sorrow and wish for you to Comfort her that is
Your Loving Sister
Han. Barton[6]

Newton's nervous breakdown meant that he was unable to reply to Hannah immediately. Within a matter of weeks, however, he made a good recovery from his illness and, not long afterwards, he sent his half-sister a hundred pounds as well as buying an annuity to be paid to her three children after his own death. His niece Catherine Barton was one of these three children. He did not know it at the time but, a few years later, Catherine would move to London to live with him as his housekeeper. Isaac Newton always retained contact with his family and he lost no opportunity to offer the medical advice which he enjoyed imparting. At a later date there is a record of Newton sending to his half-sister and her family a barrel of oysters, a delicacy which he thought would be new to them. Two years later his half-brother Benjamin Smith sought his advice for an illness from which his wife was suffering. Newton prescribed a plaster or fomentation to apply to her chest. It may have been no more than the course of nature or pure luck on Isaac's part but the remedy worked and Benjamin Smith wrote to thank him:

I reced your kind Lre dated the 31st October last, And the fomentation wee applied as soone as wee
could possible; The effects have pved very successfull; for the swelling is verry much abated, and the
blacknes quite gone. Although att certaine times shee hath still a paine in her brest; after every bathing,

shee put the same plaster to her Brest againe, you sent, I could not perswade her to take the Sowes, for since her being wth child almost every thing goes against her Stomach; But shee is resolved to try.[7]

Fortunately for Newton, despite his garbled letter to Samuel Pepys, he was soon able to renew his friendship and, on one of his visits to London, he had dinner with the diarist. Some time later a Mr Smith arrived at Cambridge with a curious letter from Pepys. It seemed that Samuel was anxious to know the solution to a probability problem which he claimed was 'more than [just] a jest'; in fact, he describes it as a matter of life and death. Peter, a criminal convict, was doomed to die. Paul, his friend, asks for one throw of the dice to spare his life. He is given three choices:

A – has 6 dice in a box, with which he is to fling a 6.
B – has in another box 12 dice, with which he is to fling 2 sixes.
C – has in another box 18 dice, with which he is to fling 3 sixes.
Q. Whether B & C have not as easy a task as A, at even luck?

Newton took up the challenge and wrote back asking for clarification. Pepys confirmed that 'A' had to throw at least one six, 'B' at least two sixes, and 'C' at least three sixes. Mathematically it was a case of binomial probability, and the solution was a simple enough matter to the discoverer of the binomial theorem. Arithmetically, however, the problem was very complex and it required raising both the numbers 5 and 6 to their sixth and twelfth powers. In the case of eighteen dice, the eighteenth powers of five and six had to be calculated. Newton drew the line at this undertaking but he worked out the expected gain if a thousand pounds were to be staked on the first two cases:

Answer: Upon six dice there are 46656 chances, whereof 31031 are for him; upon 12, there are 2176782336 chances whereof 1346704211 are for him: therefore his chance or expectation is worth 31031/46656th part of a 1000£ in the first case, & the 113346704211/2176782336th part of 1000£ in the second; that is 665£, 0s 2d in the first case and 618£, 13s 4d in the second. In the third case, the value will be found still less. This, I think Sir, is what you desired me to give you an account of, & if there be anything further, you may command your most humble and obedient servant – Isaac Newton[8]

Many of Newton's biographers claim that, after the publication of the *Principia*, he gave up his interests in science and mathematics in favour of less rigorous pursuits such as theology and chronology. It is true that he threatened to give up natural philosophy at regular intervals but, when his mathematical papers came to be published by Derek Whiteside, they were found to cover every period of his life in eight heavy volumes each of six to seven hundred pages. His prolific mathematical output did not diminish until the eighteenth century, by which time he was approaching sixty, and it continued at a lesser rate until his death.

In the 1690s Newton was working on the problem of the motion of the Moon as described in the previous chapter. It was a problem with so many complexities that he once confessed that 'his head never ached but with his studies on the moon'. His main correspondent at this time was John Flamsteed the Astronomer Royal. In one of his letters, Newton wanted to know whether or not the different colours of light travelled at different velocities. He knew that Römer had calculated the speed of light from observations on the satellites of Jupiter but Newton's own instruments and eyesight were not adequate to see the effect he sought. His eyesight was not as sharp as that of Flamsteed, and he wrote to the astronomer asking if the light from the moons of Jupiter appeared red or blue, ruddy or pale, just before the Moon moved into the shadow of Jupiter. Flamsteed obliged but his reply was non-committal:

> I am so intent whilst observing on ye moments they disappear that I seldome heed to give such circumstances as you enquire onely thus much can I say that they begin to lose their light 2 or 3 minutes before they disappear and grow fainter and duller and smaller till they diminish to a point and vanish … cannot say that I ever saw any change to a blewish colour or red but duskish when I used a glass of 27 foot.[9]

At first the *Principia* generated a slow response on the continent of Europe but, once the leading scientists and mathematicians had absorbed its contents, they found it was a veritable goldmine of new ideas. In 1693 Newton received a letter written in Latin from Gottfried Wilhelm Leibniz of Hanover. It was a very generous letter praising the work in the *Principia*:

> How great I think the debt owed to you, by our knowledge of mathematics and of all nature, I have acknowledged in public also when occasion offered. You had given an astonishing development to geometry by your series; but when you published your work the Principia, you showed that even what is not subject to the received analysis is an open book to you. I too have tried by the application of conventional symbols which exhibit differences and sums, to submit to that geometry, which I call 'transcendent', in some sense to analysis, and the attempt did not go badly. But to put the last touches I am still looking for something big from you, first how best problems which seek lines from a given property of their tangents, may be reduced to squarings, and next how the squarings themselves – and this is what I would very much like to see – may be reduced to the rectification of curves, simpler in all cases that the measurings of surfaces or volumes…[10]

Leibniz was a brilliant and active mathematician. He had spent five years in Paris in the company of Huygens and others and, during that time, he had made two visits to the

Royal Society in London. On his first visit, in 1671, he had demonstrated his calculating machine to the Society and it had generated a lot of interest. His second visit was in 1676 when he passed about ten days in London and spent time with both John Wallis and John Collins. John Collins showed him a treatise by Newton on mathematical series. Leibniz immediately recognized the treatise as a work of genius, and he took copious notes from the script. There is little doubt that Leibniz was influenced by Newton's work but his great contribution to mathematics, the differential and integral calculus, was developed independently by himself – the similarity to Newton's method of the fluxions was very striking but purely coincidental. The discovery of the calculus was to lead to the greatest ever controversy in the history of mathematics but, in the seventeenth century, the friction between the two men had not yet developed. Newton and Leibniz were corresponding amicably with each other.

The *Principia* was out in the open for all to see but Newton was still cautious about the publication of his other works. In 1695 he received a timely warning from John Wallis about his lack of publication and the problems to which it could lead. Wallis was one of the oldest and most respected members of the Royal Society. His connection went back to the Oxford days in the 1650s and, before Oxford, right back to the time of the invisible college. Wallis's publication *Arithmetica Infinitorum* was an inspiration to Newton in his early years, and his *Algebra* was published the year before Newton's *Principia*. It was also mainly due to the efforts of John Wallis that the *Opera Posthuma* of Jeremiah Horrocks was published in 1672. Wallis was eighty years old when he wrote to warn Newton about his lack of publication and the possible priority disputes which might arise – he was one of the few people mature enough to write to Newton as he did:

Sir

I thank you for your letter of Apr. 21. by Mr Conon. But I can by no means admit your excuse for not publishing your Treatise of Light & Colours. You say, you dare not yet publish it. And why not yet? Or, if not now, when then? You adde, least it create you some trouble. What trouble now, more then at another time? Pray consider, how many years this hath lyen upon your hands allready: And, while it lyes upon your hands, it will stil be some trouble. (for I know your thoughts must needs be still running upon it.) But, when published, that trouble will be over. You think, perhaps, it may occasion some Letters (of exceptions) to you, which you shal be obliged to Answer. What if so? 'twill be at your choise whether to Answer them or not. The Treatise will answer for itself. But, are you troubled with no letters for not publishing it? For, I suppose, your other friends call upon you for it, as well as I; & are as little satisfyed with the delay. Mean while, you loose the Reputation of it, and we the Benefit. So that you are neither just to yourself, nor kind to the publike. And perhaps some other may get some scraps of ye notion, & publish it as his own; & then 'twil be His, not yours; though he may perhaps never attain to ye tenth part of what you be allready master of. Consider, that 'tis now about Thirty years since you were master of those notions about Fluxions and Infinite Series; but you have

never published ought of it to this day, (which is worse than nonumque prematur in annum.) 'Tis true, I have endeavoured to do you right in that point. But if I had published the same or like notions, without naming you; & the world possessed of anothers Calculus Differenatialis, instead of your fluxions: How should this, or the next Age, know of your share therein And even what I have sayd, is but playing an After-game for you; to recove (precariously ex postliminio) what you had let slip in its due time. …You may say, perhaps, the last piece of this concerning Colours is not quite finished. It may be so: (and perhaps never will.) But pray let us have what is. And, while that is printing, you may (if ever) perfect the rest. But if, during the delay, you chance to die, or those papers chance to take fire (as some others have done,) 'tis all lost, both as to you, & as to the publike. It hath been an old complaint, that an Englishman never knows when a thing is well. (But will still be over-doing, & thereby looseth or spoils many times what was well before.) I own that Modesty is a Vertue; but too much Diffidence (especially as the world now goes) is a Fault … I hope, Sir, you will forgive me this Freedome (while I speak the sense of others as well a my own,) or else I know not how we thus forgive these delays. I could say a great deal more: But, if you think I have sayd too much allready, pray forgive this kindness of
Your real friend & humble servant
John Wallis[11]

It was very good advice for Wallis to suggest that the method of fluxions be written up and published but, by the 1690s, Newton had tired of university life. He had achieved his great aim of publishing his *System of the World*, and the inevitable anticlimax followed. He yearned for something more to occupy his mind, and he applied to his friends John Locke and Charles Montague, among others, to find a suitable public office for him. Locke suggested that he apply for the position of Master of Charterhouse which carried an income of £200 per annum plus a coach and lodgings. The way of life did not appeal to Newton, however: he complained about the London air and did not apply for the post. Charles Montague was busy advancing his career with the Whig government and, late in 1695, when he became Chancellor of the Exchequer, he wasted little time in finding a position for Isaac Newton. In March 1696 he wrote to say that he could show 'good proof of my friendship' by offering Newton the post of Warden of the Mint. The job was a very nice sinecure. Montague explained that it carried a salary of £500 a year for very little work, and declared that he 'would not suffer the lamp which gave so much light to want oil'. He assured Newton that the office of Warden 'has not too much bus'-nesse to require more attendance than you may spare'. He did not expect Newton to do much more than collect the salary. Isaac Newton accepted the job despite his having to breathe the smoky London air. At the age of fifty-three, when most men would start looking for a nice university sinecure with which to end their working life, Isaac Newton left the university which had been his home for thirty-five years and moved to his new job in London.

13

LA BARTICA

AT BARTON'S FEET THE GOD OF LOVE
HIS ARROWS AND HIS QUIVER LAYS
FORGETS HE HAS A THRONE ABOVE
AND WITH THIS LOVELY CREATURE STAYS

John Dryden (1631-1700)

THE ROYAL MINT was situated inside the walls of the Tower of London to ensure the security of the precious metals and the valuable coins produced from them. In May 1696, when Isaac Newton started his new job as Warden of the Mint, he moved into the house that came with the job. It was built against the interior wall of the Tower. The accommodation was superior to that which his friends, Oldenburg and Pepys, had endured, both of whom had been forcibly confined to the Tower in the 1670s. It was a very smoky and noisy place to live, however, particularly after many years in the quiet confines of Trinity College, Cambridge. The fumes from the smelting metals were familiar to him from his years of sweating over his furnace but the constant din of the coin-striking machinery, as the metal for the nation's currency was being hammered out into coins of the realm, was worlds apart from the peace of the university cloisters. Isaac wasted no time in searching for a more pleasant place to live.

In August, he moved to a house in Jermyn Street, a new development in the west end of London. It was near one of the finest pieces of Christopher Wren's architecture, the Church of St James' which lay between Jermyn Street and a thoroughfare named after the Piccadilly Hall of the tailors, the place where they produced the elaborate piccadill borders for fashionable collars and ruffs. The house was near the western outskirts of the London residential development of the time, with the highly sought-after St James's Square close behind. It was an excellent choice of area but it could hardly have been further away from the Mint and still claim to be in London. The Warden was not required

ABOVE The Royal Mint. The picture is later than Newton's time at the mint but it shows the same method of striking the coins. Thousands of coins were struck every day, it was a very noisy process.

to be on site every day, however, and it made good sense to live in what was, for a city with the teeming population of London, a pleasant and expanding suburb in the West End. It was common knowledge that the prevailing winds carried off the smoke and the smells of the city for the consumption of the East End where the Royal Mint was situated.

The government had so many problems to cope with and more urgent matters than the currency that the coinage of the realm had been sadly neglected and it was in a very bad state. Over many years, the coin clippers had been systematically shaving the silver coins, reducing them to a fraction of their face value. Forgers had prospered, too, for they had been able to strike coins that could be circulated as genuine, and they were busy producing more forgeries from their illegal hidden refineries. A major re-coinage was long overdue, and it had to be done as speedily as possible. New machinery was available which not only gave a clearer image on the coins but could also produce a milled edge with characters embedded in it. The words 'Decus et Tutamen' [A decoration and a safeguard], referring to the new milled edge, appeared for the first time on the new coins. (Three hundred years later the two pound coin carried the motif 'Standing on the shoulders of giants' on its milled edge.) Newton was also involved with the setting up of provincial mints to help with the re-coinage problem – there were five of these, at

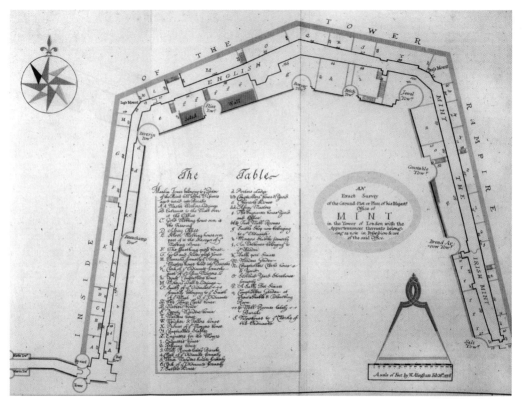

ABOVE A plan of the Tower of London by William Allington. The plan was made in 1701 at the time when Newton was Master of the Mint. The plan shows the location of the English mint on the west and the north with the Irish mint on the east. The main reason for locating the mint inside the Tower was the obvious security problem of looking after the precious metals and the coins.

Norwich, York, Chester, Bristol, and Exeter. He was able to appoint his friend Edmond Halley as Deputy Comptroller of the Mint at Chester – a position which Halley gladly accepted but which he came to regret when he had to face the many administrative problems that the job brought with it.

As Warden of the Mint, Newton answered to Thomas Neale, the Master of the Mint, and they did not always see eye to eye. Newton discovered that, as Warden, he was responsible for tracking down the forgers, of whom there were many, and prosecuting them if necessary. He did not relish the tedious task of locating and taking action against these counterfeiters but it was his responsibility and, having accepted his lot, he made a very thorough job of bringing them before the courts. The most notorious of these was William Chaloner, a very resourceful figure who had lined his pockets so well at the expense of the country that he was able to afford the best lawyers for his defence. As an experienced counterfeiter, Chaloner made a bold-faced attempt to gain control of the Mint for himself by claiming that he could mint coins that would be impossible for other coiners to forge. He exposed other forgers in the hope of saving his own skin. His plans were thwarted by Newton who quickly concluded that he was a great trickster. Chaloner was the slipperiest of customers, however, and as the net closed in on him he played every trick in the book to escape justice, including a desperate attempt to feign madness. His fellow counterfeiters then turned and gave evidence against him, and, after two years of court action, his sins finally caught up with him. The court sentenced him to death and he wrote to Newton pleading for mercy:

> *Sr*
>
> *…W[ha]t Mrs Carter swore ag[ains]t may appear direct mallice I have 3 yeares before Convicted her husband of Forgery and discovered where he*
>
> *and she were coyning for wch he is now in Newgate But I desire God Allmighty may Damne my Soule to eternity if every word was not false that Mrs Carter and her Maid swore ag[ains]t me . . . I am murderd O God Allmighty knows I am murderd Therefore I humbly begg yor Wor[shi]p will considr these Reasons and yt I am convicted without Preced[en]ts and be pleased to speak to Mr Chancellr to save me from being murtherd O Dear Sr do this merciful deed O my offending you has brought this upon me O for Gods sake if not mine Keep me from being murderd O dear Sr no body can save me but you O God my God I shall be murderd unless you save me O I hope God will move yor heart with mercy and pitty to do this thing for me I am*
>
> *Yor near murderd humble Servt*
>
> *W Chaloner[1]*

Newton could not have saved Chaloner from the court's sentence even had he wished to do so – the man was guilty and the wheels of justice could no longer be halted.

The re-coinage was completed by the middle of 1698 and, in the following year, Isaac Newton had a stroke of good fortune when the Master of the Mint, Thomas Neale, suddenly died in office. Newton was able to gain promotion from Warden to Master of the Mint, and this put everything at the Mint under his control. It was not the custom for the Warden to become Master. In fact, the move was without precedent, but the Treasury recognized that Newton had excelled in the re-coinage and he had shown himself to be the best person available for the job of Master. Financially, it was the most beneficial move which Isaac Newton made in his whole career. The Master of the Mint was allowed threepence-farthing for every pound weight of silver minted, in addition to his salary of £600 per annum. The amount he received from this source varied greatly from year

ABOVE The two-pound coin. The milled edge of the two-pound coin, struck in the third millennium, commemorates Newton's connections with the mint.

to year but it brought him an additional £1000 per annum for several lucrative years in the early 1700s when a great deal of silver coin was being minted. In addition to all the perquisites the job was a sinecure for life. Isaac Newton became a wealthy man and was well provided for in his old age.

There was an even happier side to Newton's time at the Mint. In about 1696 he acquired a new housekeeper. She was a young lady of only seventeen, or possibly a year or two older for we do not know the exact date when she moved to London. Her name was Catherine Barton and she was Isaac's niece (strictly, his half-niece), the daughter of Hannah Smith Barton and the Reverend Robert Barton, the latter being the incumbent of Brigstock in Northamptonshire. When Robert Barton died in 1693, Newton's widowed sister Hannah was anxious to find a suitable position for her daughter.

The earliest surviving correspondence between Newton and his niece dates from August 1700 but we know from some of her anecdotes that she had been in his household for at least three years before that time. The letter gives us an uncompromising picture of a young woman suffering from the ravages of smallpox, her face disfigured by the lesions. Having contracted the disease in London, Catherine left her uncle's house to recuperate in the Gyre household at Woodstock in Oxfordshire. She wrote two letters from Woodstock to her Uncle Isaac but these have not survived. Her uncle wrote back and, true to form, he could not resist giving her some medical advice. It was a warm and personal letter showing that the two had already formed a close relationship by this time:

> *Dear Niece*
>
> *I had your two letters & am glad ye air agrees with you & th[ough the] fever is loath to leave you yet I hope it abates, & yt ye [re]mains of ye small pox are dropping off apace. Sr Joseph [Tily] is leaving Mr Toll's house & its probable I may succeed him. [I] intend to send you some wine by the next Carrier wch [I] beg the favour of Mr Gyre & his Lady to accept of. My La[dy] Norris thinks you forget your promis of writing to her, & wants [a] letter from you. Pray let me know by your next how your f[ace is] and if your fevour be going. Perhaps warm milk from ye Cow may [help] to abate it.*
> *I am*
> *Your very loving Unkle*
> *Is Newton[2]*

Thus we find that Sir Joseph Tily – an attorney who had recently been knighted – was among Newton's acquaintances. The mention of Lady Norris shows that, at this time, Catherine Barton had already made some impact on London Society. Lady Norris was born Elizabeth Read, the daughter of a Bristol merchant, Robert Read, and was married to her third husband, Sir William Norris of Speke Hall on the north bank of the River Mersey, who was a Member of Parliament for Liverpool. Lady Norris was clearly an acquaintance of Isaac Newton. We do not know how well they knew each other but, in

ABOVE The picture by George Romney is thought to be Isaac Newton explaining one of his experiments with the prism to his niece Catherine Barton (centre). Note the prism, the spectrum on the wall and the orrery. On the left is a serving maid. Cambridge University Library Keynes U.4.7 p.314

Newton's correspondence, there appears a letter to her on which someone has written the words 'A Letter from Sir I. N. to…', and a different hand has written the words 'Copy of a letter to Lady Norris by…'. The letter is no less than an elaborate proposal of marriage! It was written in 1698, soon after the death of Sir William Norris. David Brewster is the only one of Newton's biographers to take the marriage proposal from the fifty-five-year-old Newton as genuine but the wording is out of character and it is certainly not written in the precise style of Newton's other correspondence. Such a hot item of gossip, however, is difficult for a biographer to pass over without comment, and it is difficult to explain how a marriage proposal to Lady Norris came to be among the possessions of Isaac Newton.

Returning to Catherine Barton, whom we left still suffering from smallpox, we find an unfortunate young woman in danger of losing her complexion for the rest of her life. Happily, because of, or perhaps in spite of, the warm milk from the cow, Catherine and her complexion survived and soon we find plenty more evidence of her entry into a London society in which she had, as said above, made some impression before her illness. The relationship between uncle and niece had advantages to both parties. Newton, in late middle age, needed someone to run his household and to help him with his entertaining and the rigours of London life. For Catherine, coming as a teenage girl from a rural vicarage to live in the big city with her famous uncle was a golden opportunity for a provincial girl and she certainly made the most of it. We have seventeen portraits of Isaac Newton, some by the finest artists of the day, such as Godfrey Kneller and James Thornhill. We also have medallions showing his profile, and three-dimensional likenesses in statues and marble busts. Unfortunately there is no authenticated contemporary likeness of Catherine Barton, and we can only guess at her appearance. We do know, however, that she was very popular with the opposite sex, not simply because of her looks but also because of her intelligence, humour, and conversation.

Despite Newton's increasingly cantankerous nature and the great disputes which marred his later years, Catherine remained with him as his housekeeper for the rest of his life. In the past he had lived on his own or in the company of male colleagues, such as John Wickins and Humphrey Newton, but now, with old age approaching, he found himself with a very attractive young woman running his house. The relationship between uncle and niece was excellent, if not perfect – certainly Newton's many detractors have been unable to find any flaw in their relationship and, though they have uncovered scandal about Catherine Barton and Lord Halifax, Catherine still emerges with her honour intact. The house in Jermyn Street was visited by many notaries wishing to seek the company of the author of the *Principia*, especially foreign visitors to the Royal Society. Far from being overawed by the visitors, Catherine readily joined in with the conversations, easily holding her own, and she befriended people in the same circle as her uncle, often captivating them with her feminine charms.

It is through Catherine that we hear little anecdotes about Newton's friends and correspondents. She tells the story, for example, of Isaac Newton's difference of opinion with Archbishop Tenison over the question of hanging pictures in the cathedral. She reported on the time that he rebuked Halley for his attitude towards religion. 'I have studied these things – you have not', said Newton to Halley. This incident was after Halley had returned from his scientific expedition to the South Atlantic in the *Paramour*. Following this voyage, he was often referred to as 'Captain Halley', and it seems that he had picked up some of the seaman's vocabulary along with his scientific data. Catherine is reputed to have told the story of Newton losing twenty thousand pounds by speculating on the South Sea Bubble. The amount has been exaggerated but Newton certainly held large sums of money in the South Sea Company.

One of the foremost of Catherine Barton's admirers was Charles Montague, the former Chancellor of the Exchequer, who had been instrumental in obtaining her uncle's position at the Mint. Montague's wife, the Countess of Manchester, died in 1698. In 1700 Montague was elevated to the peerage and he became the first Earl of Halifax so that, in the eighteenth century, he was invariably known by his new title of Lord Halifax.

Halifax was a prominent member of a London club known as the Kit-Kat Club. This was a gentleman's club run by leading members of the Whig party, and among the more notable members were Steele, Addison, Congreve, and Vanbrugh. The Club met in the house of Christopher Gate who lived in Shire Lane near Temple Bar. Gate was a pastry cook famous for his mutton pies which were known by the name of Kit-Kats. There is a rival theory for the club's name: some thought that it originated with Christopher Katt who lived at the sign of the Cat and Fiddle. A piece of doggerel was written by Dr John Arbuthnot of the Royal Society:

> *Whence deathless Kit Kat took his name*
> *Few critics can unriddle*
> *Some say from pastrycook it came*
> *And some from Cat and Fiddle*
>   John Arbuthnot

The members of the Kit-Kat Club were not without means, and portraits of all forty-two of them were painted by Godfrey Kneller, the leading portrait painter of the age, in a uniform series destined to become the property of the National Portrait Gallery. The portraits became so well known among the artists' community that Kneller's pictures became known as 'Kit-Kat' canvases. One of the customs amonst the members of the club was to engrave the name of a lady they admired on a toasting glass together with a verse in praise of her charms. Lord Halifax loved to try his hand at the poetry: he wrote odes to the Duchess of St Albans, the Duchess of Beaufort, Lady Mary Churchill, Lady Sunderland, and Mademoiselle Spanheim. In 1703 Miss Catherine Barton joined this august company. Inscribed on the toasting glass were the words:

> *Stampt with her reigning Charms, this Standard Glass*
> *Shall current through the realms of Bacchus pass;*
> *Full fraught with beauty shall new Flames impart,*
> *And mint her shining image on the Heart.*

The oblique reference to the Mint was no coincidence and 'proves' that the ode was written to Catherine Barton. If there was any ambiguity or doubt about his feelings, Halifax excelled himself by producing a second ode in which he mentions her explicitly by name:

> *Beauty and Wit strove each, in vain,*
> *To vanquish Bacchus and his Train;*
> *But Barton with successful Charms*
> *From both their Quivers drew her Arms;*
> *The roving God his Sway resigns,*
> *And awfully submits his vines.*

Catherine continued to turn heads, and she became the inspiration for yet more romantic poetry. In his *Miscellany Poems*, Dryden dedicated two verses to her:

> *At Barton's feet the God of Love*
> *His arrows and his Quiver lays*
> *Forgets he has a throne above*
> *And with this lovely Creature stays*
>
> *Not Venus' beauties are more bright*
> *But each appear so like the other*
> *That Cupid has mistook the Right*
> *And takes the Nymph to be his Mother* [3]

Lord Halifax's passion did not stop at the writing of verses to Catherine. In 1706 he added a codicil to his will in which he left her three thousand pounds and all his jewels. There evidently existed a stable and lasting relationship between them which was broken only by the Halifax's death. In 1713, when Halifax changed his will, he increased the three thousand pounds to five thousand and threw in a lodge at Bushey Park. When John Flamsteed heard this gossip, he estimated that the lodge was worth twenty thousand pounds. Catherine never took possession of the lodge but she ended up with an annuity of two hundred pounds a year instead. 'These Gifts and Legacies, I leave to her as a Token of the sincere Love, Affection and Esteem I have long had for her Person, and as a small Recompense for the Pleasure and Happiness I have had in her Conversation' reads the will of Lord Halifax.

In 1715 there came a Frenchman to visit the Royal Society. His name was Remond de Montmort and he was fortunate enough to meet Catherine while he was in London. Her attractions had been described to him before he left France. He was not disappointed by her charms. On the contrary, he was very taken with her beauty but his visit to London was all too short and soon he had to return to Paris. Catherine asked to be remembered to him through a third party. De Montmort was very touched that she still remembered him and he praised her charms in a letter to Brook Taylor of the Royal Society. Remond felt that the distance of 100 leagues (in English-speaking countries 1 league is estimated at roughly 3 miles) between Paris and London allowed him to express his passion for Catherine without compromising her in any way:

> *I am deeply stirred by the honor she does me in remembering me. I have preserved the most magnifi-*
> *cent memory of her wit and of her beauty. I loved her even before I had the honor of seeing her as the*
> *niece of Mr. Newton, predisposed by what I had heard of her charms while I was still in France. Ever*
> *since I beheld her, I have adored her not only for her great beauty but for her lively and refined wit. I*

believe there is no danger in your betraying me to her. If I had the good fortune to be near her, I would forthwith become as awkward as I was the first time we met. My awe and anxiety lest I displease her would reduce me to silence and I would conceal my feelings. But a hundred leagues away and separated by the sea, I think a lover can speak without being judged too bold, and a cultivated woman can tolerate declarations without reproaching herself for being too indulgent.[4]

Remond de Monmort believed in action as well as words, and he could hardly contain his love for Catherine Barton. On his return to Paris he displayed his Gallic temperament by sending fifty bottles of champagne to Isaac Newton with the proviso that they be drunk by '*des bouches philosophiques, et la belle bouch de Mademoiselle Barton*'.

It was not surprising that Catherine's striking entry into Society and her association with Lord Halifax attracted the notice of the gossipmongers. The Kit-Kat Club was a Whig stronghold, and any scandal was pounced upon and exaggerated by their political opponents, the Tories. In 1710 there appeared a publication by a Mrs Mary de la Rivière Manley, it was called *Memoirs of Europe, Towards the close of the Eighth Century* and purported to be written by Eginardus, secretary to and favourite of Charlemagne. The title was, of course, a spoof and the gossip therein related to the beginning of the eighteenth century rather than the eighth. Mrs Manley was a very successful writer and she had already published a similar book called *Secret Memoirs* which went to no less than seven editions. Among her characters in *Memoirs of Europe* were 'Julius Sergius' and 'Bartica', and her later editions stated openly that the former was Lord Halifax and the latter the niece of Sir Isaac Newton. Mrs Manley described a wild bacchanalian feast in the palace of Julius Sergius, in the course of which the drunken host confesses to a fictitious foreign count (who is telling the story in the first person) his great passion for the proud and beautiful Bartica.

> '*I think, my Lord Julius Sergius*', continu'd I, addresseing more closely to his Lordship, ''tis hard that of all this heavenly Prospect of Happiness, your Lordship is the only solitary Lover: what is become of the charming Bartica? Can she live a Day, an Hour, without you? Sure she's indisposed, dying, or dead.'
>
>   'You call Tears into my Eyes, dear Count', answered the Hero sobbing, 'she's a Traitress, an inconsistent proud Baggage, yet I love her dearly, and have lavished Myriads upon her, besides getting her worthy ancient Parent a good Post for Connivance.'

The 'worthy ancient Parent' is a thinly disguised description of Bartica's uncle, the Master of the Mint and the discoverer of the method of fluxions. It was perfectly true, of course, that the alter ego of 'Julius Sergius' had been instrumental in obtaining for him the 'good Post for Connivance', but the implication that 'Bartica' had been involved was false. Newton had been recommended for the post at the Mint before Montague even knew of the existence of his beautiful niece. The *Memoirs of Europe* then proceeds to enlighten us with much more gossip. In an imaginary conversation with the foreign count, Julius Sergius goes on to reveal more secrets about Bartica, his mistress. The extract sounds very effeminate and even homosexual when Julius kisses the count but allowances must be made for the period and the fact that it was all a parody:

> 'She has other Things in her Head, and is grown so fantastick and high, she wants me to marry her, or else I shall have no more of her, truly:
>
> Twas ever a proud Slut; when she pretended most kindness, when she was all over Coquet, and coveted to engage me more and more; when our Intimacy was at the height, she us'd to make my Servants wait three Hours for an Answer to a How-do-ye, or a Letter, which I sent every successive Morn.'
>
> 'As to the Letter', interrupted I, 'there may be some Excuse for that, my Lord: For what Woman, or indeed Man, can dare to write to a Person of your Lordship's Character, the Quintessence of Wit and Politeness, without copy and recopying again?'
>
> 'That's true, dear St. Girrone', answered his propitious Lordship, then kissing me close, and doing me the Favour of the Glass, to let me know he exacted I should follow his Example, he drank deeply, and after cry'd out in an Extasie
>
> > "And Wit for ever Scarlet
> > from this Vein shall flow!"
>
> Then asking my Excuse, [he said] 'twas a Flight of his own Poetry, he presented me the Wine, and continu'd his Indignation against Bartica. He told me, if he pin'd himself to Death, he was resolv'd not to marry her whilst she was so saucy.
>
> 'I don't brag, my dear Count, but methinks I have some Qualifications, besides my Wealth, and being of Consular Dignity, that deserves as good a Wife; my Person is not contemptible, and as to my Wit and Sense, look into the Writing of all those Moderns who durst deliver their Opinions, who durst presume to dedicate to me; see There, what future Ages will think of me.'[5]

Mrs Manley was a High Tory and the daughter of a cavalier; she became totally committed to making political capital out of the Whigs. Many Whigs other than Lord Halifax and Catherine Barton suffered at the pen of Mary de la Rivière Manley, and her scandals were so flagrant that eventually she was arrested and held in prison for a week without bail. Undaunted by her ordeal, Mrs Manley made the most of her experience and, like a true novelist, she described her imprisonment in her next publication, *Adventures of Rivella*:

> Her defense was with much Humility and Sorrow, for having offended, at the same Time denying that any Persons were concerned with her, or that he had a farther design than writing for her own

Amusement and Diversion in the Country, without intending particular Reflections or Characters:
When this was not believed, and the contrary urg'd very home to her by several Circumstances and
Likenesses; she said then it must be by inspiration, because knowing her own Innocence she could
account for it no other way: The Secretary reply'd upon her, that Inspiration us'd to be upon a good
Account, and her Writings were stark nought; she told him, with an Air-full of Penitence, that might
be true, but it was as true, that there were evil Angels as well as good; so that nevertheless what she
had wrote might still be by Inspiration.[6]

Mrs Manley's writings were translated into French and several other languages, and they
enjoyed a wide circulation on the Continent. By this time, the French were very interested
in 'Le Grand Newton' and, when Voltaire came to visit in 1720, he was eager to find out more
about the relations between Lord Halifax and La Bartica. The French writer and philosopher enjoyed a great following throughout Europe and his remarks were widely quoted:

I thought in my youth that Newton had made his fortune by his merit. I supposed that the Court and
the city of London named him Master of the Mint by acclamation. No such thing. Isaac Newton had
a very charming niece . . . who made a conquest of the minister Halifax. Fluxions and Gravitation
would have been of no use without a pretty niece.[7]

Voltaire's visit was in 1720. Some years after the event, the scandals were still alive but Lord
Halifax was dead and Voltaire was not able to add much to the reports in the *Memoirs of*
Europe. He published his findings many years later after the death of the
parties concerned but there is no doubt that a relationship between Lord Halifax and
Catherine Barton existed. A biography of Lord Halifax was published in 1715. It does not
admit to an author and it is a sober publication filled with poetry, speeches, and
political deeds. In direct contrast to Mrs Manley, it praises Halifax's virtues and ignores his
failings but the biographer finds it necessary to include a paragraph on Catherine Barton:

I am likewise to account for another Omission in the Course of this History, which is that of the
Death of the Lord Halifax's Lady; upon whose decease, his Lordship took a Resolution of living single
thence forward, and cast his Eye upon the Widow of one Colonel Barton, and Niece to the famous Sir
Isaac Newton, to be Super-intendant of his domestic Affairs. But as this Lady was young, beautiful
and gay, so those that were given to censure, pass'd a judgement upon her which she no Ways merited,
since she was a Woman of strict Honour and Virtue, and tho' she might be agreeable to his Lordship in
every particular, that noble Peer's Compliance to her, proceeded wholly from the great Esteem he had for
her Wit and most exquisite Understanding, as will appear in what related to her from his Will at the
Close of these Memoirs.[8]

There are minor errors in the account: Colonel Barton was Catherine's brother and not her husband but, when we find that his widow's name was Katherine Barton and that Catherine was commonly called 'Mrs' Barton according to the custom of the times, then the confusion is understandable. This passage suggests that Catherine Barton became supervisor of Lord Halifax's domestic affairs. There seems little doubt that she was a frequent visitor to his residence but it seems very unlikely that she ever actually lived in his household.

Late in 1709 Isaac Newton moved out of London from Jermyn Street to Chelsea. It may have been because the lease ran out in Jermyn Street or possibly to take advantage of the cleaner air outside the city. Whatever the reason, the move lasted only a few months and, by September 1710, he and his household were back in London living in a three-storey house in St Martin's Street just south of Leicester Fields, an area which later became known as Leicester Square. The new house was a substantial building with a rent of £100 per annum, a considerable sum for the times. The house consisted of eight rooms plus the servant's quarters. It had a cellar with wine vaults, a stable with a room above it, and a yard at the rear. The accommodation was shared between Newton and his niece and, when Catherine married in 1717, she chose to remain there with her husband. There were at least six domestic staff: a housekeeper, a cook, a footman, two maids, and a Mr Woston whose duties were unspecified. Presumably, the household staff occupied the top floor. The bedrooms of Newton and Catherine, together with his study, were situated on the first floor. The ground floor was for entertaining and it contained two parlours and a dining room.

The writer and satirist, Jonathan Swift (1667–1745), best known for his fantasy, *Gulliver's Travels*, knew Lord Halifax and Catherine Barton, and they both appear in his *Journal to Stella*, a private journal which he wrote to a lady friend called Esther Johnson in Dublin. Catherine Barton appears frequently in the journal: Swift was fortunate enough to dine with her regularly and often as her only guest. He enjoyed her company and her conversation immensely but his account throws no light on her relationship with Lord Halifax – the two never appear together in Swift's journal. One day, Jonathan Swift dined sumptuously with Lord Halifax at Hampton Court and, a few days later, he dined in pleasant intimacy with Catherine Barton but at no time does his journal suggest that a relationship existed between the two. Halifax appears less frequently in the journal as Swift became more and more disillusioned with the Whig party, and eventually he wrote a disparaging doggerel about the peer:

While Montague, who claimed the Station
To be Maecenas of the Nation,
For Poets open Table kept,
But ne'er considered where they Slept.
Himself, as rich as fifty Jews,
Was easy, though they wanted shoes.

Swift's disillusionment with Halifax made no difference to his relationship with Catherine, and he kept up acquaintance with her for several years. He creates a very engaging portrait of her and we find her mentioned in the company of other society beauties such as Lady Worsley, Miss Anne Long (who, like Catherine, was a toast of the Kit-Kat Club), and Lady Betty Germain, the daughter of the second Earl of Berkeley. On 28 September 1710, Jonathan Swift dined with Catherine at her uncle's lodgings in St Martin's Street. She entertained him with amusing and slightly risqué stories about some of her acquaintances. The first story he repeats concerned a Lady S. who, when last seen in England, pretended to have a stomach problem. The lady disappeared from society for three weeks but eventually the news came out that she was pregnant and she didn't want the society gossips to find out about her confinement.

When the rumours about Catherine Barton and Lord Halifax reached Esther Johnson in Ireland, she repeated some of the gossip and made a joke about Catherine. Jonathan Swift was not amused and he playfully upbraided his correspondent for 'twitting' him about his friend Miss Barton. 'I'll break your head in good earnest, young woman, for your nasty jest about Mrs. Barton. Unlucky sluttikim, what a word is there?' He frequently refers to Catherine as 'Mrs' Barton rather than 'Miss'. The former title was the normal custom of the times for a woman of independent means and it did not imply that she was a married woman. He saw her in December 1710 and again the following January. In March, he dined with her tête-à-tête in what he described as 'that genteel manner that MD used when they would treat some better sort of body than usual . . .'. In April he saw her again and he writes a very complimentary passage about her. 'I love her better than anybody here, and see her seldomer. Why really now, so it often happens in the world, that where one loves a body best – pshah, pshah, you are so silly with your moral observations.' This was the occasion when Catherine told him one of her more *risqué* stories. It was an old theme which he dutifully repeated to Esther Johnson:

> *An old gentle-woman died here two months ago, and left in her will, to have eight men and eight maids bearers, who should have two guineas apiece, ten guineas to the parson for a sermon, and two guineas to the clerk. But bearers, parson and clerk must be all true virgins; and not be admitted till they took their oaths of virginity: so the poor woman still lies unburied, and so must do till the general resurrection.*[9]

On 9 October 1711, Catherine heard the news that her brother, Lieutenant-Colonel Robert Barton, had been drowned on active service in Canada. She went into mourning, and the servants at St Martin's Street told Jonathan Swift that she was receiving no messages that day. The following Sunday was the first day after her period of mourning that she was prepared to receive company, and Swift came to see her. He refers to Catherine Barton as 'my near neighbour' for he, too, had moved to the Leicester Fields area at about this time. Much of their conversation on that October evening was centred around the differences between the main political parties, with Catherine playfully defending the Whigs and with Swift denouncing them in favour of the Tories. 'I made her merry enough, and we were three hours disputing upon Whig and Tory', said Swift. 'She grieved for her brother only for form, and he was a sad dog.' The cosy, intimate chats between Catherine Barton and Jonathan Swift ended soon afterwards. The two may have still remained in contact with each other a little longer but no further correspondence survives until a generation later. A single letter, dated 1733, from Catherine to 'Dean' Swift in Dublin shows that they still held a great affection for each other after a gap of more than twenty years:

> Not to be able to renew an acquaintance with who can twenty years after remember a bare intention to serve him, would be to throw away a prize I am not now able to repurchase; therefore when you return to England I shall try to excel in what I am very sorry you want, a nurse; in the meantime I am exercising that gift to preserve one who is your devoted admirer [10]

Newton's biographers have combed the journals of Jonathan Swift in vain for evidence of an illegal liaison between Catherine Barton and Lord Halifax. Many fantastic theories have been forwarded and Augustus de Morgan has suggested that Lord Halifax and Mrs Barton were secretly married and that she lived in his house. This rumour is based entirely on a remark in a letter to Sir John Newton in which Isaac Newton refers to the death of Lord Halifax. He uses the wording 'the circumstances in which I stand related to the family'. De Morgan chooses to interpret this passage to mean that Newton was actually related to Halifax through his niece, and he invents the secret marriage to create the relationship. He chooses to ignore the more direct evidence that Catherine pronounced herself a spinster on her marriage certificate.

That Catherine had some kind of affair with Lord Halifax seems fairly certain, but the intimate details were cleverly concealed from the scandalmongers. She was a single woman at the time and he was a widower – there were no wives or children involved and it is hard to see what all the fuss was about. The only real problem was the Victorian image of Isaac Newton. This required not only the man himself to have an untarnished image but also the impossible requirement that all his family must be perfect, particularly the niece who kept house for him and for whom he was in some ways responsible. Newton must have been fully aware of the physical attractions between his niece and his patron, and he wisely made no effort at all to interfere with their relationship – no doubt had he done so his detractors would have found something far worse in his character to write about.

Catherine comes out of the affair with great credit and her character is unblemished. After the death of Halifax she became a wealthy woman in her own right but she chose to stay with her uncle until he died. It was through her Uncle Isaac that Catherine Barton met John Conduitt in 1717. Once again the introduction came through the Royal Society. John Conduitt read a paper to the Society concerning the location of the Roman city of Carteia near Gibraltar. Soon afterwards the President entertained Conduitt at his house in St Martin's Street and the latter was introduced to Catherine Barton. If it was not love at first sight, then it was something akin for they married only a few weeks later. John Conduitt was a man of independent means. He had been educated at the same Cambridge college as Newton and he served several years in the British Army during the Spanish War of Succession. Catherine Barton was thirty-eight at the time of her marriage, nine years older than her husband.

ABOVE Medallion showing the profile of John Conduitt. Catherine Barton married John Conduitt in 1717 and the two lived in Newton's house during their time in London. In 1727 Conduitt succeeded Isaac Newton as master of the mint.

They were blessed with one child, Kitty, born three years later when Catherine was forty-one. Conduitt owned a country house at Cranbury Park in Hampshire but, in 1721, he became a Member of Parliament and his duties required him to spend most of his time in London where he and Catherine lived at St Martin's Street with Isaac Newton. Conduitt was immensely proud of his marital connection with Newton, and he was well pleased with himself to be married to the much sought-after Miss Catherine Barton. After the death of Isaac Newton, he succeeded his wife's uncle as the Master of the Mint.

14

A NEW CENTURY

WHAT IS NATURE? NOTHING IN RELATION TO THE INFINITE,
EVERYTHING IN RELATION TO NOTHING, A MEAN BETWEEN
NOTHING AND EVERYTHING

Blaise Pascal (1623-1662)

WHEN NEWTON BECAME INVOLVED with the coinage of the realm he had little time
in which to pursue his mathematical and philosophical interests. On 29 January 1697 a
letter arrived at the house in Jermyn Street. It was from the Swiss mathematician Johann
Bernoulli (1667-1748) – he had issued a challenge known as the brachistochrone problem to all the leading mathematicians of Europe. The problem involved finding the
curve, through two given points at different heights, which would cause a frictionless
particle to slide from the upper to the lower point in the minimum time. Bernoulli and
Leibniz were very pleased with their brachistochrone problem: no other person had
managed to find a solution, and they felt justified in claiming that only those with a
knowledge and understanding of the calculus would be able to solve it.

'I do not love…to be dunned & teezed by forreigners about Mathematical things…',
wrote Newton to Flamsteed soon afterwards. He saw his duties at the Mint as his first
priority but the mathematician in him could not resist the allure of what was a fascinating and creative problem. Arriving home at four in the afternoon after a hard day at the
Mint, he set to work straight away trying to solve it. According to his niece, he was still
engrossed in the problem at midnight and he did not solve it until four in the morning.
He did not want to encourage further discussion on the problem and he therefore sent
the solution anonymously to Bernoulli. His secrecy was to no avail, however, and
Bernoulli recognized the author immediately. 'The lion is recognized by his paw', said
Bernoulli as soon as he read Newton's solution.

Isaac Newton's parliamentary career seemed to have ended in 1690 when he decided not to stand for re-election. In 1701, however, by which time he was well established in London, he was persuaded by Lord Halifax to stand again for a seat in the Commons. The result of the election was that Henry Boyle and Isaac Newton were returned with comfortable majorities. There was a complaint from the defeated candidate, Mr Hammond, that the East India Company had been buying votes but, in spite of this, the result was allowed to stand. Newton took his seat again in the Commons but only for a very short spell. He seems to have been completely inactive in the 1701 Parliament, and he did not stand again at the next election in the following year.

ABOVE Newton by Charles Jervas, 1703. The artist shows Isaac Newton in his London days shortly after his election as President of the Royal Society, formally dressed with his fine periwig. Newton retained the post until his death in 1727, when the portrait was presented to the Society.

Now that he had become a permanent resident in London, Newton was able to attend the regular meetings of the Royal Society. At one meeting in 1699 he described a new sextant of his own design, only to find that in the last thirty years one thing at the Society had not changed. Robert Hooke claimed to have invented a better sextant some years before. Newton gained no pleasure from the Royal Society as long as Hooke was there to thwart him. He was happy to remain a member but he did not contribute very much and he immersed himself instead in the problems of the Mint. Robert Hooke was a sick man, however, and he had not long to live. He survived until the first years of the eighteenth century but his wealth and his health had declined so rapidly that he presented a sorry figure 'rendered sordid by poverty'. Poverty apart, Newton was not prepared to seek office with the Royal Society as long as Hooke remained a member but Hooke died in the March of 1703 and, later in the same year, Lord Somers retired from the Presidency. Newton was at last willing to become more active and he was persuaded to stand for the post of President. He was elected in November 1703 and he held the position until his death in 1727. His first decision after becoming President was to change the regular meeting day from Wednesday to Thursday, because Wednesday was the day when he had to attend to his duties at the Mint. The previous president, Lord Somers, had not attended a single Royal Society council meeting but Newton took his position very seriously, and the records show that he attended

161 out of a possible 175 meetings in his twenty-four years as President. The Royal Society was delighted to have the greatest scientist of the age for their President. He ruled the Society with a rod of iron. He would allow no levity or misconduct of any kind during the meetings:

> Whilst he presided in the Royal Society, he executed that office with singular prudence, with a grace and dignity – conscious of what was due to so noble an Institution – what was expected from his character... There were no whispering, talking, or loud laughters. If discussions arose in any sort, he said they tended to find out truth, but ought not to arise to any personality...Every thing was transacted with great attention and solemnity and decency; nor were any papers which seemed to border on religion treated without proper respect. Indeed his presence created a natural awe in the assembly, they appear'd truly as a venerable consessus Naturae Consiliariorum, without any levity or indecorum.[1]

John Evelyn described one meeting at the Royal Society when the President demonstrated a burning glass which focused sunlight so sharply that it could be used to melt metals:

> I went to the R: Society, where were Tryals with Sir E [sic] Newton's Burning-glasse: which did strange things as to mealting whatever was held to it in a moment: One of the most difficult was common slate, which lasted longer than Iron, Gold, brasse, Silver, flint, brick etc which it immediatly mealted, calcined and Vitrified: The glass was composed of 7 round burning glasses of abourt a foote diameter, so placed in a frame, as to cause all their Sun-beames to meete in one focus onely[2]

Thus the suggestion that Newton had, in his old age, given up on practical science or natural philosophy could hardly be further from the truth. It was true that his contributions were no longer the great original thoughts from his years at Cambridge but, in the new century, he went on to produce second and third editions of the *Principia*, and he finally published his work on optics which he had held in abeyance for over thirty years! He admitted that his reluctance to publish the *Opticks* earlier was because he had no wish to become 'engaged in Disputes about these Matters' – there seems little doubt that he was admitting that he had waited thirty years for the death of his old adversary, Robert Hooke.

The *Opticks* was a less demanding book than the *Principia*. It did not require the same level of mathematics. The book was written in English and this obviously made it easier for the English-speaking countries to understand but a Latin edition followed in 1706 and, soon afterwards, came editions in French, German, and Russian – it soon became widely read on the European continent. The early part of the *Opticks* followed very closely the paper he had written for the *Philosophical Transactions* thirty years before in 1673. He dealt with his classical experiments on the prism, leading on to the properties of light and the nature of colour. Even though the *Opticks* had taken over three decades to find its way into print, he admitted that the work was incomplete and he made an apology to his readers:

> When I made the foregoing Observations, I deigned to repeat most of them with more care and exact-
> ness, and to make some new ones for determining how the Rays of Light are bent in their passage by
> Bodies, for making the fringes of colour with the dark lines between them. But I was then interrupted,
> and cannot now think of taking these things into farther Consideration. And since I have not finish'd
> this part of my Design, I shall conclude with proposing only some Queries, in order to a farther
> search to be made by others.[3]

The *Queries* were a list of questions and suggested experiments for future physicists. This
was another contrast to the *Principia*: far from spurning hypotheses the *Queries* was full
of them. He included suggestions and ideas for new experiments which would help to
prove, one way or another, the various assertions about light. The evidence for light as a
wave motion was very strong but there were certain properties which he felt could only
be explained by a stream of particles (the 'corpuscular' theory), and he refused to be
drawn into making an hypothesis on which of the two theories was correct. The *Opticks*
also contained 'two Treatises of the Species and Magnitude of Curvilinear Figures'. These
had nothing at all to do with light and they did not appear in the later editions. Newton
put them there to help with his claim on the discovery of the calculus – at last he was

ABOVE A formal meeting of the Royal Society with Newton in the chair. The picture shows the mace presented by Charles the Second.

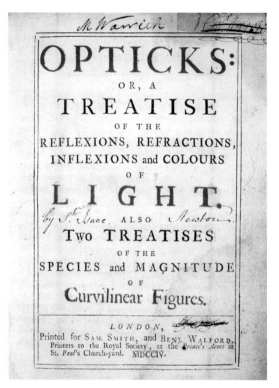

beginning to heed the warnings given by John Wallis and others to establish his priority.

In April 1705 Isaac Newton made a rare visit to his old college at Cambridge. Queen Anne was making a visit to Cambridge after a day at the races in Newmarket and it had been arranged for her to confer a knighthood on Isaac Newton together with John Ellis, the university's vice-chancellor, and James Montague. This was a unique occasion for the university because it was the first time that a knighthood had been conferred for services to science.

Her Majesty went up into the Regent-House; where, as is usual upon so great and extraordinary a Solemnity, Degrees in the several Faculties were by Her Majesty's Special Grace conferred upon Persons of High Nobility and Distinguishing Merit…From the Schools Her Majesty went to Trinity College, the Master whereof, Dr Bentley, received Her Majesty likewise with a very dutiful Speech; and Her Majesty was pleased to Confer the Honour of Knighthood upon John Ellis Esq; Doctor in Physick, and Vice-Chancellor of the University, James Montague Esq; Council for the University, and Isaac Newton Esq; formerly Mathematick Professor, & Fellow of that College.[4]

A month later, in May, Newton was in Cambridge again. His friend Charles Montague, then known as Lord Halifax, persuaded Newton to run again as a Member of Parliament for Cambridge University. Perhaps Newton was no longer interested in having a seat in the House of Commons for he spent only the minimum of time trying to obtain votes. The ceremony of the knighthood, which must have done much for his popularity in Cambridge and elsewhere, did not sway the voters. They knew perfectly well that the new knight no longer spent any time at the university. The first time he was able to use his new title in public was the 1705 election when he came last in a field of four.

At the age of sixty-two, this was the end of Isaac Newton's political career but it was by no means the end of his scientific career. After the publication of the *Opticks*, Newton set to work on the second edition of the *Principia*. The first edition, already over twenty years old, was in very short supply, and a number of minor errors had been pointed out by the few who were able to understand it. He wanted to include a better model for the motion of the Moon, showing the theory and also the correct values for the constants of the motion. Many accurate observations of the Moon were needed to determine the constants, and the only man who could supply these observations was John Flamsteed at Greenwich. Newton began to think that Flamsteed would never publish his stellar catalogue, the *Historia Coelestis*, and that, even if he finally did so, it would be too late to perfect and publish the theory of the Moon.

As President of the Royal Society, Newton was in a position to make noises in high circles. He approached Prince George of Denmark, the husband of Queen Anne, and he found that the prince was willing to finance the publication of *Historia Coelestis*. In December 1710, Queen Anne issued a warrant to Isaac Newton, written in the royal 'we': it gave him the authority to visit Flamsteed at Greenwich and to force his hand :

Anne R

Trusty and Well beloved

We Greet you well. Whereas We have been given to understand that it would contribute much to the Improvement of Astronomy and Navigation if We should appoint constant Visitors of our Royal Observatory at Greenwich, with sufficient Powers for the due Execution of that Trust . . .

Authorising and requiring you to demand of Our Astronomer & Keeper of Our said Observatory for the time being to deliver to you within six months after every Year shall be elapsed a true & fair Copy of the Annual Observations he shall have made. And Our further Will and Pleasure is, that you do likewise from time to time Order and Direct our Said Astronomer…to make such Astronomical Observations as you in your Judgement shall think proper…

Given at Our Court of St James's the Twelfth day of December 1710.

In the Ninth Year of Our Reign.

By her Majties Command   H. St. John[5]

It was a big mistake to upset John Flamsteed but, with the Crown and the Royal Society backing him, Newton's will prevailed and the *Historia Coelestis* was prepared for publication. Newton made another blunder by appointing Edmund Halley as editor to see Flamsteed's work through the press. Technically speaking, Halley was the best-qualified person for the job but everyone knew about his strained relations with Flamsteed, and it was hardly surprising that Halley's proof-reading and checking was not backed up by a disgruntled Astronomer Royal who would not co-operate.

In December 1711 Flamsteed was summoned before the Royal Society at the Crane

Court premises off Fleet Street. He was suffering from gout and he had a struggle to climb the stairs to face a three-man committee consisting of Isaac Newton, John Arbuthnot, and Hans Sloane. In a letter to his assistant at Greenwich, Flamsteed described the terrible scene as he confronted Isaac Newton:

I have had another contest with ye Pr[esident] R[oyal] S[ociety] who had formed a plot to make my instruments theirs and sent for me to a Comittee where onely himselfe & two Physitians, Dr. Sloane & another, as little skillful as himselfe were present. Ye Pr[esident] ran himself into a great heat & very inde-cent passion. I had resolved aforehand his Kn[avei]sh talke should not move me shewed him yt all ye Instrumts in ye Observatory were my owne the Murall Arch & Voluble Quadrant haveing been made at my own charge the rest purchased with my own Mony, except ye sextant & two clocks which were given me by Sr Jonas Moore, with Mr Towneleys Micrometer, his gift some yeares before I came to Greenwich.[6]

The Royal Society was claiming through the Secretary of State that the instruments at Greenwich were Crown property. This was certainly true of some of them, but not all because, as we have seen earlier, Flamsteed had been obliged to purchase a number of instruments with his own money. Flamsteed then complained about his catalogue being printed by Halley and that he had been robbed of the fruits of his own labours. The insinuation angered Newton who rose to the bait and hurled names at Flamsteed:

At this he fired & cald me all the ill names Puppy &c. that he could think of. All I returnd was I put him in mind of his passion desired him to govern it & keep his temper, this made him rage worse, & he told me how much I had receaved from ye Govermt in 36 yeares I had served. I asked what he had done for ye 500lb [sic] per Annum yt he had receaved ever since he setled in London. This made him calmer but finding him goeing to burst out againe I onely told him: my Catalogue half finished was delivered into his hands on his own request sealed up. He could not deny it but said Dr Arbuthnot had procured ye Queens order for opening it. This I am persuaded was false, or it was got after it had been opened. I sayd nothing to him in return but with a little more spirit than I had hitherto showed them, that God (who was seldom spoke of with due Reverence at that Meeting) had hitherto prospered all my labours & I doubted not would do so to an happy conclusion, took my leave and left them.[7]

The '500lb' a year was a reference to Newton's salary as Master of the Mint. The only other witnesses to this heated confrontation were John Arbuthnot and Hans Sloane. Dr Arbuthnot rose to support Newton but Sloane wisely kept his silence:

Dr Sloan had sayd nothing all this while, the other Dr. told me I was proud & Insulted the Presidt & run into ye same passion with ye Pr[esiden]t. At my goeing out I called to Dr Sloan, told him he had behavd himsef civilly & thankt him for it. I saw Raymer after, drunk a dish of Cofe[e] with him & told him still calmly of the Villainy of his conduct & called it blockish since then they let me be quiet but how long they will do so I know not nor am I solicitous;...[8]

It was a very ugly scene. Two distinguished scientists, who had known each other for over forty years and who at one time had happily played backgammon together, were transformed into red-faced old men with raised blood pressure shouting at each other. The mysterious 'Raymer' in Flamsteed's account is known to be his derogatory name for Edmund Halley who, together with Dr Sloane, are among the few people to come out of this deplorable incident with any credit. Halley could be a great diplomat when he chose but it was still a miracle that he managed to persuade the irate Astronomer Royal to calm his nerves by taking coffee with him. The *Historia Coelestis* was printed a few months later and it was greatly despised by Flamsteed as a parody of his lifetime's work. It was not long before the Royal Society had to agree with him – the work was so full of errors that it was of little value.

When George I succeeded Queen Anne to the throne, Flamsteed at last found friends at Court and he was allowed to purchase the bulk of the 300 printed copies of *Historia Coelestis*. He ceremoniously burnt the parts that offended him. His own publication, with the almost identical name of *Historia Coelestis Britannica*, was eventually published by his assistants in 1726, six years after his death. After the scene at Crane Court in 1711, the book was a worthy memorial to the first Astronomer Royal. A lighter side of the controversy was provided by Caroline of Anspach who, when she met John Flamsteed at Greenwich, found herself regaled with a list of complaints against the Royal Society and, in particular, the President whom Flamsteed described as 'a great rascal' who had stolen two of his stars. Caroline's response to this grave charge was a fit of giggles.

Caroline of Anspach was married to the future George II of England. Therefore, she had a position in the Courts of both London and Hanover. She met Isaac Newton in London and Gottfried Leibniz at Hanover, and, a few years later, she became marginally involved when the greatest controversy ever to be associated with the history of mathematics flared up.

Gottfried Wilhelm Leibniz was about four years younger than Newton. He was born in Germany and spent most of his life at the Court of Hanover. He also spent many years in Paris, where he befriended Huygens and Bernoulli, and became very well known for his remarkable mathematical skill. His connection with the Royal Society went back many years and, as we saw earlier, on his first visit in 1673 he exhibited a mechanical calculating machine to the Society. The calculator was greatly admired by those present and, though Mr Hooke declared that he could build a better and simpler machine, it never materialized. Leibniz visited the Royal Society again about three years later.

Leibniz knew something of Newton's work but, because none of it had been published, his progress on the calculus was independent of the work done by Newton. The question of priority did not become a contentious issue until 1710 when John Keill in the *Philosophical Transactions* charged Leibniz with publishing material which had originated with Newton. Leibniz, who was himself a member of the Royal Society, wrote to Hans Sloane to complain that the charge was untrue. Leibniz had published an account of his own version of the calculus but the British school of mathematics was anxious to prove that his methods were essentially the same as those discovered by Isaac Newton many years before.

The Royal Society set up what they claimed was an independent committee to examine the dispute. The committee consisted of six members of the Society, namely John Arbuthnot, Abraham Hill, Edmund Halley, William Jones, John Machin, and William Burnett, all of whom were pro-Newtonian so that their findings were almost a foregone conclusion. The committee's report, called the *Commercium Epistolicum*, was published in January 1713. The facts of the report were very accurate as far as they went but it was not unbiased and it made very little allowance for the claims of Leibniz. The report concluded that Leibniz had had access to Newton's work and that Newton's priority in the matter was affirmed.

After his visits to London in the 1670's Leibniz had communicated with John Collins and Henry Oldenburg at the Royal Society, and Collins had shown him the work of Newton and Gregory. The committee claimed that he had also been shown a work by John Pell which described a method known as 'Mouton's Method' which Leibniz subsequently published as his own discovery. *The Commercium Epistolicum* claimed that Newton's discovery of the fluxions was clearly documented in manuscripts from as early as 1669 and 1671. This was true enough but the manuscripts had never been published and they were certainly not available to Leibniz. A letter of Newton's, dating from 1676, was quoted which implied that he had his method of fluxions about five years earlier, in 1671. It was generally agreed that the fluxions and the calculus differed only in name and mode of notation. *The Commercium Epistolicum* was a hastily assembled document and, though it claimed to be impartial, Newton could not keep himself out of the controversy. He had vetted and edited some of the text.

The response from Leibniz's supporters was an anonymous fly-sheet called the *Charta Volans*. Leibniz was prepared to accept Newton's word on the development of the calculus but he insisted on his own priority of publication. In an article called '*Remarques sur la différence entre M. de Leibniz et M Newton*', published in the *Journal Litéraire de l'Haye*, Leibniz took a harder line and claimed that Newton's fluxions could do nothing that his own work could not do. He went on to claim that Newton knew nothing of the differential calculus when the *Principia* was published in 1687. Matters continued to escalate and Leibniz prepared a long discourse to which Newton replied at great length.[9]

The dispute grew into a long and bitter controversy which marred the last years of both men's lives. It was true that Newton had invented the calculus before Leibniz, but it was also true that Leibniz had discovered the calculus independently and that he was therefore also an inventor. Newton had used his method of fluxions to derive many of the results in the *Principia* but, because of the difficulty of the method, he had deliberately reworked the results by classical methods. Leibniz could claim to be the first to publish many of the results. Newton had only himself to blame for not publishing his ideas earlier: his friends had warned him many times about the priority of publication, and he had taken no action until it was far too late. The controversy continued after the death of Leibniz until it became so prolonged that everyone except the participants longed in vain for the issue to come to an end.

The second edition of the *Principia* was published in 1713 with Roger Cotes and David Gregory as editors. In common with the first edition, it contained a generous reference to 'that most excellent geometer, G. W. Leibniz' stating that 'that most distinguished man' had fallen upon a method of determining maximum and minimum values, and drawing tangents by a method very similar to that of the author. A third edition of the *Principia* followed only thirteen years later, ten years after the death of Leibniz and a year before the death of Newton. The editor was Henry Pemberton, and the passage about Leibniz had been expurgated.

Far from being the reserved university academic of his earlier life, Newton later became the complete autocrat in the way that he ruled the Royal Society and, through it, the scientific life of the whole country. Despite the controversies which raged around his scientific life, he had many friends and supporters in London and he still seemed to manage a contented social life in his final years. Catherine Barton was indebted to her uncle for launching her career in London society but, after the death of Lord Halifax, she had her own fortune and independent means so she did not owe the rest of her life to her uncle. He certainly gained a lot of pleasure from the company of his niece. Perhaps he found in her the daughter he had never had and he treated her with a gentleness and respect which outsiders did not see.

The last ten years of Newton's life were the first decade of John and Catherine Conduitt's married life. John Conduitt was very proud to be associated with the great scientist and he performed a very valuable service to posterity by drawing out the elderly Isaac Newton to tell stories of his childhood. Conduitt recorded anecdotes about Newton's early years which would otherwise have been lost. Some of these anecdotes, such as the story of his birth, when he was small enough to fit inside a quart pot and when the need for a bolster to hold his infant head, were recalled by Isaac Newton as stories he had been told by his mother. Conduitt also had the foresight to write to elderly people in the neighbourhood of Woolsthorpe and Grantham for information about the Isaac Newton they had known in their youth. He wrote, too, to those who knew Newton in his days at Cambridge. He received two letters from Humphrey Newton, the amanuensis who lived with Newton during the writing of the *Principia*, and also from the son of John Wickins with whom Newton shared his rooms at Trinity College for twenty years. He collected biographical detail from Newton's earlier and later life, as well as anecdotes, such as that of the brachistochrone problem, which were supplied by his wife, Catherine.

William Stukeley must also be mentioned in the same context as John Conduitt.

He was born at Holbeach in Lincolnshire, he completed his medical education in London, and opened a medical practice in Boston. In 1717 he moved to London and became a member of the Royal Society. He met Newton the following year and the two became close friends, drawn together by their common background despite their age difference.

> *According to my own observation, tho' Sir Isaac was of a very serious and compos'd frame of mind, yet I have often seen him laugh, and that upon moderate occasions . . . He usd a good many sayings, bordering on joke and wit. In company he behavd very agreeably; courteous, affable, he was easily made to smile, if not to laugh . . . He could be very agreeable in company, and even sometime talkative.*[10]

On 20 February 1721 the annual Lincolnshire feast was held at the Ship Tavern in Temple Bar. As usual, the class differences were very evident and William Stukeley, himself a Lincolnshire man, went upstairs to where the more affluent company was assembled. Gossip filtered through that there was an old gentleman downstairs whom they thought was Isaac Newton. Stukeley, who at this time knew Newton well, went down to confirm the story. The elderly gentleman was indeed Sir Isaac Newton, and Stukeley chose to remain downstairs chatting with him. When the upstairs company discovered the situation, they invited the two men to come up and join them but Newton preferred to remain where he was. The upstairs company came downstairs – they decided that the better sort of company was in the room that held the great philosopher.

Stukeley became a regular visitor to the house in St Martin's Street and he came to know the Conduitts very well. In 1726 William Stukeley changed his career from saving bodies to saving souls, and he moved to Grantham to take up a living as a clergyman. He searched the countryside around for elderly people who had known Newton in his youth, and he was fortunate enough to find a few octogenarians still with good memories. His best find was Mrs Vincent, the Miss Storer of Newton's schooldays, who told him the valuable account of the 'sober silent thinking lad' she remembered from her youth. Having lived in the same lodgings, Mrs Vincent recalled many stories of Isaac Newton as a boy, and she even claimed that she was engaged to be married to him. It is through William Stukeley that we have the fullest account of the famous story of the apple tree. The story is such a simplified version of the discovery of gravitation that it seems it must be apocryphal, but it came from Newton himself and Stukeley described the summer evening when Newton, then in his eighties, recalled his thoughts from sixty years before:

> *After dinner, the weather being warm, we went into the garden and drank tea, under the shade of some apple trees, only he and myself. Amidst other discourse, he told me, he was just in the same situation, as when formerly, the notion of gravitation came into his mind. It was occasion'd by the fall of an apple, as he sat in a contemplative mood. Why should that apple always descend perpendicularly to the ground, thought he to himself. Why should it not go sideways or upwards, but constantly to the earth's*

centre? Assuredly the reason is, that the earth draws it. There must be a drawing power in matter: and the sum of the drawing power must be in the earth's centre, not in any side of the earth. Therefore does the apple fall perpendicularly, or towards the centre. If matter thus draws matter, it must be in proportion of its quantity. Therefore the apple draws the earth, as well as the earth draws the apple. That there is a power, like that we here call gravity, which extends itself thro the universe.[11]

In 1724, when Newton was in his eighty-second year, he was advised by his physicians to move out of London and seek the more salubrious country air. He went to the village of Kensington. His residence was known as Orbell's Buildings and it stood to the west of Kensington Church Street. The change of air improved his health but he kept on his old residence and he insisted on making regular visits back to London. In March 1727 the rector of St Martin-in-the-Fields, Zachary Pearce, found him back at his old house still studying at the age of eighty-four, only a few days before he died:

I found him writing over his Chronology of the Ancient Kingdoms, *without the help of spectacles, at the greatest distance of the room from the windows, and with a parcel of books on the table, casting a shade upon the paper. Seeing this, on my entering the room, I said to him. 'Sir, you seem to be writing in a place where you cannot so well see.' His answer was, 'A little light serves for me.' He then told me that he was preparing his Chronology for the press, and that he had written the greatest part of it over again for that purpose. He read to me two or three sheets of what he had written, (about the middle, I think, of the work) on occasion of some points in Chronology, which had been mentioned in our conversation. I believe, that he continued reading to me, and talking about what he had read, for near an hour, before the dinner was brought up.*[12]

By this time Newton was terminally ill and he had contracted a violent cough which refused to leave him. On his return to Kensington, the Conduitts sent for his physicians and they diagnosed a stone in the bladder. There was no hope of any recovery and Newton was suffering from great pain. The sweat ran in beads from his face, and he knew that he was dying, but he held his Unitarian beliefs to the end and he refused to receive the last sacrament. He had plenty of time in which to think up a suitable epitaph by which the world would remember him. It has been used by most of his biographers but the source remains unknown:

I do not know what I may seem to the world, but, as to myself, I seem to have been only like a boy playing on the sea shore, and diverting myself in now and then finding a smoother pebble or a prettier shell than ordinary, whilst the great ocean of truth lay all undiscovered before me.

On 15 March he recovered slightly but the relief was only temporary. On 19 March he fell asleep in the evening and he died in the small hours of Monday morning, 20 March, 1727.

EPILOGUE

WHEN YOU AND I BEHIND THE VEIL ARE PAST,

AH, BUT THE LONG, LONG WHILE THE WORLD SHALL LAST,

WHICH OF OUR COMING AND DEPARTURE HEEDS

AS THE SEA'S SELF SHOULD HEED A PEBBLE-CAST.

Omar Khayyam (1048-1131)

BEARING IN MIND THAT in the seventeenth century London was the smokiest and probably the most unhealthy place to live in the whole of England, the longevity of the members of the Royal Society was remarkable. Robert Boyle died in 1691 at the age of sixty-four but many of the prominent members who knew London before the Great Fire were still alive in the eighteenth century. Hooke died in 1702 aged sixty-six; Samuel Pepys and John Wallis died in the following year aged seventy and eighty-seven respectively. John Evelyn was eighty-six when he died in 1706 and Flamsteed lived until 1719 when he was seventy-two. Newton died in 1727 having reached the venerable old age of eighty-four; Halley survived him by fifteen years and reached the age of eighty-five. Halley needed to live another for ten years to see his comet return. The oldest member of the group was Christopher Wren who died in 1723 in his ninety-first year.

It was a remarkable circumstance for the architect of a great cathedral to live long enough to see his work completed. In 1710, when the final stone was placed on St Paul's Cathedral, the architect's son described the scene in his book *Parentalia*. It was a moving ceremony high above the streets of London when Christopher Wren helped to place the last and highest stone of the cathedral into position – but the highest man in London on that day was not the seventy-eight-year-old architect but his son of the same name:

> *The highest or last Stone on the Top of the Lantern was laid by the Hands of the Surveyor's Son, Christopher Wren, deputed by his Father, in the Presence of that excellent Artificier Mr Strong, his son, and other Free and Accepted Masons, chiefly employed in the Execution of the Work...*
>
> *Thus was this mighty Fabric, the second Church for Grandeur in Europe in the space of 35 Years, begun and finished by one Architect, and under one Bishop of London, Dr Henry Compton: The*

charge supported chiefly by a small and easy Imposition of Sea-coal brought to the Port of London.[1]

It had to be acknowledged that St Paul's Cathedral was smaller than St Peter's in Rome but Londoners made capital from the fact that it had been completed in a much shorter time and under one architect and one bishop. St Peter's took 145 years to build and saw nineteen popes during its construction.

Christopher Wren was one of the few people old enough to remember the medieval cathedral of old St Paul's and London before the Great Fire. Many of the houses in the new city had been completed even before the new cathedral was started, and the Monument to commemorate the fire was built only eleven years after the event. It was St Paul's, however, that represented the completion of the rebuilding of London after the terrible conflagration of 1666. The

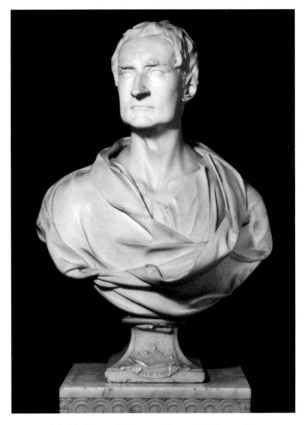

RIGHT Marble bust of Newton. The marble bust of Isaac Newton by Roubiliac in Trinity College Chapel at Cambridge. This was the bust which inspired Wordsworth's lines on Newton 'the marble index of a mind, voyaging on strange seas of thought alone'.

new London was a much safer and healthier place than the old city: the houses were of stone, regulations governing open fires were much stricter, and, thankfully, the plague of 1665 was the last visitation of its kind. London Bridge had changed very little, and it remained the only crossing of the Thames until the completion of Westminster Bridge in 1750. The bridge retained its character until 1758 when the houses were removed over a period of four years to leave a more efficient but much less interesting river crossing.

In the early decades of the eighteenth century, the first signs of the Industrial Revolution had already appeared. At Coalbrookdale Abraham Darby had solved the problem of smelting iron by the use of coke. The first Newcomen atmospheric engine was erected at Dudley Castle in 1712, and the engine solved the problem of pumping water from mines. The Industrial Revolution was not centred on London. Most of the major developments were made in distant parts of the kingdom and, in many cases, the

practical men of the Industrial
Revolution owed little to the
armchair philosophers at the
Royal Society. But, as the
Revolution gained momentum,
it was obvious that an understanding of the basic laws of science became more and more of a
necessity for technological
progress and understanding.

There is no scale on which to
measure the value of the knowledge passed on to us by previous
generations, yet we must
acknowledge our great debt to
those who first formulated the
laws of physics and mechanics,
and who opened up the understanding of nature so that
humanity could use the knowledge to further its ends. The seventeenth-century philosophers
were born in an age of supersti-
tion, astrology, and alchemy
when the common people still

ABOVE Newton's death mask. It was quite common in the
eighteenth century and earlier to take a cast of the face and to
produce a death mask for posterity.

believed in magic and witchcraft. They left behind them laws of nature and the scientific method by which those following after them could discover other laws and refine the
existing ones. They had human failings, and they squabbled frequently among themselves, but they all had a common end in view and they still managed to grope forward
to a deeper understanding and mastery of nature. As a result of their findings, quality of
life improved steadily towards an age when every household could enjoy a living standard that surpassed that of even the wealthiest of the seventeenth-century nobility.

Newton's driving force was a passionate desire to discover the system of the world
and the basic truths of the universe. *The Principia* came as close as was possible in his
times to explaining the mechanism of the Solar System. But this was not enough for
him. He was searching for the truth behind the Creation which he believed could be
found in theology and in the chronology of the ancient kingdoms. All this and much
more was needed to master the system of the world. His writings on scientific and mathematical subjects amounted to more than a million words. His writings on theology and

chronology were greater than this by half-a-million more. His alchemical researches were greater yet again and, if we include his work at the Mint and his miscellaneous manuscripts, he must have written more than four million words in his eighty-four years.

We know far more about Newton than we know about any other genius before him but we must ask the question: how long would it take to read and understand all of his works? To understand the *Principia* requires a fluency in Latin as well as mastery of obsolete branches of mathematics that are no longer in the school curriculum. How many of the few who understand his science and his unique mathematical demonstrations also understand his millions of words on theology? If it is possible for anybody to master all these then life is not long enough to take in his millions of words on alchemy as well. It is scarcely possible to understand the mind of Isaac Newton. Its depths have never been plumbed, and a genius working for a whole lifetime would not have the time to read and comprehend all his work.

The posthumous son of an illiterate, unknown farmer mastered the whole of the natural philosophy of his time. He had no peers. He pushed the boundaries of knowledge as far as they could go, and he invented the scientific method for those who followed after him. His thoughts were often too deep to put into words and to share with others. He was in a world of his own with his thoughts and his philosophy. William Wordsworth, when he first saw Roubiliac's marble bust of Newton at Trinity College, found a form of words which was very close to the truth:

Newton with his prism and silent face,
The marble index of a mind
Voyaging on strange seas of thought
Alone.
William Wordsworth

REFERENCES

Andrade E N: *Isaac Newton* (London 1950)

Ashmole, Elias: *Autobiographical and Historical Notes*
(Ed C H Josten, Oxford 1966)

Aubrey, John: *Brief Lives*
(Ed: Richard Barber; Boydell Press 1982)

Aughton, Peter: *Endeavour* (Windrush Press, 1999)

Bailey, Francis: *An account of the Rev John Flamsteed,*
the First Astronomer Royal (London 1835-7)

Birch, Thomas: *The History of the Royal Society of London for Improving Natural Knowledge* (London 1756-7)

Boyle, Robert: *Robert Boyle on Natural Philosophy*
(Ed Maria Boas Hall, London 1966)

Brewster, Sir David : *The Life of Sir Isaac Newton* (London 1831)

Bryant, Arthur: *Samuel Pepys – The Man in the Making,* (London 1933)

Bryant, Arthur: *Samuel Pepys – The Years of Peril,*
(London 1935)

Cohen, I B: *Introduction to Newton's Principia*
(Cambridge 1971)

Cohen, I B: *The Newtonian Revolution*
(Cambridge 1980)

Cook, Alan: *Edmond Halley, charting the Heaven's and the Seas* (Oxford 1998)

Correspondence:
(The) Correspondence of Isaac Newton,
Eds: H W Turnbull, J F Scott, A R Hall, L Tilling
Vols I to VII (Cambridge 1959 to 1977)

De Morgan G H : *Newton: his Friend: his Niece*
(London 1968)

Downes, K: *Christopher Wren* (London 1988)

'Espinasse, Margaret: *Robert Hooke,*
(London 1956)

Evelyn, John: *The Diary of John Evelyn: Vols I to VI*
(Ed. E S de Beer: Oxford 1955)

Fauvel J, Flood R, Shortland M, Wilson R:
Let Newton be (Oxford 1988)

Feuer, L S: *The Scientific Intellectual,* (New York & London 1963)

Gjertsen, Derek: *The Newton Handbook* (London & New York 1986)

Hall, A R: *Isaac Newton, Adventurer in Thought*
(Oxford 1992)

Hall, A R: *The Scientific Revolution 1500-1800*
(London 1954)

Hutchinson, Harold F: *Sir Christopher Wren:*
(London 1976)

Lyons, Henry : *The Royal Society 1660-1940*
(Cambridge 1944)

McGuire J E & Tamny, Martin: *Newton's Trinity Notebooks* (1983)

Manuel F: *A Portrait of Sir Isaac Newton* (London 1980)

More, L T: *Isaac Newton,* (New York & London 1934)

Newton, Isaac : *Opticks: or a Treatise of Light*
(1st edition London 1704)

Newton, Isaac: *Philosophiae Naturalis Principia Mathematica* (1st edition London 1686)

Pepys, Samuel: *Diary of Samuel Pepys,* (11 volumes,
Ed R C Latham and W Matthews, London 1970-83)

Purver, M: *The Royal Society: Conception and Creation,* (London 1967)

Robinson and Adams (ed): *The Diary of Robert Hooke* (London 1935)

Sobel, Dava: *Longitude* (London 1995)

Sprat, Thomas: *The History of the Royal Society of London for the Improving of Natural Knowledge* (London 1667, reprint London 1959 Ed: J I Cope & H W Jones)

Stukeley, William: *Memoirs of Sir Isaac Newton's Life* (Ed A Hastings White, London 1936)

Swift, Jonathan : *Journal to Stella* (Ed Harold Williams Oxford 1948)

Villamil, Richard de: *Newton: The Man* (London 1931)

Westfall R S : *Never at Rest* (Cambridge 1980)

Whatton, Rev A B: *Memoir of the Rev Jeremiah Horrox* (London 1849)

White, Michael: *Isaac Newton. The last Sorcerer,*
(London 1997)

Whiteside D T: *The Mathematical Papers of Isaac Newton* (Vols I to VIII, Cambridge 1967-80)

Wolf, A: *A History of Science, Technology, and Philosophy in the 16th & 17th Centuries* (London 1935)

Wood, Anthony : *Life and Times of Anthony à Wood*
(Ed. Llewelyn Powys, London 1932)

Wren, Christopher: *Parentalia, or Memoirs of the Family of Wrens* (London 1750, facsimile reprint London 1965)

NOTES BY CHAPTER

CHAPTER ONE
1   Keynes MS, King's College Library: 130 (2) 18
2   Stukeley 46
3   *ibid* 39
4   *ibid* 43
5   *ibid* 42
6   *ibid* 46

CHAPTER TWO
1   Anthony Wood 68
2   Dorothy Stimson: Ballad of Gresham Colledge ,
ISIS XVIII (Oxford 1932)
3   Sprat 53
4   Anthony Wood 40
5   *ibid* 59

6   Walter Pope: *The Life of the Right Reverend Father in God, Seth, Lord Bishop of Salisbury,* (London 1697)
7   Anthony Wood p 81
8   Sprat 52
9   Francis Bacon: *Advancement of Learning Book I* (London 1605)
10   John Wilkins: *Discourse on The Discovery of a New World in the Moone* (London 1638)
11   Evelyn III 110-111
12   Robert Hooke: *Posthumous Works,* ed Richard Waller (London 1705)
13   Anthony Wood 255

CHAPTER THREE
1   Wren p 254
2   Evelyn III, 266
3   *ibid* 332
4   Lyons 41
5   *Ibid* 41
6   *Ibid* 41-42
7   Hooke : *Micrographia* (1665)
8   Wren 210
9   Pepys IV 223
10   *ibid* IV 226
11   *ibid* VI 36
12   Aubrey 166-169
13   Pepys VII 239
14   *ibid* VI 120
15   *ibid* VI 208
16   *ibid* VI 213
17   Evelyn III 421

CHAPTER FOUR
1   More 53
2   Fiennes, *Celia: The Journeys of Celia Fiennes* (Ed Christopher Morris London 1949) 78
3   Correspondence I 1
4   More 206
5   *ibid* 206
6   Stukeley 53
7   More 53
8   Correspondence I 2
9   Westfall 143
10   Correspondence I 92
11   *ibid* 92-102

CHAPTER FIVE
1   Evelyn III 448
2   *ibid* 449
3   Pepys VII 268
4   *ibid* 271-272
5   Evelyn III 453-454
6   *ibid* 455-456

7   *ibid* 457
8   Anthony Wood 131/132
9   Pepys VII 274-275
10   *ibid* 276
11   Evelyn III 458-459
12   ibid 460-461
13   ibid 461-462

CHAPTER SIX
1   Evelyn III 462-463
2   Pepys IX 146
3   Lyons 66
4   Correspondence I 13
5   *ibid* 14
6   *ibid* 15
7   *ibid* 53
8   *ibid* 73
9   *ibid* 79
10   *ibid* 79
11   *ibid* 120
12   *ibid* 80
13   *ibid* 92-102
14   *ibid* 92-102
15   *ibid* 169
16   *ibid* 394
17   *ibid* 198-203

CHAPTER SEVEN
1   More 54
2   Ashmole 84
3   *ibid* 84
4   *ibid* 85
5   *ibid* 85
6   E J Holmyard (Ed): *Works of Geber,* Translated by Richard Russell 1678
7   Correspondence I 84
8   Portsmouth Papers (Cambridge University Library) Add MS 3795,115
9   Correspondence I 262
10   *ibid* 412
11   *ibid* 416
12   *ibid* 27
13   *ibid* 262
14   Stukeley 59

CHAPTER EIGHT
1   Correspondence II 301
2   *Philosophical Transactions.* 16 (1686-7), 7
3   Anthony Wood 233
4   Evelyn IV 359
5   *ibid* 360
6   *ibid* 361-362
7   *ibid* 363
8   Correspondence I p442
9   Westfall 403

10   Westfall 404

CHAPTER NINE
1   More 206
2   *ibid* 247
3   *ibid* 249
4   *ibid* 247
5   *ibid* 249
6   Correspondence II p431
7   *ibid* 431
8   *ibid* 436
9   *ibid* 438
10   *ibid* 437

CHAPTER TEN
1   *Dictionary of Scientific Biography* (Ed C C Gillispie: Scribners 1970)
2   Aubrey 169
3   Correspondence II p 441
4   *ibid* 443
5   *ibid* 444
6   *ibid* 472
7   *ibid* 474
8   Newton, Preface to book III of the *Principia*
9   Correspondence III 253-254
10   *ibid* 483
11   *Philosophical Transactions* 16 1686/7
12   Keynes MS 130.5, 2-3 Kings College Library, Cambridge

CHAPTER ELEVEN
1   Cook 378
2   Calendar of State Papers 1675-6
3   Correspondence IV p68
4   Dorothy Stimson: *Ballad of Gresham Colledge ,* ISIS XVIII (1932)
5   P Aughton: *Endeavour* (Windrush Press 1999)
6   Correspondence IV 58
7   *ibid* 77

CHAPTER TWELVE
1   Correspondence III 214
2   *ibid* 230
3   *ibid* 231
4   *ibid* 279
5   *ibid* 280
6   *ibid* 278
7   Correspondence IV 187
8   Correspondence III 300
9   *ibid* 202
10   *ibid* 258
11   Correspondence IV 116

CHAPTER THIRTEEN
1   Correspondence IV 307–308
2   *ibid* 349
3   Dryden, *Miscellany Poems* V 61
4   Brook Taylor: *Contemplatio Philosophica* (London 1793)
5   Mary de la Riviere Manley: *Memoirs of Europe Towards the Close of the Eighth Century*, Written by Eginardus (London 1710) p 294
6   Mary de la Riviere Manley: *Adventures of Rivella; or the History of the Author of Atalantis, with Secret Memoirs and Characters of several Considerable Persons, her Contemporaries* (London 1714) 113
7   Dictionnaire Philosophique; *Oeuvres completes de Voltaire* (Paris 1785–9)
8   *The Works and Life of the Right Honourable Charles late Earl of Halifax* (London 1715)
9   Swift 229
10 More 541

CHAPTER FOURTEEN
1   Stukeley 78
2   Evelyn V 592
3   Newton: *Opticks* (London 1704) 338
4   *London Gazette*, number 4116, Thursday 19th April to Monday 23rd April
5   Correspondence V 79
6   *ibid* 210
7   *ibid* 209–210
8   *ibid* 210
9   Correspondence VI 341–342
10 Stukeley 57
11 *ibid* 19
12 Westfall 869

EPILOGUE
1   Wren: *Parentalia*

INDEX

Page numbers in *italics* indicate illustrations.

ACKNOWLEDGEMENTS

The author would like to thank the following: his wife, Dilys, and Victoria Huxley, Lesley Grayson, Miranda Harvey, John Taylor for their help while working on this book.

The publishers would like to thank the following sources for their kind permission to reproduce the pictures in this book. In particular they would like to thank Christine Woollett at The Royal Society, Lynne MacNab at the Guildhall Library, Ann Ronan, and Anne Marie Robinson at Cambridge University Library for their help.

PICTURE CREDITS

The Portrait facing the Contents page by kind permission of the Trustees of the Portsmouth Estates

Back jacket images: gravity map Royal Observatory, Edinburgh/Science Photo Library. Telescope Science & Society Picture Library

Ann Ronan Picture Library opposite title page; 7; 10; 44; 53; 62; 89; 94; 125; 132; 142; 150; 152; 154; 195; 196

Peter Aughton 57

Board of Trustees of the National Museums and Galleries on Merseyside (Walker Art Gallery, Liverpool) 161

The Bridgeman Art Library/Museum of London 118; /Philip Mould Historical Portraits Ltd, London 148

Guildhall Library, Corporation of London 35; 36; 65; 81

Mary Evans Picture Library 16

© Museum of London 47; 77; 111

© National Maritime Museum, London 157

By kind permission of the Provost and Scholars of King's College, Cambridge 15; 99

Reproduced courtesy of the Royal Mint 177; 178; 179; 191

© The Royal Society 29; 30; 42; 62; 66; 75; 79; 115; 123; 130; 165; 193; 205; 206

Science Photo Library/ Alfred Pasieka 58; /Simon Marsden 126; /NASA 145; /Eckhard Slawik 158

By permission of the Syndics of Cambridge University Library 49; 85; 120; 137; 166; 181

John Taylor for the map on page 12.

First published in Great Britain
by Weidenfeld & Nicolson in association with
The Windrush Press in 2003
A division of The Orion Publishing Group Ltd,
Orion House, 5 Upper St Martin's Lane,
London WC2H 9EA

The Windrush Press
Windrush House
Adlestrop
Moreton-in-Marsh
Gloucestershire GL56 0YN

Copyright © Peter Aughton 2003

First published 2003

British Library Cataloguing-in-Publication Data
A catalogue record for this book is available from the British Library

ISBN 0-29784321-4

Printed and bound in Italy

PETER AUGHTON was born in Southport
and educated at King George V School and
Manchester University. He has lived in the Bristol
area since 1967, working firstly on the Concorde
supersonic airliner and now at the University of
the West of England. He is a member of the British
Computer Society and an Associate Fellow of the
Institute of Mathematics and its Applications. He is
married with two children and a granddaughter.

also by Peter Aughton

Endeavour: The Story of Captain Cook's
    First Great Epic Voyage

North Meols and Southport

Liverpool - A People's History

Bristol - A People's History

Image opposite title page Newton investigating
the nature of light. An engraving after the painting
by J A Houston.

Image opposite contents Isaac Newton at the age of 46 by
Godfrey Kneller. One of the earliest of many portraits
of Newton, Kneller was the leading portrait painter
of the times and this is probably a good likeness.